TABLE OF CONTENTS

Chapter 1

IN THE BEGINNING

"Dr. Apocalypse, Dr. Apocalypse......my roommate just showed me his tentacles!" shrieked my patient as she held a chair over her head. But I was confused, my name was in fact Dr. Aliapoulios and my patient didn't have a roommate. Not only that…did she actually mean tentacles or testicles? My primeval day as a Psychiatric resident ALREADY wasn't adding up and it wasn't even 8AM. My first Psychiatric patient was a paranoid schizophrenic and in retrospect she was my Baptism by fire into the world of the human mind. Her behavior told me everything I needed to know about her condition…she was highly disorganized (but then again no one else pronounces my name right) and she was actively psychotic (delusional and paranoid). I was naive at the time to think I could simply convince her that she had no roommate and that she was safe. Unfortunately, that strategy had about as much chance of success as talking someone out of a heart attack. An increase in her Prolixin however ultimately provided the lucidity she needed. The same cause and effect took place countless times during those educationally formative years for me. It was becoming quite clear that just like any other organ in the human body, the brain could become sick. And just like any other sick organ, it could be medicated. She thankfully improved but still couldn't get the name right. The following week she said she felt safe but insisted that my name was Dr. Alienpolice. At least I wasn't single handedly responsible for "The End of Days" anymore.

My foray into Psychiatry starts even earlier however. Flashback to the early 1970's….1973 to be specific. I was still in my single digits, but I can remember the news maelstrom that surrounded William Friedkin's "The Exorcist" quite clearly. It was an irreverent and terrifying film depicting an alleged demonic possession of a little girl and a Jesuit Priest/Psychiatrist's attempt to help. Their introduction is as follows:

> Father Karras: "Well, then let us introduce ourselves...I'm Damien Karras."
>
> Regan: "…and I'm The Devil!!…now kindly undo these straps!"
>
> Father Karras: "…If you're The Devil, why not make the straps disappear?"

Regan (in a gravelly voice): "That's much too vulgar display of power Karras"

As I watched motionless with my heart palpitating……I felt like my mind was a steel trap…capturing anything that meandered into its orbit. My adrenaline level was so high that I experienced one of the first crystal clear moments of thought clarity I had ever experienced. No disorganized thoughts, no distractibility…just pure concentration. In retrospect, I was experiencing a catecholamine induced reversal of what I'm quite sure is my own attention deficit disorder. Nowadays we give exogenous catecholaminergics (Ritalin and the like) to mimic the same "adrenaline rush" focusing effect. In the attention deficit world...fear is focus, but I digress.

Heretical or not, I was fascinated that this man was designated the task of sorting out schizophrenia from Satan. This movie undoubtedly represented our human struggle in distinguishing the soul from the body. A Shaman physician treats all illnesses as a form of demonic possession; whereas, the modern-day physician never considers the possibility of a body snatching incubus. Clearly, modern day society and conventional Medicine dictates that bodily disease is in fact physiologically driven. If someone we love has a heart attack, is it caused by a demon or more reasonably the logical conclusion of years of nutritional and recreational neglect (or even bad genes)? The latter makes more sense I think. But what about our behavior….in the modern day do we give the brain the same latitude? Not really. We designate bad behavior as either moral insufficiency, reaction to a problematic childhood or "the person needs to deal with their demons". I once listened to a Christian radio station when a person calling in was experiencing the symptoms of a garden variety panic attack. The caller however described it as "spiritual warfare". The host of the show agreed with him and his only sage advice was to "repent". After spitting up a bit in my mouth, I then proceeded to ponder if the show's host had decent malpractice insurance or if Jesus was just going to pony up the lawyer's retainer fee on that one. I'll describe the concept of the "blind leading the blind" later.

The misery (or hell?) experienced by Psychiatric patients must be the MOST overwhelming of all Medical pain as it represents the vast majority of suicides (Chart 1). I think it's because Psychiatric disease, unlike any other Medical illness, alters our sense of "self". The concept of suicide is undoubtedly considered "bad behavior" to many and even considered "evil" by some. This book is about explaining the origins of "bad" behavior in humans and thus we initially need to attempt to understand the difference in the semantic meaning of the words "bad" versus "evil". There are material distinctions between those two terms. Before I delve into talking about that however ...we must first address some basic concepts about the brain and define the word "behavior".

The human brain (including cerebral cortex, subcortical regions, brain stem and cerebellum) (Chart 2) has only three functions. It thinks, it feels and it behaves...that's it. Often times these functions overlap as far as the particular brain anatomy and neurochemistry is concerned. For example, the frontal lobe serves to "feel" and "think" and singular neurochemicals such as dopamine play a role in both "feeling" and "behavior". My definition of BEHAVIOR is the physiological interpretation of the environment and the subsequent physiological response to it. An example of behavior NOT mediated by conscious THINKING is the regulation of body temperature. We physiologically interpret the cold from our skin and it travels to "unconscious" centers in our brain to initiate shivering (heat generation). We don't decide to shiver; it just happens on its own. An example of behavior mediated by conscious THINKING would be if my patient thinks she hears a voice threatening her and subsequently holds a chair over head to defend herself. THINKING is a deliberate set of processes that sizes up a situation (so we can behave appropriately) and is mediated by our own individual capabilities of insight, judgment and calculation. "Thinking" truly varies from person to person as this book will address. And finally, FEELING is the emotional impression that is left in response to the topics we think about. Or in other words, it represents our global sense of well-being at any particular time.

In Psychiatry we deal with all three functions of the brain.... abnormal thinking (ex schizophrenia), abnormal feeling/mood (ex major depression, manic depression) and abnormal behavior (obsessive compulsive disorder). Truth be told.... almost all Psychiatric disorders have elements of all three functional deficits. For instance, manic depressives "feel" moody and have erratic "behavior" (often times due to their irrational and disorganized "thinking"). Neurologists/ Neurosurgeons (two other specialists that treat the brain) will deal much more with the sensory and motor aspects of the brain (illnesses such as multiple sclerosis and cerebral vascular strokes). In addition, they will deal with primary medical causalities of brain dysfunction such as infections or tumors (meningitis or a meningioma). There are exceptions to this distinction but this suffices for now.

Defining "behavior" is easy but defining "evil" is much more difficult. The term "evil" can be defined as any quality or behavior that defies God. The only problem is, there are too many different religions espousing too many different definitions of what God expects from us. Thus, what is considered "evil" to one religion might not be considered "evil" to another. A Christian might say a divorce defies God and therefore may be considered an "evil" sin, but another person may see divorce as a logical conclusion to a ghastly decision in Vegas. The reason we all agreed that Regan (In The Exorcist) might be possessed by an "evil" demon was that the end result of her behavior was unequivocally "anti-God" in that she allegedly threw her caretaker out the window (thou shall not kill). However, she had numerous other behaviors which clearly were "bad" (based on our own sense of moralities) such as urinating on the rug and intentionally vomiting on a priest…. but technically speaking those behaviors are not considered "evil" as there is no verse in doctrine defying them. But if one is a granular hard core Bible thumper, one COULD make the argument she "dishonored" her Mother per the 5th commandment (Honor thy Father and Mother). The only problem with that argument is that's a whole lot of "adding" to the text which Biblically speaking is prohibited (Deuteronomy 4 2…"Ye shall not add unto the word which I command you…"). This type of confusion happens all the time when contemplating "right and wrong" as it pertains to Religious Doctrine.

As we can see, we all unconsciously blur the definition distinguishing "evil" behavior from just "bad behavior". I had a female teenage manic depressive seek an evaluation for agitation and depression after a break-up with her boyfriend. She broke down while she explained how her friend "stole" her ex-boyfriend …….she described her friend as being "evil". Since there is no Biblical law specifically preventing ex-boyfriend stealing, we can start to see that humans loosely use the term "evil" to simply describe a person or person's behavior that is objectionable on a personal level, but not necessarily on a theological one. By using the term "evil", we try to unconsciously convince ourselves (and the listener) that not only do "I" not like this person or person's behavior…. but God doesn't either. It's the ultimate justification for hatred towards others. It's a cheap and dirty attempt to bolster our own ego by condemning our adversary as ALSO an enemy to God. Quite often, people can't get past their own insecurities and as a result, they simply call someone "evil" just because that person is different in some way (race, creed, socio-economics, New England Patriots fan etc.). Everyone likes to think that they are basically good, righteous, and acceptable to God or The Universe....to think otherwise would be a death sentence for our sense of self (ego). As a result, if we as an individual feel we are good (righteous), then anyone different from us must be "bad" (evil) and somehow objectionable to God. You can now see how we quickly we assign the term "evil" to define those we dislike, but also to those who are simply "different" from us as well. I've always said the best way to bring world peace would be to have the Earth be invaded by aliens.... then everyone would feel equally persecuted then hopefully allied. Maybe that's what The Apocalypse is all about.... who knows.

So now we are still left with finding a consensus standard to define "bad behavior" because defining "evil" differs from person to person and religion to religion. "Evil" seems to be a useless term. Unfortunately, the best we can do in defining "bad behavior" is trust our own innate sense of right versus wrong which is loosely defined by how we are raised, the health of the chemicals in our brain, our own spiritual enlightenment, the governmental laws of our land and religious expectations. As a former Medical advisor to The Palm Springs SWAT team.... we have always defined "bad behavior" as anything that gets us a ticket or arrested. It's the only domestically consistent criteria base to define unacceptable behavior. Clearly, we are at the mercy of the sensibilities of current and past law-makers to assist us in defining "bad behavior", but at least we have a starting point. This definition essentially ignores Biblical laws and "human moral codes" as there is profoundly significant inter-religious and inter-individual variability of said standards. As expected and hoped, at least there are several "religious" laws that do overlap with societal ones such as condemnation towards murder (thou shall not murder) and stealing (thou shall not steal).

The word "Apocalypse" comes from the Greek word "to unveil". It is an unveiling of The Truth about God and His judgment towards human kind and its behavior (bad behavior). Satan allegedly also plays a central role in "The End Days". I will attempt to prove that our "bad behavior" has predictable substrates of causality......some chemical and some "spiritual". The vast majority of our bad behavior comes from my Four Horseman of The Apocalypse: Mental Illness, Substance Abuse, Hormones and Flawed Logic. Psychiatric Apocalypse will show how all four of these elements conspire to foment the bad (aka "evil") behavior seen on our planet. If we can make a case that bad (or evil) behavior has reasonable origins, maybe "evil" doesn't exist at all......and neither does Satan. Disproving the existence of Satan would provide a huge step in creating world peace as we could no longer justify any bad behavior, either original or retaliatory, whose intention was to defend Gods providence over "Evil".

In moving forward, it will be important to emphasize that not all Psychiatric conditions will be appropriate for this manuscript. My goal is to only concentrate on Psychiatric disorders that have secretly participated in the deterioration of society both domestically and globally. Conditions such as social phobia, panic disorder, most "alleged" personality disorders, autism, anorexia, bulimia, post-traumatic stress disorder, unipolar major depression, obsessive compulsive disorder and others, may obviously be important to individuals and their loved ones.... but their social/criminal influences are limited. The painful experiences these types of patients suffer through are far more private and limited to the self and loved ones. Also, in my experience, they are not quite as common as previously conceptualized. Chances are, you won't find these conditions on an episode of the TV show "COPS" (a show that showcases bad behavior), unless they are caught self-medicating with illicit drugs. This is in contrast to attention deficit disorder, bipolar disorder (manic depression), and cluster B Axis II personality disorders (narcissism and sociopathy specifically) which all have left a far greater imprint on modern day philosophy and ethos (see Chart 3 of DSM-IV-TR MultiAxial system). The reason is, these later conditions in my opinion are far more prevalent in our population than previously recognized, and their behavioral manifestations bleed more heavily into society. Incidentally, in this manuscript I will be referring to DSM-IV-TR classifications instead of the more recent DSM-V. The newer DSM-V classification system is not that much different from the old one for our purposes.

Many of these un-included conditions are not only not as prevalent as once believed, but several may not even exist. Contrary to the APA's (American Psychiatric Association) DSM-IV-TR, I contend post-traumatic stress disorder (PTSD) (Chart 4) is not even a "real" disorder. It is considered to be a reactive/anxiety disorder that is manifested by flashbacks, exaggerated startle reflex and avoidance behavior as a result of a profoundly stressful event. The problem is, there is a substantial difference inter-individually as to what is considered to be a painful or offending experience. I once had a patient who claimed she had PTSD from her father unintentionally walking in on her while she was dressing. She simply couldn't get over it even after 20 years. I think the overwhelmingly vast majority of PTSD cases have a previous Psychiatric condition that is undiagnosed, and this underlying condition simply exacerbates as a result of the alleged stressful event. Please keep in mind throughout this text that ALL Psychiatric conditions worsen with stress, as do most "physical conditions" (myocardial disease, asthma, psoriasis for example). In this patient's case, she felt much less "traumatized" after I treated her diagnostically presumed obsessive compulsive disorder (OCD) with Lexapro. "Miraculously" her past "post-traumatic stress", which she held onto so obsessively, was no longer interpreted as being so traumatic. As an added benefit, the need to pick her acne also disappeared thus confirming a probable singular diagnosis of OCD (and not PTSD). Alleged PTSD patients may also have a cluster B Axis II personality disorder such as sociopathy or narcissism as these types of patients perpetually see themselves as victims and have very little tolerance for mental discomfort. As a result, they tend to feel easily traumatized and victimized. These patients frequently initiate frivolous law suits as they feel unjustly persecuted by everyone AND by life in general. They don't have the "mental" tools to comprehend that life is "post traumatic" by nature. Perhaps PTSD might be a legitimate diagnosis in an extraordinary case of an individual actually watching a loved one die violently, but I still maintain this is a well over-diagnosed condition that drains our insurance/entitlement systems and more importantly, masquerades the true nature (and diagnosis) of a patient.

The vast majority of personality disorders may not even exist either (except sociopathy, narcissism and dependent personality). Reasons for this will be addressed in the chapter "Born as a Beast". Of all the well-known personality disorders, I will most notably adjust the definition of the so called "borderline personality disorder" defined by Adolf Stern in 1938 who described impulsive, mood labile, identity disturbed patients as being on the "borderline" of neurosis and psychosis. Glenn Close made the condition famous in her bunny boiling role in "Fatal Attraction". This is an enigmatic disorder that just might combine both chemical and "spiritual" deficiencies as I will later discuss.

Chart 1

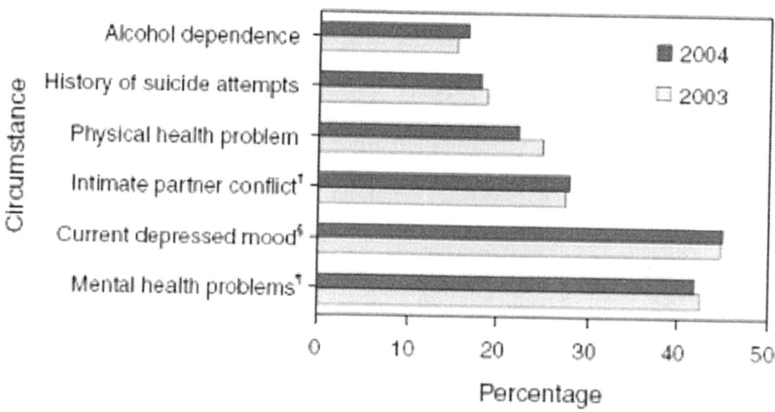

* Percentages might total to more than 100% because certain incidents involve multiple circumstances.

† Includes separation, major argument, or violence.

§ Current depressed mood was based on the family or friends' impression of the decedent's mood.

¶ Includes any mental illness diagnosis of the decedent (e.g., clinical depression, dysthymia, bipolar disorder, or schizophrenia).

Graph showing circumstances that contributed to suicide cases in 2003 and 2004

Chart 2

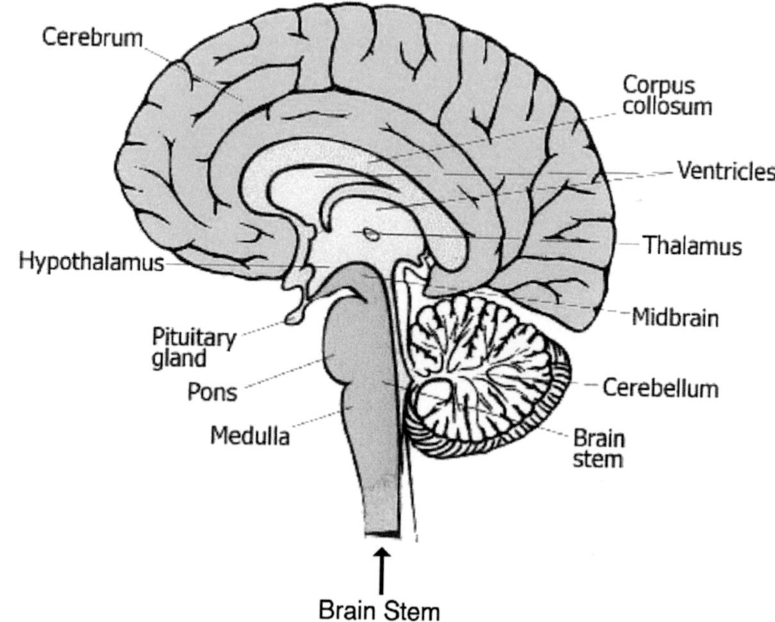

Chart 3

DSM (Diagnostic and Statistical Manual of Mental Disorders) -IV-TR: Multiaxial Assessment System (2000-2013)

(Note: As of 2013, the APA [American Psychiatric Association] has replaced the DSM-IV-TR with the DSM 5. It combines the first 3 axes into a single non axial system. The change was probably made for coding (billing) improvements and ease of clinical diagnostics/care. For purposes of this book, we will still refer to this axial system as it helps delineate between "chemical" and "spiritual" disorders. The APA no longer endorses this "multiaxial system" and for all intents and purposes does not codify diagnoses of "spirituality". I'm on my own on this one).

Axis I: Major mental and learning disorders. (ex. depression, bipolar disorder, ADHD, phobias, schizophrenia, anxiety, etc).

Axis II: Conditions of personality and mental retardation. (ex. antisocial personality disorder, narcissistic personality disorder, dependant personality disorder etc)

Axis III: Physical disorders and acute medical conditions (ex. meningioma, , meningitis, traumatic brain injury etc)

Axis IV. Psychosocial and environmental factors contributing to the clinical presentation.

Axis V. Global assessment of functioning (a numerical value reflecting functionality (0 - 100)

Chart 4

DSM-IV & DSM-IV-TR: Posttraumatic Stress Disorder (PTSD)

When an individual who has been exposed to a traumatic event develops anxiety symptoms, reexperiencing of the event, and avoidance of stimuli related to the event lasting more than four weeks, they may be suffering from this Anxiety Disorder.

Diagnostic criteria for 309.81 Posttraumatic Stress Disorder
(cautionary statement)

A. The person has been exposed to a traumatic event in which both of the following were present:

(1) the person experienced, witnessed, or was confronted with an event or events that involved actual or threatened death or serious injury, or a threat to the physical integrity of self or others
(2) the person's response involved intense fear, helplessness, or horror. **Note:** In children, this may be expressed instead by disorganized or agitated behavior

B. The traumatic event is persistently reexperienced in one (or more) of the following ways:

(1) recurrent and intrusive distressing recollections of the event, including images, thoughts, or perceptions. **Note:** In young children, repetitive play may occur in which themes or aspects of the trauma are expressed.
(2) recurrent distressing dreams of the event. **Note:** In children, there may be frightening dreams without recognizable content.

Chart 4 (continued)

(3) acting or feeling as if the traumatic event were recurring (includes a sense of reliving the experience, illusions, hallucinations, and dissociative flashback episodes, including those that occur on awakening or when intoxicated). **Note:** In young children, trauma-specific reenactment may occur.
(4) intense psychological distress at exposure to internal or external cues that symbolize or resemble an aspect of the traumatic event
(5) physiological reactivity on exposure to internal or external cues that symbolize or resemble an aspect of the traumatic event

C. Persistent avoidance of stimuli associated with the trauma and numbing of general responsiveness (not present before the trauma), as indicated by three (or more) of the following:

(1) efforts to avoid thoughts, feelings, or conversations associated with the trauma
(2) efforts to avoid activities, places, or people that arouse recollections of the trauma
(3) inability to recall an important aspect of the trauma
(4) markedly diminished interest or participation in significant activities
(5) feeling of detachment or estrangement from others
(6) restricted range of affect (e.g., unable to have loving feelings)
(7) sense of a foreshortened future (e.g., does not expect to have a career, marriage, children, or a normal life span)

D. Persistent symptoms of increased arousal (not present before the trauma), as indicated by two (or more) of the following:

(1) difficulty falling or staying asleep
(2) irritability or outbursts of anger
(3) difficulty concentrating
(4) hypervigilance
(5) exaggerated startle response

E. Duration of the disturbance (symptoms in Criteria B, C, and D) is more than 1 month.

F. The disturbance causes clinically significant distress or impairment in social, occupational, or other important areas of functioning.

Specify if:

Acute: if duration of symptoms is less than 3 months
Chronic: if duration of symptoms is 3 months or more

Specify if:

With Delayed Onset: if onset of symptoms is at least 6 months after the stressor

Chapter 2

THOU SHALL NOT BE BORED

Attention deficit disorder (ADD) and attention deficit hyperactivity disorder (ADHD) are essentially the same condition (Chart 1). As per the DSM-IV-TR, both of these Psychiatric conditions symptomatically present in childhood and are manifested by inattentiveness and impulsivity, but ADHD is associated with these qualities plus hyperactivity. Interestingly, ADHD fetuses are frequently "hyperactive" in the womb and tend to be profound "kickers" in utero. This early "mobility" also translates into earlier than expected walking and talking compared to age appropriate peers (now we know who ends up being child actors 1-4 years old!). In reality, there is a spectrum of presentation with ADD/ADHD patients, and it is up to the diagnostician to decide which diagnosis is most accurate. Regardless, treatment is generally the same as we will address later.

The story of ADD/ADHD starts in our DNA. It is a highly genetic condition to the extent that if a child has the condition....in my opinion it's almost 100% certain that one of the parents has it as well. Just as we inherit our facial features from our parents, we also inherit the chemicals in our brain. Now remember, if you ever read an article stating that maternal "substance abuse" (such as cigarette smoking while pregnant) CAUSES ADD/ADHD in their children, the truth is that the mother already had the condition for which she self-medicated with that nicotine in the cigarette (nicotine helps focus). The nicotine exposure didn't cause the child to have the condition, but the mother's genes did (which she in turn passed onto child). The faulty gene (or genes) causes disruptions in the management of chemicals norepinephrine, epinephrine and dopamine in the pre-frontal cortex of the brain and related sub cortical structures (Chart 2). Simply put, the front of the brain which manages focus and alertness doesn't work properly. As a result of this chemical derangement.... we feel bored (under stimulated). ADD/ADHD is based on boredom. If you have a child who frequently uses the term "bored" or "boredom" to describe how he/she routinely feels.... think ADD/ADHD. Having a sense of boredom foments numerous symptoms of this condition including inattentiveness, poor focus, procrastination, distractibility and day dreaming. All of these will contribute to poor school and social performance. Impatience is another sign of boredom. Impatient kids often can't wait their turn and impatient adults while driving their cars usually tailgate, weave in and out of traffic, and speed. I saw a lot of ADD "ticketing" when patrolling with The Palm Springs Police Department (I can tell they were ADD by the rate of their speech…more to come).

Now, for some reason, not all ADD patients have symptoms of hyperactivity. However, they all tend to have racing thoughts. These racing thoughts in ADD children might simply cause fidgetiness as seen in the kid sitting down who's foot just won't stop bobbing, or in ADHD patients who are patently hyperactive. One can easily observe racing thoughts by the rate of an ADD/ADHD's speech. They tend to be "motor mouths" and "chatty Cathy's". Racing thoughts can also promote sleep initiation problems ("Night owling" [staying up late]). This can wreak havoc with an ADD's daily functioning as it tends to compromise a full night's sleep. They also can be quite difficult to awaken in the morning.

As the hyperactive kids grow up, their hyperkinesis tends to become less of a problem but they can become more irritable instead. It's almost as if their physical hyperactivity transforms into chaotic mental hyperactivity (perceived as irritability). This irritability, racy thinking and unchanged inattentiveness, continue to alter focus well into adulthood and participate in the patient's sense of daily overwhelment, especially when chronically stressed. Nobody outgrows ADD/ADHD…they just at a minimum become less hyperactive. As will be a constant theme throughout this book, when our thoughts are disorganized, racy or generally not in order, we tend to feel helpless, out of control and terribly unsettled. We will never make good, qualified decisions when we are in these states. I guess you could say we could make "evil" decisions.

ADD/ADHD's are also quite impulsive. Impulsivity is defined as "doing without thinking". Since ADD/ADHD's have compromised patterns of thinking, they tend to make very impulsive decisions (such as faulty business ventures, suspect marital decisions or criminal behavior) that tend to further complicate their lives. When these patient's conditions are finally improved by medications, they often require psychotherapy to make sense of a lifetime of bad decisions (and bad behavior) generated by these unfettered thoughts. To make matters worse, these patients as they progress through life, occasionally present to the mental health professional with primary complaints of depression. The reasoning is as follows. If one can't focus, then one can't complete projects. And if one can't complete projects then one tends to fail at project completion. Perpetual failure results in being endlessly scolded by teachers, parents, bosses and self. This in turn leads to feelings of hopelessness and depression. If an ADD/ADHD is not properly medicated, and they have repeated failures.....they also become "paralyzed" by a fear of failure and hence stop trying. Homer Simpson from "The Simpsons" said it best..."Trying is the first step towards failure."

Often times these patients are not pharmacologically treated properly because this symptom of depression is taken at face value, and chemically inappropriate antidepressants are prescribed. Unfortunately, when these patients don't respond to antidepressant therapy (they aren't pharmacologically depressed) they again feel like failures. Even worse however, is that the original condition is still left untreated. These kinds of repetitive personal failures pillage an ADD/ADHD child's developing sense of self-esteem. I've evaluated countless adult ADD/ADHD patients who simply can't remember their childhood as they have unconsciously deleted their uncomfortable life's memories secondary to the mental pain associated with them. This forgetfulness of childhood could also be a direct result of the ADD/ADHD itself as well.... if one can't focus, then one can't encode the information for future memory. Many ADD/ADHD's use copious post it notes and "lists" to combat this memory problem.

Another frequent scenario for many ADD/ADHD's is that their ego is so fragile from repeated failures, that they are simply too embarrassed to talk about their self-perceived insufficiencies when conversing with their physician. They feel stupid and don't feel like advertising it. Either way, the cycle of non-treatment worsens upon itself as now the detective (the Psychiatrist) does not have the proper historical facts to work with secondary to the patient's amnesia of the facts or embarrassment to talk about them.

Many people disregard ADD/ADHD as a legitimate Psychiatric condition and their argument usually sounds like this, "well, how can my kid have ADD if he focuses just fine on that Nintendo game". To answer this, please recall my experience watching The Exorcist in Chapter 1. Each individual has a unique repertoire of activities or interests that naturally fascinate and excite them. One person might like golf whereas another person could be horrifyingly bored by it. When we find an activity that interests us, we tend to have an adrenaline rush which originates from our adrenal glands located on top of our kidneys. When this occurs, epinephrine (adrenaline), dopamine and norepinephrine (noradrenaline) (all collectively known as catecholamines: Chart 3) are released by the adrenal glands and bolster the deficient catecholamine activity in the frontal lobe as previously discussed. When this happens, we focus. Simultaneously, systemic adrenaline is perfusing our heart and skeletal muscle to increase blood pressure, heart rate and muscle oxygenation (as I experienced watching the movie). Interestingly, ADD/ADHD patients will sometimes OVER focus on activities to the point where they act obsessively. It's a consequence of too much adrenaline causing too much interest. Obsessiveness is defined as "too much thinking when making decisions" which is the exact opposite of impulsivity ("too little thinking when making decisions"). In essence, ADD and OCD are the exact opposite of each other chemically.

In an attempt to feel less racy, less confused and more organized, ADD/ADHD's will unconsciously choose activities that manufacture these focus inducing adrenaline rushes. Unfortunately, this is quite frequently associated with risky behavior such as dare-deviling, gambling or otherwise reckless pursuits that ultimately result in "bad behavior". This bad negligent behavior often ends up with an injury, an arrest or a detention. However, not all is lost. This sense of need for adrenaline clearly helps us decide what type of profession is most suitable. Without ADD/ADHD, professions such as piloting, military/fire/police, news reporters, extreme athletes (skiers, car racers, x-games), CEO's, disc jockeys and stock brokers would all be at jeopardy. Yours truly for the most part was chronically under stimulated in Medical School and found solace in only 2 specialties.... Emergency Medicine (an ADD's dream.... lots of excitement that's always changing) and Psychiatry (you never know when you'll get The Universe's second best interview...Satan, like in The Exorcist. This is a fear producing yet potentially adrenalizing thought to most).

ADD/ADHD is the only Psychiatric condition that has temporary remission of symptoms with this ACUTE stress (stress=fear=adrenaline), whereas all other Psychiatric conditions worsen with stress. I'm sure there are plenty of readers out there who only could address term papers or studying for tests when "under the gun" (aka cramming) and now you know why. The fear of failing got your brain working. The caveat to this story however is that PROTRACTED stress typically causes WORSENING of ADD/ADHD symptoms resulting in disorganized thoughts (look at all the half-done projects), irritability (look at everyone avoiding you) and worsening sleep patterns from increasingly racing thoughts (look at the bags under your eyes).

In seeking treatment for ADD/ADHD, a Psychiatric or Pediatric exam is recommended to size up the situation in its totality, combining the knowledge base of both physical and mental health disciplines. In doing so, much can be accomplished including ruling out any other Medical explanations for the symptoms (hypothyroidism, lead poisoning), teasing out coexisting Psychiatric conditions (which affects treatment options) and determining if the ADD/ADHD exists at all, and if so, to what degree (having the condition is not an all or nothing proposition). Not all ADD/ADHD variants require medications. Strategies for those cases include stress reduction through psychotherapy or children's play therapy. Don't forget, chronic stress worsens every Psychiatric condition and the majority of Medical conditions. Unfortunately, younger children have difficulty "self-observing" and making sense of their stress.... it's easier with adults. I'm far more likely to medicate a child presenting with ADD/ADHD as opposed to an adult. Adults can pick and choose their environments and tailor them to their needs in order to reduce stress. They also can pick the vocational pursuits that interest them. A child, on the other hand, is forced to complete "general" studies of which one class might promote excitement (an adrenaline rush), but another promote boredom.

It should be of no surprise that the chemicals we use to focus naturally, such as dopamine, epinephrine and norepinephrine, are the lynchpin of medicinal treatment as well. Medicinal stimulants enhance these catecholamines in our system and can be sorted out into amphetamine based (Dexedrine, Adderall, Adderall XR, Vyvanse) and Methylphenidate based (Focalin, Focalin XR, Ritalin, Ritalin SR, Ritalin LA, Metadate CD, Metadate ER, Concerta, Daytrana) (Chart 4). Although they all act to enhance catecholamine activity in the brain, they do so differently. In my experience, amphetamine based drugs are more potent (less is needed for the same effect).

A physician picks his/her initial medication based typically upon comfort with its use. I find most patients or parents become frustrated with the medications (and the Psychiatric process) due to the length of time between dosage changes and the perceived lack of effect. As long as the patient is healthy with good cardiac status, I see no reason to waste time between dosage increases. Aggressive dosing however should be avoided in patients taking other medications, those who are medically complicated, or the elderly. When starting stimulants, for the most part, whatever response is observed from the medication on day 1 is pretty much the response you will have on day 10. It doesn't take days or weeks for stimulants to "kick in", that's a fallacy. Now, once the appropriate dosage for that particular person is achieved....one will see an immediate effect. Psychiatry has had a bad "rap" in the past for not improving patients, but I find the unnecessarily lengthy medication changes does not promote noticeable changes for the patient and they subsequently give up on the process. Physicians quite frequently are apprehensive to raise dosages quickly as this is not part of the pharmaceutical company's insert protocol. Subsequently, physicians don't want to be sued if something goes awry during a rapid dose titration. The problem is, if a conservative dose escalation is employed, Junior may be on the medication for 3 months and still no-one can tell a difference. A quick phone call on day 1 to the patient can ascertain improvement, non-improvement or side effects. If there is no improvement and are no side effects...the patient should increase the medication the next day per physician specification. This process of upward titration can be adjusted daily, but modestly, until there is a remission of symptoms or development of side effects. If there is a remission of symptoms...... care should be taken to make sure the entire day is symptom free which may require a second (or third) dose. Remission of symptoms means "calm and focused." "Irritable and focused" doesn't count! That usually means the patient has a second condition (anxiety disorder or bipolar) or the stimulant preparation they are using doesn't agree with them.

Side effects of stimulants can include nausea, irritability, sedation, decreased appetite, weight loss, headache, or insomnia. If a patient is sedated with a stimulant (and that applies to cocaine, crystal methamphetamine, and caffeine use too) ......that's a good sign that the patient has uncomplicated ADD/ADHD and has an excellent chance of improvement with the right dose of prescribed stimulant medication. Failing 3 or 4 stimulants for reasons other than fatigue means a new diagnosis should be entertained. But before one gives up on a stimulant, be certain caffeine (coffee, tea, colas, Mountain Dew, chocolate, energy drinks etc.) hasn't been co-administered. The combination may alter the medication trial outcome secondary to irritability. If a prescribed stimulant has been successful in the past but is already at a maximum dosage, augmentation with a "stimulating" antidepressant such as Wellbutrin (IR, SR, XL), Effexor (IR/XR), Pristiq, Strattera, Provigil or Nuvigil can be a powerful tool for symptom resolution. Only Strattera is FDA approved for ADD/ADHD however. The others are FDA approved for depression (Wellbutrin, Effexor, Pristiq) and daytime fatigue (Provigil, Nuvigil) but not ADD/ADHD. Please keep in mind that just because a medication is not FDA approved for a particular condition, that doesn't mean it won't work. However, there are legal and insurance company ramifications for the physician in the event they are tried and an untoward event occurs.

The purpose of briefly spelling out treatment objectives is three-fold. Firstly, it illustrates that ADD/ADHD is chemically based and not a result of a moral or spiritual deficiency. Secondly, it also should illustrate that Psychiatry is tricky business. Not only does the correct diagnosis need to be made, but also other conditions need to be ruled out as causality or having co-morbidity. Once that's done, the correct medication (or combination of medications) needs to be chosen and given at the proper time in a dosage which isn't too large or too small. The medication needs to be compatible with the other medications the patient might be taking, must not exacerbate another medical condition the patient might have, and the effect of the medication needs to remain consistent despite the ebbs and flows of the condition itself. And Thirdly, it helps legitimize the point that if the medications we prescribe help the patient feel better.... it's not a reach to imagine that ADHD'ers haphazardly stumble upon various illicit and potentially harmful recreational substances to help them feel better as well (illicit drugs).

Imagine that you suffered from the physical symptoms of nasal congestion, insomnia and itchy eyes (aka environmental allergies). Let's say hypothetically that you went to your local store and bought some Mylanta (an antacid). If you used it, you would quickly discover it wouldn't relieve your symptoms and you would in turn discontinue it. The next day if you went back to the store, but this time bought St John's Wort (a naturopathic antidepressant), you would again realize this would also fail to promote improvement and you would discontinue it. Finally, if you sauntered back to the store a third time, but bought and tried some Benadryl (an antihistamine) your symptoms would quickly resolve and my guess is you would continue to use the Benadryl that day...and the next ....and the next. This is the nature of substance abuse. Each Psychiatric condition has a unique imbalance of brain chemicals which makes patients feel poorly. In order to feel "normal", they routinely experiment with drugs and substances and quite frequently stumble onto one or two that temporarily "normalize" their brains. It therefore should not be a stretch of the imagination that if we know the drugs that the patient likes to abuse, we can work backwards and have a very good idea what the initial Psychiatric condition might be. A proper diagnosis in turn guides treatment and subsequently improves the outcome for the patient.

This phenomenon occurs quite frequently with ADD/ADHD patients. These patients are attracted to and tend to abuse stimulating substances such as cocaine, crystal methamphetamine, nicotine (cigarettes, chew tobacco, cigars) and caffeine (coffee, energy drinks, DARK chocolate, tea) to improve their focus and racing thoughts. The term "energy drink" is a misnomer and it should probably be called a "focus drink". One can routinely peg an ADD/ADHD early in the exam by the color of their teeth. Years of dark caffeinated colas, coffee and cigarettes routinely cause a dingy yellow color to the enamel. ADD/ADHD patients also can OCCASIONALLY be abusers of alcohol and marijuana as well. It's usually a vicious cycle. The ADD/ADHD uses copious amounts of stimulant in the first half of the day to improve their focus, but EXCESSIVE dosing can tend to worsen anxiety by the end of the day. As a result of overshooting the right dosage to focus, they end up using "depressive" type chemicals such as alcohol or marijuana later in the day to calm down and sleep. This is especially true if they suffer from a coexisting Psychiatric disorder such as anxiety or bipolar disorder. Ironically and unfortunately, alcohol in particular tends to worsen memory and focus the NEXT day, which in turn promotes more stimulant abuse.

So, as you can see, ADD/ADHD causes numerous "evil" problems for individuals and society in general. The baseline condition causes dysregulations in behavior as manifested by impulsivity (generically bad decisions such as traffic accidents and inappropriate spending), inattentiveness (injuries to self and others while operating heavy machinery) and thrill seeking behavior (gambling and criminality). This bad behavior is also exacerbated by chronic substance abuse as illustrated by the above self-medication algorithm. Not only can the use of these substances cause further alterations in behavior and sensorium through toxicity, but they also cause extensive medical issues such as cardiac problems seen with cocaine and liver problems seen with alcohol. Furthermore, many of these substances are illegal which can result in the further deterioration of society through arrest and incarceration.

The next logical question would be "aren't the medications you give just as dangerous as the drugs they abuse". The answer is yes and no. Cocaine and Ritalin have similar modes of action as do methamphetamine and amphetamine. The difference however lies in four domains. Firstly, drug addicts usually snort, inhale or inject their illicit drugs. This delivers far greater toxic concentrations to the brain. Whereas in Psychiatry, we use slow release gastric absorption preparations or a patch (Daytrana). Secondly, the amounts used by drug abusers are substantially larger (100 mg-5000 mg) compared to medicinal dosages starting at 5mg daily potentially as high as 60mg of Ritalin equivalent (sometimes higher if the patient is a "rapid metabolizer"). Thirdly, drug abusers alter their illicit chemicals to increase the rate it is absorbed by the brain. Cocaine users "freebase", and meth labs "methylate" to produce products that readily transport through the blood brain barrier and increase the "high". Finally, abused substances can have toxic "fillers" such as lidocaine, ephedrine and cyanide. On the other hand, medications prescribed by a physician are approved by the FDA for purity. In short, if the physician screens the patient carefully for initial health (no cardiac instability or history of stroke) and the patient takes the medications as prescribed (method and dosage) …there shouldn't be a problem. Instead of people being deterred from proper ADD/ADHD treatment due to potential side effects of taking the medications…. patients and parents should also be balancing out "the side effects" of NOT taking the medications as well (Chart 5. Barkley. Biederman).

Many people also assert that medications are unhealthy due to the fact that they are "not natural" …. I hear that one all the time. With that logic, consuming arsenic and cyanide shouldn't be a problem because they are both natural …. right? Nope…. that's flawed logic and natural substances are not always healthy for us. From a personal perspective, If I don't wear my synthetic contact lenses to treat my God given nearsightedness, I can't drive or function properly in my personal/professional life. Should I not wear them because they are not natural?

Chart 1

DSM-IV & DSM-IV-TR: Attention-Deficit/Hyperactivity Disorder (ADHD)

When problems with attention, hyperactivity, and impulsiveness develop in childhood and persist, in some cases into adulthood, this mental disorder may be diagnosed.

Diagnostic criteria for Attention-Deficit/Hyperactivity Disorder
(cautionary statement)

A. Either (1) or (2):
(1) *inattention:* six (or more) of the following symptoms of inattention have persisted for at least 6 months to a degree that is maladaptive and inconsistent with developmental level:
(a) often fails to give close attention to details or makes careless mistakes in schoolwork, work, or other activities
(b) often has difficulty sustaining attention in tasks or play activities
(c) often does not seem to listen when spoken to directly
(d) often does not follow through on instructions and fails to finish school work, chores, or duties in the workplace (not due to oppositional behavior or failure to understand instructions)
(e) often has difficulty organizing tasks and activities
(f) often avoids, dislikes, or is reluctant to engage in tasks that require sustained mental effort (such as schoolwork or homework)
(g) often loses things necessary for tasks or activities (e.g., toys, school assignments, pencils, books, or tools)
(h) is often easily distracted by extraneous stimuli
(i) is often forgetful in daily activities

(2) *hyperactivity-impulsivity:* six (or more) of the following symptoms of hyperactivity-impulsivity have persisted for at least 6 months to a degree that is maladaptive and inconsistent with developmental level:

Hyperactivity
(a) often fidgets with hands or feet or squirms in seat
(b) often leaves seat in classroom or in other situations in which remaining seated is
(c) often runs about or climbs excessively in situations in which it is inappropriate (in adolescents or adults, may be limited to subjective feelings of restlessness)
(d) often has difficulty playing or engaging in leisure activities quietly
(e) is often "on the go" or often acts as if "driven by a motor"
(f) often talks excessively

Impulsivity
(g) often blurts out answers before questions have been completed
(h) often has difficulty awaiting turn
(i) often interrupts or intrudes on others (e.g., butts into conversations or games)

B. Some hyperactive-impulsive or inattentive symptoms that caused impairment were present before age 7 years.

Chart 1 (continued)

C. Some impairment from the symptoms is present in two or more settings (e.g., at school [or work] and at home).

D. There must be clear evidence of clinically significant impairment in social, academic, or occupational functioning.

E. The symptoms do not occur exclusively during the course of a Pervasive Developmental Disorder, Schizophrenia, or other Psychotic Disorder and are not better accounted for by another mental disorder (e.g., Mood Disorder, Anxiety Disorder, Dissociative Disorders, or a Personality Disorder).

Code based on type:

314.01 Attention-Deficit/Hyperactivity Disorder, Combined Type: if both Criteria A1 and A2 are met for the past 6 months
314.00 Attention-Deficit/Hyperactivity Disorder, Predominantly Inattentive Type: if Criterion A1 is met but Criterion A2 is not met for the past 6 months
314.01 Attention-Deficit/Hyperactivity Disorder, Predominantly Hyperactive-Impulsive Type: if Criterion A2 is met but Criterion A1 is not met for the past 6 months
Coding note: For individuals (especially adolescents and adults) who currently have symptoms that no longer meet full criteria, "In Partial Remission" should be specified.

Also: ADD, ADHD, hyperkinetic child syndrome, hyperkinetic reaction of childhood, minimal brain damage, minimal cerebral dysfunction, minor cerebral dysfunction

Chart 2

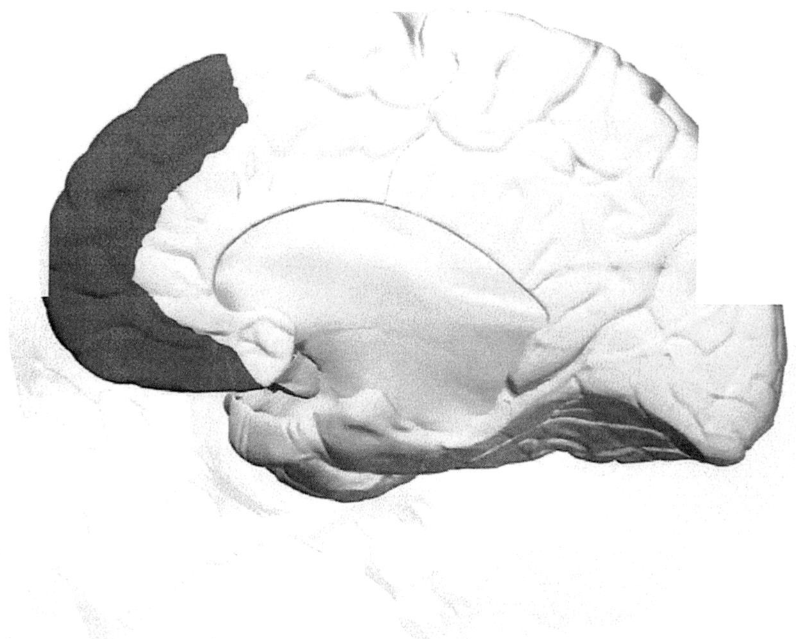

Medial view.

Polygon data were generated by Database Center for Life Science(DBCLS) [2]. - Polygon data are from BodyParts3D[1]

Prefrontal cortex of left cerebral hemisphere. Shown in red.

Permission details

Chart 3

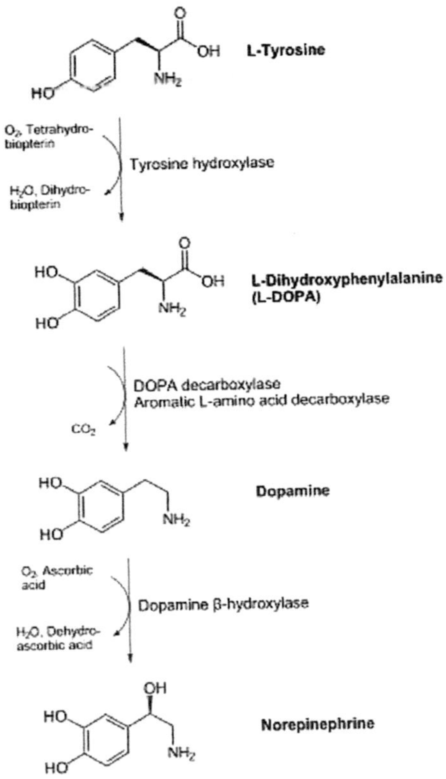

L-Tyrosine

O_2, Tetrahydro-biopterin

H_2O, Dihydro-biopterin

Tyrosine hydroxylase

L-Dihydroxyphenylalanine (L-DOPA)

DOPA decarboxylase
Aromatic L-amino acid decarboxylase

CO_2

Dopamine

O_2, Ascorbic acid

H_2O, Dehydro-ascorbic acid

Dopamine β-hydroxylase

Norepinephrine

The biosynthesis of adrenaline involves a series of enzymatic reactions.

NEUROtiker - own work

Biosynthesis of catecholamines adrenaline (epinephrine) and noradrenaline (norepinephrine), intermediates DOPA and dopamine

Permission details

Chart 4

ADD/ADHD Medication List

Levoamphetamine class: Adzenys XR ODT, Evekeo (rarely used)

Dextroamphetamine/ Levoamphetamine (mixed salts) class: Adderall, Adderal XR

Dextroamphetamine class: Dexedrine

Methylphenidate class: Ritalin, Ritalin SR, Ritalin LA, Methylin, Methylin ER, Metadate CD, Metadate ER, Concerta, Daytrana Patch

"Dextro" methylphenidate class: Focalin, Focalin XR (Dexmethylphenidate)

Non Stimulant Antidepressant class: Strattera (Atomoxetine)

Non Stimulant Alpha 2 Agonist class: Clonidine (Kapvay), Guanfacine (Intuniv)

Non Stimulant Histamine Agonist class (non FDA approved): Nuvigil/Provigil

Non Stimulant Antidepressant class (non FDA approved): Wellbutrin/Effexor/Effexor XR/ Pristiq/Imipramine/Desipramine/ Other Tricyclics /Fetzima?/ Cymbalta?

Chart 5

Why treat ADHD?

Functional Impairment in Patients with ADHD

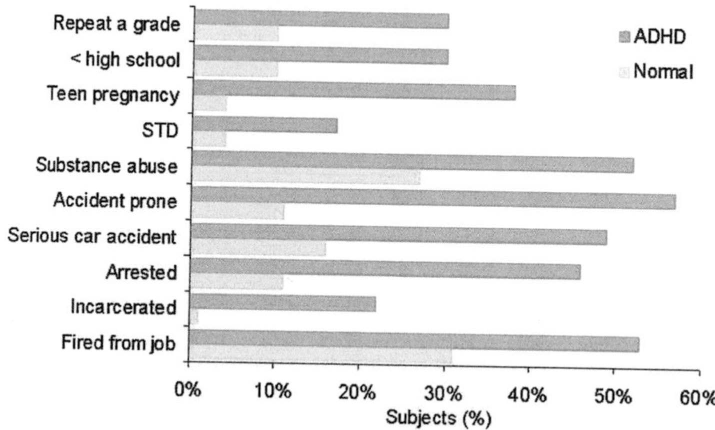

Barkley RA. *Attention-Deficit Hyperactivity Disorder. A Handbook for Diagnosis and Treatment*, 1998. Barkley RA, et al. *JAACAP*. 1990;29:546-557. Biederman J, et al. *Arch Gen Psychiatry*. 1996;53:437–446. Weiss et al. *J Am Acad Child Psychiatry*. 1985;24:211-220. Satterfield, Schell. *JAACAP*. 1997;36:1726-1735. Biederman J, et al. *Am J Psychiatry*. 1995;152:1652-1658.

Chapter 3

JOHN'S NEW REVELATION: ADRENALINE BEGETS THE WEST

I always wondered why the youngest of all the Earth's prominent migratory regions (The United States) has technologically evolved at a rate eclipsing regions that had a 2-Million-year head start (like North East Africa and The Middle East). Clearly, over the last 400 years, "The New World" has spawned the planet's most prized inventions such as the light bulb, computer/semiconductor technology, the airplane, the telephone and the modern automobile. As a result, monumental advancements in medicine, transportation, engineering, communications systems, military and commerce just to name a few, were fueled by The New World's innovative processes. Only America's NASA could have pulled off the picture on the cover of this book......"Venus transit of The Sun on 6/6/12".... are you kidding me?... people in The Middle East still live in mud huts for God's sake. How did the "new kid on the block" precipitate so much change and influence on the world landscape? Look no further than our human prefrontal cortex.

The people that initially migrated from "older" regions to "newer" regions have for years been termed "explorers". One could also define an "explorer" as an "adventurer" which in turn could be called a "risk taker" or a "gambler". As we discussed, ADD/ADHD's are legendary risk takers that actually perform better with fear. In order for a person to hop on a boat bound for an unknown place with an unknown conclusion……clearly that person practices a sense of reckless abandon that is a hallmark of ADD/ADHD. This adrenaline rush craved by ADD/ADHD's tends to obviate the sense of boredom and inattentiveness that is seen in the condition. As I mentioned in the beginning of the book, to have unfettered thoughts like this is a fairly uncomfortable state of being. This "risk taking" therefore tends to pacify the ADD/ADHD brain. It's a form of endogenous self-medication. So, in summation, what we are demonstrating here is a concept that the people that emigrated out of the "older places" and immigrated into the "newer places" were ADD/ADHD!

The risk taking demonstrated by these explorers also represents an element of impulsivity as well. Impulsivity is defined as "doing without thinking". If an early explorer was to truly think out all the possible uncertainties and outcomes of a boat ride to nowhere, it's more than likely that this person wouldn't take the trip. Impulsivity (thinking too little) is the opposite of obsessiveness (thinking too much). As a result, the obsessives or anxiety prone people probably stayed behind. Of note, epidemiological studies show a lower prevalence of ADD/ADHD in African Americans in the US (Footnote 1). This makes perfect sense as the original Africans brought to this country were not of the "explorer" ADHD variety.... but rather represented a VARIETY of Psychiatric genetics as they were brought against their will through slavery. However, current epidemiologic studies also possibly show lower ADD rates in Africa itself (Footnote 2) thus ADD/ADHD genes may be lower in Africans in general. The other possibility is that they counted an African population who has since lost many of its ADD's via modern day post slavery emigration preferentially to other countries.

Now, back to the US. Once all these ADD/ADHD's arrived to The New World…true innovation was about to take place. The explorers brought their ADD/ADHD genes with them, they procreated with other ADD/ADHD's, and produced magnificent strains of more severe cases of the condition (Biederman has confirmed this differential distribution in the US…Footnote 3). A more severe case means that a greater amount of boredom is experienced and thus a greater chance the person will behave in a more "extreme way" (to produce an adrenaline rush which makes them feel normalized). Luke Aikins jumped from 25000 feet without a parachute into a tiny net on 7/31/16. This unofficially makes him in my opinion the most ADD person on the planet! The bigger the risk, the bigger the ADD.

The extreme behavior of ADD/ADHD can range from the very bad or unfavorable (criminal behavior such as battery, stealing or recklessness) to the very favorable (innovations and business risk taking). With all these increasing cases of ADD/ADHD's in the US…there should be no surprise that The US quite logically became the cocaine capital of the world (Chart 1). It was a collective attempt to self-medicate the focus problem. On another chart, we also see similarly that the US would lead the world in tobacco usage (Chart 2). Interestingly, more ancient cultures such as The Middle East and China have less usage of these substances (particularly cocaine) due to Attention Deficit DEPLETION. Coca Cola was a huge domestic hit undoubtedly due to the original ingredients of cocaine and caffeine which quenched our domestic craving for focus.

Once in the US, the more "severe" cases of ADD/ADHD then continued "the adrenaline RUSH" by migrating FURTHER West to California via the Mid-West during the allurement of The Gold RUSH. It's also quite possible that Florida was also a magnet for the condition as I will discuss later. As time progressed, more and more of the MOST severe ADD/ADHD's flocked westward as a reaction of feeling bored and or dissatisfied with wherever they lived previously (whether from another country or the Eastern areas of the US). California's entertainment industry and "extreme" recreation options (beautiful whether, "the beautiful people", endless outdoor activities) were now the draw. Just as we can follow the ADD/ADHD trail to the US via its cocaine consumption.... we see a similar inordinate consumption of crystal methamphetamine on the west coast compared to the east coast (presumably from a higher incidence of ADD/ADHD as well) (Chart 3). We can further make sense of the craving for "energy drinks" (Red Bull, Monster) as another proxy for ADD/ADHD migration. Once again, they are best termed "focus drinks". The US quite predictably originated these caffeinated drinks due to the obvious domestic demand, but I wouldn't be surprised if the west was the leading consumer per capita. "Google trends" is an application of Google that allows one to determine the frequency and origination/location of a particular Googled term. Monster Drink is an "energy drink" and if the former term is applied to Google trends...one learns that the top four areas of inquiry are in fact on the west coast (Chart 4). This is not surprising at all...west coasters crave their focus and they know where to look to find it. Starbucks Coffee if you think about it WAS DESTINED to originate in Seattle. It's a west coast city thus the ADD/ADHD's used their product for focus, and the lack of sunshine drove the dark sensitive depressives to crave it for mood regulation (will discuss sunlight issues later). It's a perfect storm. I think we can all officially say farewell to the explanation that The Devil is responsible for substance abuse. Illicit drug abuse is not a Satanic temptation.... it's a chemical craving.

California clearly has given us all the clues that it is the attention deficit capital of the world. It is the "newest" of "The New World". ADD/ADHD's are inattentive and tend to be very forgetful. This would explain why Californians are seen as being "flaky". The condition also renders people bored which would explain all of the extreme sports and the fact that The Holy

Grail of gambling is right next door in Las Vegas, Nevada. This boredom is also seen in the lack of tradition in California. Remember, ADD's are bored with convention and this translates into a rejection of tradition. They tend to be much more futuristic. As a result, Californians have very unusual first names (Rainbow, Sierra instead of Jane or John) and it has been impossible for Los Angeles to maintain an NFL Football team unless it's winning. In other states......a losing football team will remain because their fans aren't bored with the losses. In addition, the team is part of the regions tradition. The Detroit Lions had a losing record for decades and the losing was tolerated. This wouldn't have happened in ADD saturated Southern California.... they are not loyal to concepts that are boring or don't work. All I can say is that the "new" LA Rams stadium in Los Angeles better look like a shiny space ship, have frequent controlled explosions, and have Red Bull in the drinking water.

The traditional east coast is very different. These folks take their holidays very seriously and prepare months in advance. While living in Medford, Massachusetts I noticed residents would start adorning their homes with Halloween paraphernalia almost as early as the end of Sept. On the procrastinating and disinterested West Coast, Holiday adornments might pop up the week before the Holiday if at all.

Now back to California...... but in a good way this time. California appears to be the epicenter of ADD/ADHD and because of that, our American way has been a beneficiary of its scientific vision. ADD's tend to be bored with convention, so they keep innovating new products. Silicon Valley south to San Diego is filled with many of the World's leaders in Technology and Biotech companies for this very reason. Interestingly, CEO's of said tech companies are at a particularly high risk of having ADD as not only are they innovators of the new product, but they also assume the financial RISK needed to start a company. As an aside.... I refer to the business channel cNBC as the "television Mecca" of ADD as it combines the gambling behavior of the stock market and interviews featuring ADD news reporters with ADD CEO's. I always laugh when they keep interrupting each other since they are all so impatient and talk so fast.

When I think of the traditional views of Satan, I think of temptation, deception and generically stated "bad behavior". I will discuss temptation at a later time when discussing hormones, and deception will be addressed subtly in the last chapter (Apocalescence). For now though, we reinvestigate "bad behavior". We now see that a substantial amount of the country's (and smaller amount of the Worlds bad behavior) could be as a result of ADD/ADHD. Everything from accidents, battery, stealing, divorce, primary drug abuse and the bad behavior that occurs in the procurement of this drug abuse all could be adrenaline related.

But let's apply the concept of ADD/ADHD to The Apocalypse or the so called "End Times" (which we are now allegedly experiencing via the events of 9/11). Clearly, a lot has been said of the tensions between The US and Middle East (ISIS and Al-Qaeda in particular) as part of those End Times. The number "11" is biblically known as the number of Revelation and I find it interesting that The downed Twin Towers appeared to have morphologically look like an "11" and the date was 9/11 (9+1+1=11) (Chart 5). The Book of Revelation is also the 66th Chapter in The Bible (11x SIX= 66). Just to be clear, I'm not being duplicitous in downplaying "The Devil" yet referencing The Book of Revelation. I do believe in a Supreme Being who may use "other" means (mentally ill brains by His Own Creation for example) to fulfill prophecy.

It's not hard to imagine that the efflux of ADD/ADHD to the New World left a huge chasm in FUNDAMENTAL IDEALS between it and the newly ADD/ADHD DEPLETED Middle East. We have already established that ADD/ADHD's tend to be easily bored. This boredom translates into a rejection of convention/tradition, which in turn leads to change. Ancient cultures like The Middle East virtually never change and are all about tradition. They have no ADD/ADHD's left and they don't get bored! This can be observed by just looking at where they live (except Dubai and maybe Israel) and how they dress.... very little change occurs and conditions stagnate. The same applies to their devotion to Religious Doctrine. They live their lives TRADITIONALLY (around Religious Doctrine) and there is very little departure from their religious beliefs. These more ancient cultures will justify their subscription to tradition as simply an issue of "loyalty" though. The concept of loyalty is a very important quality to have in places like the Middle East and not so much in the US. Loyalty means "sticking with something regardless of whether it makes sense or not". Clearly, there is an unconscious antagonism that exists between the traditionalist ADD depleted Middle East and The futuristic ADD saturated United States. The United States is seen as disloyal (non-traditional), gluttonous (from our need to always CHANGE and improve what we have) and morally corrupt from said indulgence. It's easy to now see how The United States is seen as

"The Great Satan" in the eyes of many.

Once this schism occurred, further deterioration in relations was inevitable as defense of that nation slowly became a "spiritual" issue as each side accused the other of being "evil" (because they are so different...VERY DIFFERENT!). Don't forget my point at the beginning of the book, we as humans quite frequently and simplistically see others as being "evil" just because they are perceived as being different. Once an assignment of a nation as being "evil" is made, "bad behavior" is then seen as "good behavior" when it's in defense of themselves or God (like Al Qaeda's view point of 9/11). There is obviously more to the diplomatic problems that exist between these regions, but I've simply added a twist which may unknowingly contribute to hostilities. I'll discuss this concept of "Good versus Evil" more in Apocalescence. Further evidence of an ADD/ADHD depleted ancient culture would be China. When a culture has difficulty innovating, they just copy. The Greek Financial crisis is another example. Many postulate that an overly traditional, non-adaptive, bureaucratic Greek Government caused a choke hold on business growth and the entrepreneurial spirit. This apocalyptic financial downfall however has a very different mechanism of action than that which we have seen in the US (see below).

World Geopolitical tensions are only one aspect of "The End Days". Much has been said of the recent turmoil of the World's financial markets as well. I will investigate this "fiduciary Armageddon" more extensively in "The Sun of God" chapter...but I'd like to touch on one ADD related hook. It's been said that the 2008 financial turmoil originated in the US subprime mortgage debacle (a consumer issue, not a governmental one like in Greece). Although the phenomenon can be seen throughout the country, clearly the lion's shares of foreclosures per capita were in California, Nevada, Arizona and Florida (Chart 6). Could this be an ADD/ADHD issue? These states are prime ADD/ADHD migratory destinations and it would make sense. This condition is heralded by inattentiveness to detail and impulsivity. Inattentiveness could account for the lack of understanding of terms in a contract, and impulsivity dictates that we behave in a way that ignores ramifications (such as buying a home that is too expensive). It's no different than when an ADD/ADHD child states he/she is hungry and proceeds to fill the plate with three times the food needed. ADD/ADHD's are usually not slaves to details and as a result they miscalculate situations all the time. Also, don't forget the concept of "tradition". ADD/ADHD's have less proclivity for traditions as non-ADD/ADHD's. The Traditionalists

Psalm is "Be happy with what you have" (stated out of a lack of boredom). ADD/ADHD's on the other hand DO get bored with what they have. They "need" more change to stay stimulated. As you can see, a very fine line is being drawn of "being happy with what you have" ....and stagnation as a society. There is also an element of "entitlement" in buying objects that one can't afford, but this will be discussed in the chapter pertaining to personality disorders. In conclusion, I contend the US debt crisis is much more reckless "consumer" based (too much ADD), whereas the recent financial instability in older societies (like Greece) is more of a non-adaptive, overly traditional Government based failure (too little ADD).

In a case of "The Universe has a sense of humor" section of this book, I would be remiss to not add one more irony to Apocalyptic ADD/ADHD. From my personal experience of seeing innumerable Psychiatric cases, many left-handers have a high probability of being diagnosed with ADD/ADHD. The opposite however is not true, in that most ADD/ADHD's are actually right-handed. It's a percentage issue. Anyway, Christian doctrine has Jesus sitting on the Right Hand of The Father. However, who is sitting on the left hand? It has been speculated that Satan in fact sits on The Left Hand. The comical irony is that both Satan and ADD are associated with "left" .... a highly tangential and obnoxiously loose supportive statement of my original thesis that mental illness mimics evil. Forgive me for indulging myself, but I'd like to take this sinister lefty chit chat one step further. We see this left verses right distinction in Organic Chemistry as well. Many single compounds have a collection of molecules with identical bond structure, but different geometrical positioning. In other words, the two molecules that make up the compound look exactly alike but are "mirror images" of each other (much like your hands are identical, but cannot be superimposed on each other) (Chart 7). One "isomer" is considered the R (right or dextro) isomer.... the other.... The S (left or levo) isomer. The "S" stands for the "sin isomer". The rationale was that the Left isomer implied The Devil (because he sits on the left hand of The Father), and The Devil represents "sin". Who knew such spirituality had a home in organic chemistry? Furthermore, maybe on a cosmic unconscious level we interchange in our minds "right versus left" for "right versus wrong" (i.e. left=-Satan=wrong)? I really can't say for sure, but it definitely was a "spiritually responsible" deed for Novartis Pharmaceutical to choose the "R" isomer of Ritalin to formulate its product Focalin....and not the "sin" isomer (I know, I know.... I apparently have too much time on my hands).

ADD/ADHD represents two of my Four Horseman of The Apocalypse…… Mental Illness and Substance Abuse. However, since this publication is supposed to be a "feel-good" story, don't forget that without ADD/ADHD, we wouldn't have: "new and improved" anything, demand for SIX Flags amusement parks, and anybody to join us for a reckless trip to Vegas. Did you know all the numbers on a roulette wheel add to 666?

Chart 1

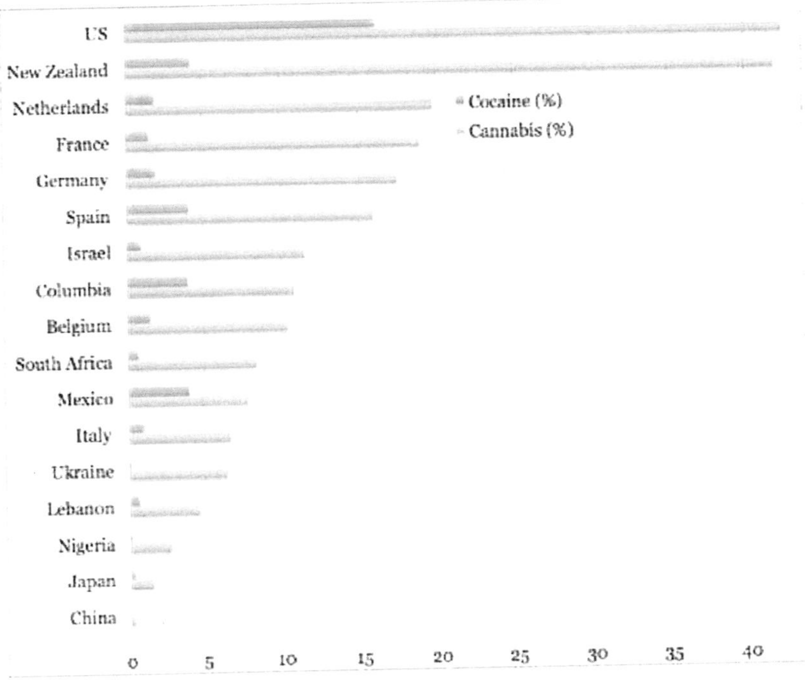

Chart 2

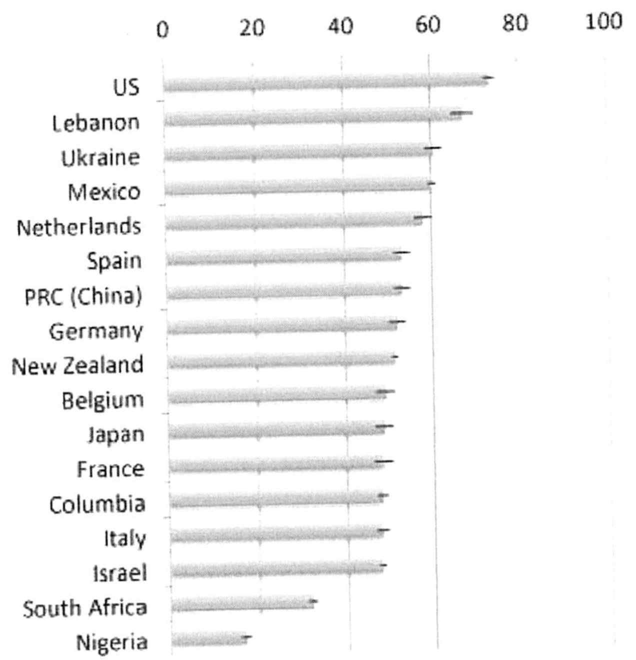

Chart 3

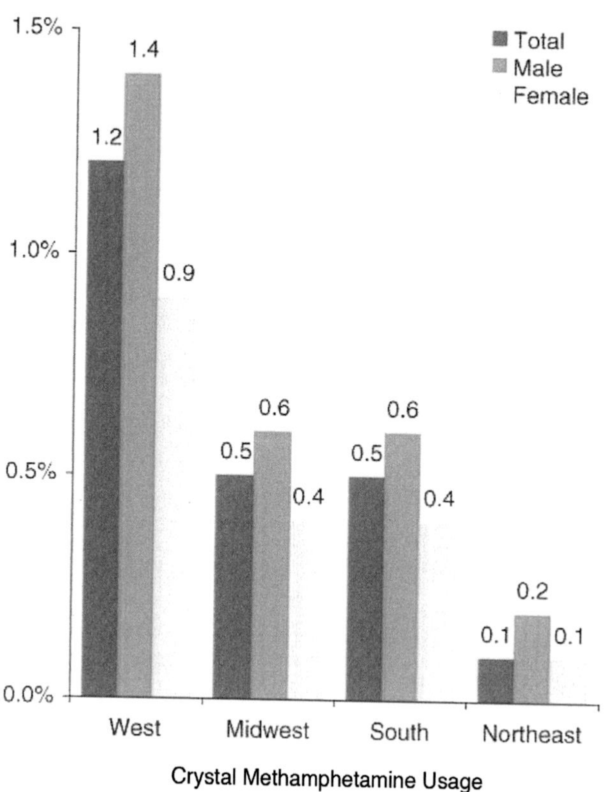
1.5%
1.0%
0.5%
0.0%
Total
Male
Female
1.4
1.2
0.9
0.6
0.5
0.4
0.6
0.5
0.4
0.2
0.1
0.1
West
Midwest
South
Northeast
Crystal Methamphetamine Usage

Chart 4

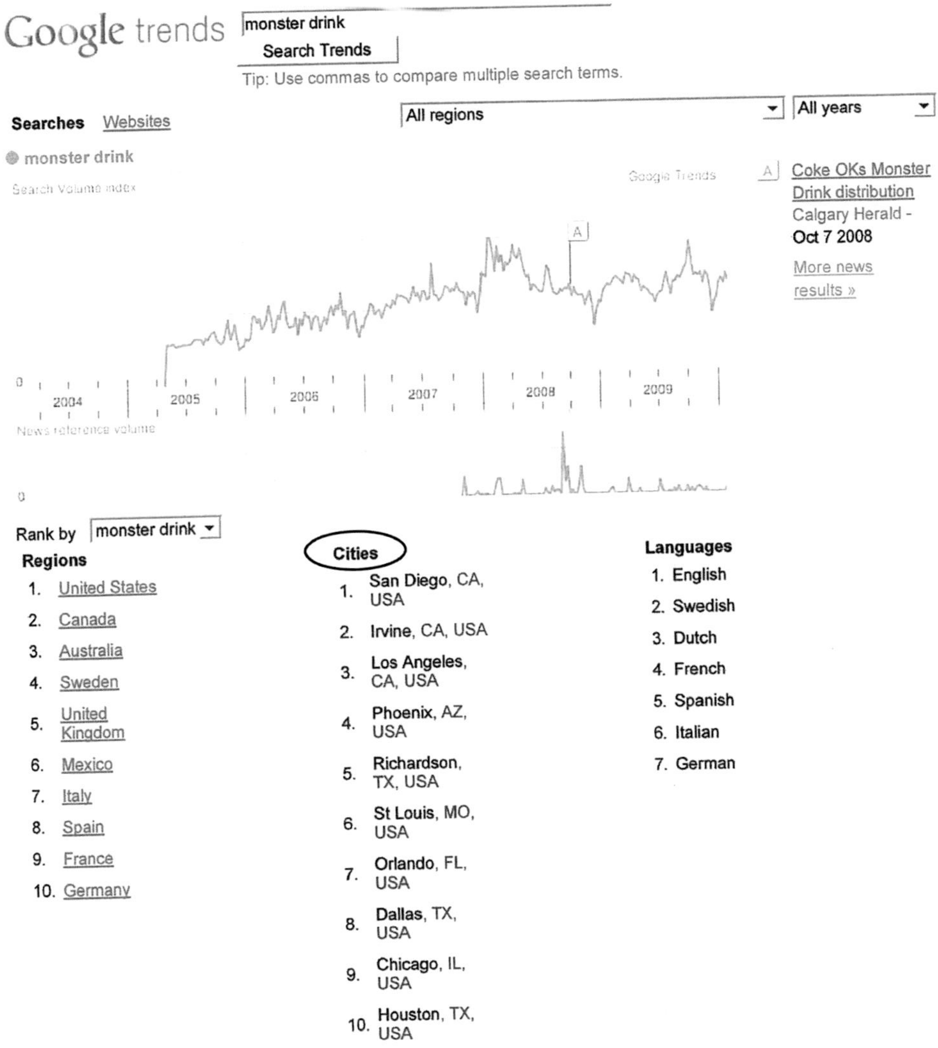

Google trends | monster drink | Search Trends

Tip: Use commas to compare multiple search terms.

Searches | Websites | All regions | All years

● monster drink

Search Volume index

Google Trends

0 | 2004 | 2005 | 2006 | 2007 | 2008 | 2009

News reference volume

0

A | Coke OKs Monster Drink distribution
Calgary Herald - **Oct 7 2008**

More news results »

Rank by monster drink

Regions

1. United States
2. Canada
3. Australia
4. Sweden
5. United Kingdom
6. Mexico
7. Italy
8. Spain
9. France
10. Germany

Cities

1. **San Diego**, CA, USA
2. **Irvine**, CA, USA
3. **Los Angeles**, CA, USA
4. **Phoenix**, AZ, USA
5. **Richardson**, TX, USA
6. **St Louis**, MO, USA
7. **Orlando**, FL, USA
8. **Dallas**, TX, USA
9. **Chicago**, IL, USA
10. **Houston**, TX, USA

Languages

1. English
2. Swedish
3. Dutch
4. French
5. Spanish
6. Italian
7. German

Chart 5

Spiritual Numbers

1 Number of Unity (God)

2 Number of Division (ex. Light and Dark, Heaven and Hell)

3 Number of Divine Perfection (Holy Trinity)

4 Number of Creation and Creative works on Earth (ex. 4 Seasons)

5 Number of Divine Grace

6 Number of Man (666)

7 Number of Spiritual Perfection or Completeness

8 New Beginnings or Resurrection

9 Number of Judgment and Finality (Related to 6. Upside down 6=9, 3+3=6 but 3x3=9)

10 Number of Divine Perfection

11 Number of Revelation and Disorder

Chart 6

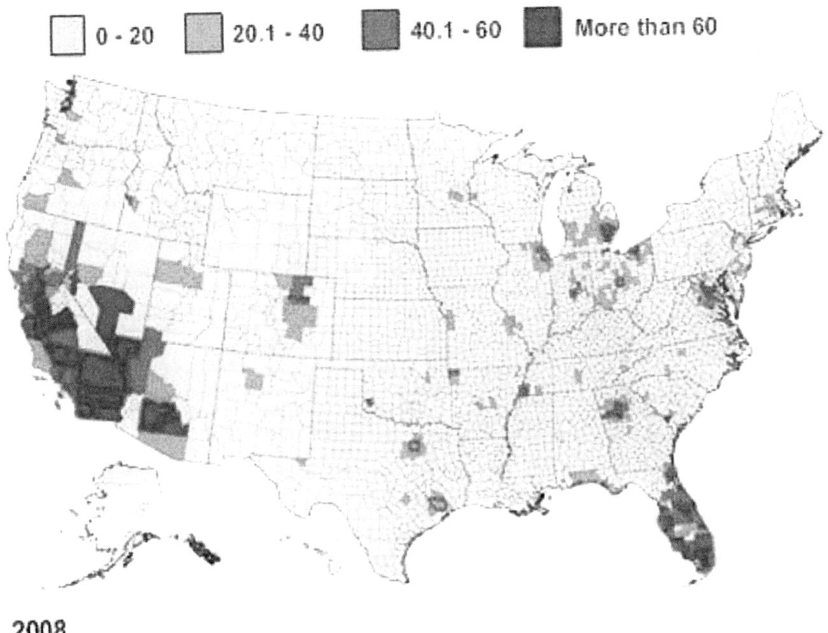

Chart 7

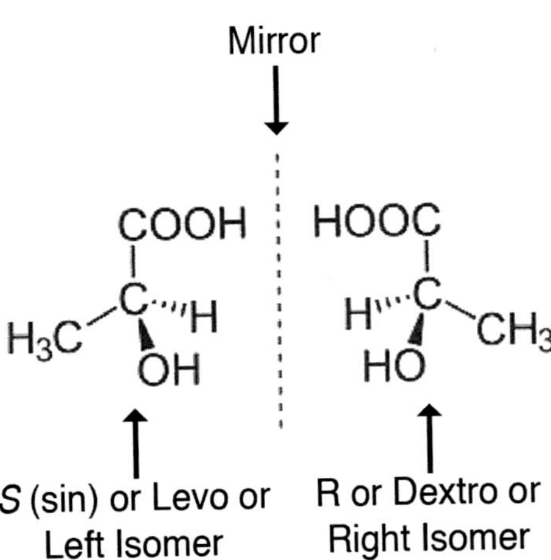

(*S*)-(+)-lactic acid (left) and (*R*)-(–)-lactic acid (right)

NEUROtiker (talk) - Own work

Both enantiomers of lactic acid displayed mirrored; left: (*S*)-lactic acid, right: (*R*)-lactic acid

Chapter 4

THOU SHALL NOT BE MOODY

Bipolar disorder is also known as manic depression…they are one in the same. Like ADD/ADHD, it is a "chemically" based condition and it is handed down genetically from our biological family tree. Also like ADD/ADHD, it is substantially under diagnosed and plays an important part in the overall health and behavior of the world society. Routine misdiagnosis of bipolar disorder exists because it is a heterogeneous disease that symptomatically appears to be the "weigh station" between depression and schizophrenia. Many patients at one bipolar extreme can look very unipolar depressive (just depressed…. Chart 1), and at another extreme can even look schizophrenic (Chart 2). The ramifications of this can be profound as successful treatment for all three conditions (bipolar disorder, unipolar depressive disorder, schizophrenia) pharmacologically can be very different. Prognoses are also very different. Unipolar depression is treated primarily with SRI's (Serotonin Reuptake Inhibitors), SNRI's (Serotonin-Norepinephrine Reuptake Inhibitors), Dopamine Reuptake Inhibitors, Serotonin modulators, Monoamine Oxidase Inhibitors and Tricyclics (Chart 3). True schizophrenia is rare, and manifests typically in the late teens/early 20's with symptoms of social isolation, cognitive dysfunction, bizarre disorganized/delusional thinking and primarily hallucinations of the auditory type (like my patient in the first paragraph of the book). These symptoms always persist and have little cyclicity (in contrast to bipolars, who always cycle or change). Despite medications like the new generational antipsychotics (will describe later), the condition only has a fair prognosis whereas bipolar disorder (even when it looks "schizophrenic-like") not just gets "better" with treatment, but actually can get "well". If a depressed patient comes to see me and they say they have a sibling with schizophrenia, I usually tell them that sibling is more than likely bipolar just based on the similar family genetics involved.

Bipolar disorder can be subtle, not so subtle, look more like depression in some cases or more like schizophrenia in others. This condition is so vast, that it's also possible that ALL mood disorder diagnoses could simply be variants of manic depression with the various bipolar poles weighted disproportionately from patient to patient. This would make total sense as it would be more consistent with the "up and down" seasonal nature of the animal kingdom (more in chapter The Sun of God). As you will learn, "bipolarity" is actually considered "normal" in the animal kingdom (hibernation/mating season) and very well may be normal in humans as well. In short, bipolar disorder encompasses a huge proportion of Psychiatric cases due to its variable presentations and varying severities, not to mention its analogous "normalcy" in much of the animal kingdom.

Bipolar disorder is not only a condition of changing moods (moodiness), but also should philosophically be considered a disorder of fluctuating "energy" (Chart 4). There are two high energy symptom states and one low energy symptom state (the term "state" is also equivalent to the word "pole" or "phase"). A period of low energy is manifested by depression, FATIGUE, slow thoughts, low energy and poor motivation. It resembles the symptoms of patients with so-called unipolar or melancholic depression. These patients are always tired, unmotivated, and routinely sleep (or wish they could sleep) most of the day. This fatigue can last anywhere from a few hours to a few weeks. Patients during this period of time typically will abuse substances that enhance energy such as "energy" drinks, coffee, tea, dark chocolate, stimulants like cocaine or crystal methamphetamine, or an old prescription of antidepressants. We already mentioned in "Adrenaline Begets The West" that Seattle's Starbucks coffee is a beneficiary of ADD/ADHD migration. But the aforementioned "fatigued phase" of bipolarity has also contributed to Starbucks success. The cloudiness/darkness associated with this region can induce lethargy and depression in those who are mood vulnerable, which in turn drives caffeine usage. This double dose of needy patrons appears to be the business equivalent of "form following function". In any case, alcohol may also be abused for its immediate euphoric effects during these "lower phases", but the alcohol is not necessarily habituated as it tends to make the fatigued patient even more tired.

It was once thought that "the depressed" patient is the one that commits suicide, but these patients truly don't have the energy to kill themselves. Bipolar patients who are in a depressive state will routinely go to see a mental health professional and complain primarily of their depression, however if the patient isn't properly diagnosed as manic depressive, and an antidepressant is prescribed (because the patient looks depressed), the patient may actually go on and attempt suicide. That antidepressant took the patient from a low energy non-suicidal depressed state to a high energy suicidal dysphoric manic state. This dysphoric manic state is brutal because it leads to irritability, mental discomfort, possible central nervous system depressant drug abuse (because of the irritability), and suicidality/homicidality (more to come). This concept holds true with children as well. Routinely, a depressed child will be given an antidepressant for treatment of "depression", but then that child goes onto either talk about suicide or actually go on to attempt suicide. This occurred because the child wasn't suffering from depression to begin with, but rather bipolar disorder. A history of epic temper tantrums (or better described as "wailing sessions" based on profound emotional sensitivities) in childhood would have assisted to make the correct diagnosis. The pharmaceutical companies get a very bad rap for this. It wasn't the medication that caused this suicidality, it was an inaccurate diagnosis. Upon completion of this chapter, you will have a better understanding that suicidality (and possibly homicidality) is not the end result of depression per se, but rather a consequence of depression with IRRITABILITY (the dysphoric manic pole). Similarly, if an allegedly "depressed" patient does well with an antidepressant for a few months but it then stops working regardless of a dosage increase.... think bipolarity. In this case, the anti-depressant helped the depression, but the natural cycle of the illness now requires a different balance of chemicals for stabilization.

As mentioned, there are two different high energy poles. They occur at different times and individually can last for hours to weeks. A patient who is diagnosed with bipolar disorder can as far as I'm concerned experience one, or the other, or both (but at different times). The first type of high energy presentation is the "classic" mania as described in Psychiatric literature and diagnostic manuals (Chart 5). It is characterized not surprisingly with symptoms that are the exact opposite of the low energy phase.... high energy (not low energy), racing thoughts (not slow thoughts) and too little sleep (not excessive sleep). But in addition, these patients experience an intoxicating euphoria for which they will rarely see a doctor (unless forced to). They will routinely stay up at night engaged in: gratuitous obsessive behavior, partying, intense spiritual thoughts, promiscuity, talking, cleaning, writing, gambling, traveling, or simply being creative. People with mood disorders (ESPECIALLY bipolar disorder) are profoundly artistic and these highs can turn out great works of artistry. It is not hyperbole when I say that bipolarity is the seed of much Earthly genius. Bipolars tend to be musicians (and so was Satan…Ezekial 28:13), poets (lead singers!!... people in the "the industry" call a lead singers notorious bad behavior as "LSD" …lead singer's disease), photographers, writers, actors, comedians (especially ones preoccupied by sex and incorporating music in their show), designers, hair stylists, makeup artists, painters, actors, architects, sculptors or any profession that demonstrates creativity. It differs from "ADD creativity" in that ADD/ADHD innovate through boredom, whereas bipolars create out of "emotional expressiveness". Not surprisingly, just as I can see an ADD a mile away (a fast talking, sloppy writing, off-white toothed patient who is always late for an appointment), I can usually identify a bipolar by their multiple tattoos (Axyl Rose?), piercings/hair tinting (Amy Winehouse?), and either black clothing (Johnny Cash?) or colorful clothing (Lady Gaga?) depending on their mood. The rest of the manic pole can be manifested by hyper-sexuality, hyper-spirituality, and lots of spending. Thorough Psychiatric evaluations for Tiger Woods, Harvey Weinstein, Kevin Spacey and Bill Cosby would serve them well by carefully ruling out bipolarity in these ALLEGEDLY hyper sexual individuals. Now, in this manuscript I might hint at various people who MIGHT have elements of a Psychiatric condition, but please keep in mind I've never examined or treated any of them. The criteria I'm using is unusual, and a kin to modern day witchcraft. Please do not assume any of the people I mention are definitively diagnosable. However, many of the people I have cited are either deceased (which is considered "fair game" as far as the American Psychiatric Association is concerned), or they have already made their diagnosis public. Everyone else is pure speculation on my part so I ask you to interpret them accordingly.

The manic pole can be quite persistent and thus it often shapes what the person does on a day to day basis. As a result, in my opinion, there is an unusually high percentage of bipolars in the sex industry (hyper sexual) as well as the Church (hyper religious). Is SeX,SeX,SeX the true number of the beast? I don't know about that, but If you see a Porn actor/actress with numerous tattoos .... you now probably know the diagnosis! And if a Church leader is caught in a sex scandal.... you now know the possible diagnosis again (especially if they are an alcoholic). And if a Porn star or actor/musician goes onto become a preacher or preoccupied with religion .... third time is a charm! There shouldn't be a surprise that bipolar entertainers could become persuasive spiritual preachers and visa versa.... preaching can be very theatrical (Sam Kinison, the deceased comic, comes to mind on that one). The previously stated manic pole quite often renders bipolar patients into substantial trouble in that they are more likely to have affairs, be a vector for STD's, cause unwanted pregnancies and go bankrupt. Manic states can also include delusions (often religious) and auditory hallucinations (schizophrenic like) and these patients need to be promptly seen by a Psychiatrist. Unlike the other bipolar phases, mania is a "high" in of itself and is infrequently "self-medicated" by the patient because they already feel euphoric. In fact, if they are already on medications, they have a high likelihood of unilaterally stopping them because they "feel great and don't need pills anymore".

The other high energy state is known as the dysphoric manic state (Chart 6). Many professionals refer to it as a "mixed state" as it combines the depressive discomfort of a low phase with the high energy of a manic phase. Just like a manic state, these patients have high energy, racing thoughts and a decreased sleep. But unlike mania, they are irritable! This is the stage that usually results in most arrests, Psychiatric evaluations and Psychiatric hospitalizations. This is typically code for a "Mental Breakdown". These states are characterized by agitation, fighting, contentious behavior, violence, "throwing things", worsening obsessions, panic attacks and most importantly suicidality and homicidality. This is by far the most dangerous phase of bipolarity. Dysphoric manics usually have racing and disorganized thoughts and they subjectively feel as though they are going "crazy" (patients use that exact word to describe it). It is in this frenzied state that they kill themselves (or others) …. often violently by hanging, firearm or jumping. This tumultuous means of suicide represents the intense frenzy they feel internally. If a bipolar has a killing spree, it usually occurs during this phase and it typically occurs over a short period of time (minutes to a few weeks at most). It is a time limited, nonsensical, frenzied, and chaotic. If a sociopath has a killing spree, it's much more methodical and typically is over a longer period of time (years). Sociopathic murderers tend to savor their moments of playing God and thus time elapsed during killing sprees is protracted.

Manic depressives, like ADD/ADHD's, are legendary substance abusers. As previously mentioned, low energy states are routinely self-medicated with caffeine, stimulants, antidepressants, and maybe alcohol (it has a brief euphoric effect). The problem is, when bipolars ingest these activating substances, it forces them up to a high energy (usually dysphoric manic) state. The bipolar then invariably and unfortunately experiences the irritability associated with this dysphoric manic state. As a result, they self-medicate AGAIN but with calming drugs like alcohol, marijuana, benzodiazepines like Valium or Xanax to help with their sleep, or most notably opiate based pain killers like Codeine, Vicodin or Heroin (Chart

7). Heroin abusers in my opinion are manic depressives until proven otherwise. Incidentally, the reverse frequently happens too. A Bipolar may start off self-medicating a dysphoric manic phase with central nervous system depressants (Xanax etc.), then plunge into the depressive phase with self-medication of these calming/depressing substances. They then use "uppers" to feel less depressed. Not surprising, bipolars tend to abuse two opposite acting drugs SIMULTANEOUSLY, like Crystal Meth/alcohol or Cocaine/Heroin (Speedball) for example. The two opposite acting drugs taken at the same time seems to ensure they won't stay in any annoying pole for any given period of time, but it clearly ensures massive acceleration and higher frequency of the cycles themselves. They never really retain the feeling of "centeredness" or homeostasis because the drugs they are abusing aren't designed to collapse the poles into a level horizontal line as seen with bipolar medications (Chart 8). In my experience, bipolars also tend to be the patients who actually like exotic drugs such as mushrooms, mescaline or ecstasy. Mostly anyone else who uses them might use them a few times, but then call it quits. There is something about the constantly shifting bipolar brain and its complicated neurochemistry, that promotes this unusual tolerance and drug craving. It is also possible that the HYPER SPIRITUAL nature of bipolarity is somewhat satiated by hallucinogens as these substances may serve as a portal to another more interesting spiritual dimension.

The dysphoric manic phase is so uncomfortable, that this phase single handedly makes bipolars the largest group of intractable alcoholics and pain killer/heroin addicts (at least in my practice). These dysphoric manics also can't sleep, and "sleeping pills" are also chronically abused. With all of this self-medication, you now know why those "evil" tattooed MUSICIANS are notorious drug abusers (especially when it comes to Heroin or Pain killers) .... they are bipolar! "Sex, Drugs and Rock'n Roll" is everything a bipolar musician stands for (oops....and don't forget hyper-spirituality, they sing of God and Satan...just ask one of my favorite artists, Ozzy Osbourne). We'll discuss the bipolar patients (and musicians) that actually go on to kill themselves later in the next chapter, but I'd like to make one comment on the subject now. It would make total sense that many patients go on to kill themselves AFTER drug rehab because the "original" SELF-MEDICATED dysphoric manic state is in an actively undiagnosed and NON-SELF MEDICATED dysphoric manic state at discharge. As a result, the addicted bipolar is off the drugs and alcohol.... but remains symptomatically bipolar (usually dysphoric manic). They somehow need to still cope with the condition's symptoms, and suicide unfortunately is sometimes the only "drug free" solution these patients can think of to definitively deal with the pain. Proper medication in most cases should improve outcome, but some substance treatment programs just see physician prescribed medications as just another "addiction" to be avoided.

Now that you understand the cyclical nature of the condition, you can imagine that properly medicating a "moving" up and down target is a challenge. It is a delicate game of applying "gas" and "brakes" during the different energy poles, which requires great tolerance and meticulous follow through on the patient's part. Patients must realize that not every medication or combination of medications will initially work, but they need to commit to trying new treatments until the interventions foment stabilization. As with ADD/ADHD, the physician should be proactive in raising medication levels every few days (NOT every few weeks). As long as there are no side effects and proper medical monitoring is done (EKG, Blood Labs) …this is a good strategy to either prove a medication as effective, or ineffective (but in a far shorter period of time!). However, a more conservative approach should be taken with the elderly and those patients on multiple medications. Long spans of unchanging medications do nothing more than frustrate the patient and increase the chance they will go back to feeling better with drugs or alcohol, or possibly ditching the medications altogether. Psychotherapy is usually great for relieving stress, but psychotherapy won't really be helpful for the bipolar patient until the faulty chemical "lenses" they have been looking through are fixed. Medications allow patients to think clearly, be more functional, feel less overwhelmed and be less reactive in their daily lives. Imagine how much more productive therapy would be under such circumstances. Having said that, truth be told, once a bipolar patient feels better with medications, they have less to rehash in psychotherapy and are less confused about life in general. As a result, they spend that extra time not in therapy but simply enjoying their lives and making sense of it on their own.

Complete text books have been written on the technical aspect of medication management for bipolar disorder. However, for the sake of brevity and my impatient sense of being, let's try to outline it in just a few far from adequate paragraphs. If the reader has ADD, is easily bored, or could not care less about it, one can easily bypass to the second to last paragraph in this chapter and not lose the overall understanding of the manuscript.

Now, for those self-proclaimed non-ADD readers that remain, this outline is not intended to be an absolute "cookie cutter" solution to treat the highly cantankerous condition that is bipolar disorder, and should not be utilized as such. It's simply added to provide a sense of balance to the bipolar story. I'd first like to say that many of the strategies I employ are not necessarily endorsed by the APA (American Psychiatric Association) or FDA (Food and Drug Administration). Sometimes I might use medications that are indicated for a certain non-Psychiatric condition (like epilepsy), but then use them Psychiatrically (like for bipolar). Also, many bipolar meds have particular FDA indications for a CERTAIN POLE of bipolarity, and not for other poles. But this lack of FDA approval doesn't prevent me from using them in a variety of unapproved poles. The fact is, these poles can change so quickly that it's difficult to ascertain which pole is the most problematic anyway. In addition, I will sometimes find myself prescribing a certain medication for a child that is only FDA approved for an adult. My feeling on that subject is that if properly dosed and monitored.... children have a much better chance of "beating" their condition if they have a whole palette of agents to choose from. Trial and error is unfortunately part of the treatment process. Quite often, conventional "FDA approved" medications for children won't treat the condition in its entirety or the child might experience side effects. In which case, we need to weigh the risk/benefit ratio of not treating the young patient compared to using a medication that is not FDA approved for a particular childhood condition (but is of course is approved for use in other conditions or ages). Interestingly, children's livers are metabolically more active than adults, thus they tend to metabolize medications with greater facility which means in aggregate less side effects (especially for the older kids). Having said all of this, your best bet is to always work with a physician you know and trust, and use strategies that work for the both of you.

The key with treating bipolar is to fix the dysregulation of wakefulness. Keep in mind the triad of mood, sleep (or wakefulness) and sunlight.... they are all related and will be further detailed in the next chapter. Fixing the sleep, whether it is too much or too little, is critical to treating mood as a whole. If the patient is sleeping too much (a depressed phase), you must wake them up with an activating anti-depressant such as Wellbutrin, Provigil (not FDA indicated for depression), Nuvigil (not FDA indicated for depression), Pristiq, Effexor XR, Strattera (indicated only for ADD not depression), Prozac, Zoloft, Fetzima or Cymbalta. If the patient has a history of bipolar induction with antidepressants (i.e. they have become manic or dysphoric manic with treatment of their depression), more gentle ones like Paxil, Remeron, Trintellix, Viibrid, Lexapro, Celexa, or Luvox should be initially used. BUT BEFORE AN ANTIDEPRESSANT CAN BE ADDED, a mood stabilizer should be started to prevent induction into a manic or dysphoric manic state. Lithium and Depakote are effective "mood stabilizers" and are FDA approved for bipolar disorder, but frequent blood draws and annoying side effects tend to cause on occasion as many problems as they solve. In which case, the anticonvulsant Lamictal is an excellent FDA approved choice. Symbyax, a combination pill of Prozac and Zyprexa, is FDA approved for the depressive pole of bipolarity. However, one pill with two separate medications sometimes makes it difficult to "fine tune" a patient. Seroquel and Seroquel XR are also approved for this pole and are excellent "sleepers".... but these patients are already tired and care needs to be taken not to make them more so. Many other antipsychotics in addition to Seroquel can also be used to initially to stabilize the patient prior to antidepressant treatment such as very low dose Zyprexa, Abilify, Rexulti, Vraylar, Latuda (all technically "protective" AND indicated for a "depressive" pole). Consideration, can also be given to non-FDA approved anticonvulsant treatment which could include Trileptal, Topamax, Neurontin, Lyrica, Gabitril or Keppra. As mentioned, FDA approval for medications and development of new medications is ongoing and CONSTANTLY changing, so please do not use this list as gospel. As a reiterated point of interest, if one suffers from symptoms of "depression" and the doctor prescribes anti-depressants, one is more than likely bipolar if there is a failure of two or three antidepressants due to side effects such as agitation, panic attacks or insomnia. What this means is that the medication induced a low pole into a high pole. Most of the time, patients who present with depression and who have failed numerous anti-depressants are eventually diagnosed with bipolar (or infrequently ADD/ADHD as mentioned).

IF a patient presents manic......the new generational antipsychotics that induce sleep (Geodon, Seroquel, Seroquel XR, Zyprexa, Saphris, Risperdal, Invega, Latuda, Fanapt) are theoretically appropriate. Initiating and maintaining nocturnal sleep is a must in these upper poles....so I give these sedating medications at night. One can also prescribe "benzos" but sedating antidepressants like Trazodone and Remeron should be avoided. Once the sleep is fixed, then the addition of Lithium, Depakote or Lamictal is considered, but not always needed.

In those dangerous and uncomfortable dysphoric manic states, we once again (like with mania) need to fix the sleep first. I primarily use the above sedating night time antipsychotics as used in mania, but due to a side effect called akathisia (a subjective feeling of restlessness and fidgetiness), I'm very careful NOT to make these edgy patients EVEN MORE irritated. If this side effect becomes a problem, the antipsychotic is discontinued. We need to keep hacking away at the sleep though, so sedating agents such as Lunesta, Belsomra, Ambien, Ambien CR, Sonata, Xanax, Ramelteon (melatonin), Restoril, Ativan, Klonopin (to name a few) may be considered. Be careful however of the lack of focus, and depression felt the next day with benzodiazepine based "sleepers". There are also issues of dependency (physiological withdrawal when "benzos" are discontinued) and tolerance (ever increasing doses needed for stabilization when used habitually). Sedating antidepressants like Trazodone or Remeron should probably be avoided. Once the patient is sleeping properly, core treatment can include any combination of medications such as Depakote/Lamictal/Lithium/Trileptal or any other calming anticonvulsant.

One way that I know the medication or combination of pills I've chosen is working for a patient is if he/she has an absence of cravings for their traditionally abused substances. Also, it should also be kept in mind that medication treatment becomes much more challenging if the patient also suffers from a second condition like ADD/ADHD or panic disorder. The treatment of one disorder (like stimulants for ADD) will invariably effect the treatment of the second disorder (like bipolar or panic). Therefore, it's vitally important that an initial accurate diagnosis is made, as this has a "butterfly" effect on the rest of treatment and sets the tone for a positive patient experience.

Like ADD/ADHD, manic depression represents two Horseman of my Apocalypse.... Mental Illness and Substance Abuse.

Chart 1

DSM-IV & DSM-IV-TR: Major Depressive Episode

When an individual experiences a discrete episode of persistent and pervasive emotional depression, this term may be applied. The individual may be diagnosed with one of the Mood Disorders, either Major Depressive Disorder or a Bipolar Disorder.

Criteria for Major Depressive Episode
(cautionary statement)

A. Five (or more) of the following symptoms have been present during the same 2-week period and represent a change from previous functioning; at least one of the symptoms is either
  (1) depressed mood or
  (2) loss of interest or pleasure.
Note: Do not include symptoms that are clearly due to a general medical condition, or mood-incongruent delusions or hallucinations.

(1) depressed mood most of the day, nearly every day, as indicated by either subjective report (e.g., feels sad or empty) or observation made by others (e.g., appears tearful). **Note:** In children and adolescents, can be irritable mood.
(2) markedly diminished interest or pleasure in all, or almost all, activities most of the day, nearly every day (as indicated by either subjective account or observation made by others)
(3) significant weight loss when not dieting or weight gain (e.g., a change of more than 5% of body weight in a month), or decrease or increase in appetite nearly every day. **Note:** In children, consider failure to make expected weight gains.
(4) Insomnia or Hypersomnia nearly every day
(5) psychomotor agitation or retardation nearly every day (observable by others, not merely subjective feelings of restlessness or being slowed down)
(6) fatigue or loss of energy nearly every day
(7) feelings of worthlessness or excessive or inappropriate guilt (which may be delusional) nearly every day (not merely self-reproach or guilt about being sick)
(8) diminished ability to think or concentrate, or indecisiveness, nearly every day (either by subjective account or as observed by others)
(9) recurrent thoughts of death (not just fear of dying), recurrent suicidal ideation without a specific plan, or a suicide attempt or a specific plan for committing suicide

B. The symptoms do not meet criteria for a Mixed Episode (see p. 335).

C. The symptoms cause clinically significant distress or impairment in social, occupational, or other important areas of functioning.

D. The symptoms are not due to the direct physiological effects of a substance (e.g., a drug of abuse, a medication) or a general medical condition (e.g., hypothyroidism).

E. The symptoms are not better accounted for by Bereavement, i.e., after the loss of a loved one, the symptoms persist for longer than 2 months or are characterized by marked functional impairment, morbid preoccupation with worthlessness, suicidal ideation, psychotic symptoms, or psychomotor retardation.

Chart 2

DSM-IV & DSM-IV-TR: Schizophrenia

Schizophrenia, a term introduced by Bleuler, names a persistent, often chronic and usually serious mental disorder affecting a variety of aspects of behavior, thinking, and emotion. Patients with delusions or hallucinations may be described as psychotic. Thinking may be disconnected and illogical. Peculiar behaviors may be associated with social withdrawal and disinterest.

Diagnostic criteria for Schizophrenia

(cautionary statement)

A. *Characteristic symptoms:* Two (or more) of the following, each present for a significant portion of time during a 1-month period (or less if successfully treated):

(1) delusions

(2) hallucinations

(3) disorganized speech (e.g., frequent derailment or incoherence)

(4) grossly disorganized or catatonic behavior

(5) negative symptoms, i.e., affective flattening, alogia, or avolition

Note: Only one Criterion A symptom is required if delusions are bizarre or hallucinations consist of a voice keeping up a running commentary on the person's behavior or thoughts, or two or more voices conversing with each other.

B. *Social/occupational dysfunction:* For a significant portion of the time since the onset of the disturbance, one or more major areas of functioning such as work, interpersonal relations, or self-care are markedly below the level achieved prior to the onset (or when the onset is in childhood or adolescence, failure to achieve expected level of interpersonal, academic, or occupational achievement).

C. *Duration:* Continuous signs of the disturbance persist for at least 6 months. This 6-month period must include at least 1 month of symptoms (or less if successfully treated) that meet Criterion A (i.e., active-phase symptoms) and may include periods of prodromal or residual symptoms. During these prodromal or residual periods, the signs of the disturbance may be manifested by only negative symptoms or two or more symptoms listed in Criterion A present in an attenuated form (e.g., odd beliefs, unusual perceptual experiences).

D. *Schizoaffective and Mood Disorder exclusion:* Schizoaffective Disorder and Mood Disorder With Psychotic Features have been ruled out because either (1) no Major Depressive, Manic, or Mixed Episodes have occurred concurrently with the active-phase symptoms; or (2) if mood episodes have occurred during active-phase symptoms, their total duration has been brief relative to the duration of the active and residual periods.

E. *Substance/general medical condition exclusion:* The disturbance is not due to the direct physiological effects of a substance (e.g., a drug of abuse, a medication) or a general medical condition.

Chart 2 (continued)

F. *Relationship to a Pervasive Developmental Disorder:* If there is a history of Autistic Disorder or another Pervasive Developmental Disorder, the additional diagnosis of Schizophrenia is made only if prominent delusions or hallucinations are also present for at least a month (or less if successfully treated).

Classification of longitudinal course (can be applied only after at least 1 year has elapsed since the initial onset of active-phase symptoms):

Episodic With Interepisode Residual Symptoms (episodes are defined by the reemergence of prominent psychotic symptoms); *also specify if:* **With Prominent Negative Symptoms**

Episodic With No Interepisode Residual Symptoms

Continuous (prominent psychotic symptoms are present throughout the period of observation); *also specify if:* **With Prominent Negative Symptoms**

Single Episode In Partial Remission; *also specify if:* **With Prominent Negative Symptoms**

Single Episode In Full Remission

Other or Unspecified Pattern

Chart 3

Antidepressant List

SSRI's (Selective Serotonin Reuptake Inhibitors): Celexa (Citalopram). Lexapro (Escitalopram). Prozac (Fluoxetine). Luvox (Fluvoxamine). Paxil/Paxil CR (Paroxetine). Zoloft (Sertraline).

Tricyclics (TCA): Elavil (Amitriptyline). Ascendin (Amoxapine). Anafranil (Clomipramine). Norpramin (Desipramine). Sinequan (Doxepin). Tofranil (Imipramine). Ludiomil (Maprotiline). Pamelor (Nortriptyline). Vivactyl (Protriptyline). Surmontil (Trimipramine).

SNRI's (Serotonin and Noradrenaline Reuptake Inhibitors): Pristiq (Desvenlafaxine). Cymbalta (Duloxetine). Fetzima (Levomilnacipran). Effexor/Effexor XR (Venlafaxine).

Noradrenergic and Specific Serotonergic Antidepressant: Remeron/ Remeron Sol Tab (Mirtazapine).

Norepinephrine Reuptake Inhibitor: Strattera (Atomoxetine).

5HT2 Antagonist: Desyrel (Trazodone).

Serotonin 5HT 1A Agonist/SSRI: Viibryd (Vilazodone).

Serotonin Modulator: Trintellix (Vortioxetine).

NDRIs (Norepinephrine and Dopamine Reuptake Inhibitor): Wellbutrin SR/XL (Buproprion)

MAOIs (Monoamine Oxidase Inhibitors): Marplan (Isocarboxazid). Nardil (Phenelzine). Parnate (Tranylcypromine). Emsam (Selegiline).

Atypical Antipsychotics ?: Rexulti (Brexpiprazole). Seroquel/Seroquel XR (Quetiapine). Vraylar (Cariprazine). Latuda (Lurasidone). Abilify (Aripiprazole). Zyprexa (Olanzapine).

Chart 4

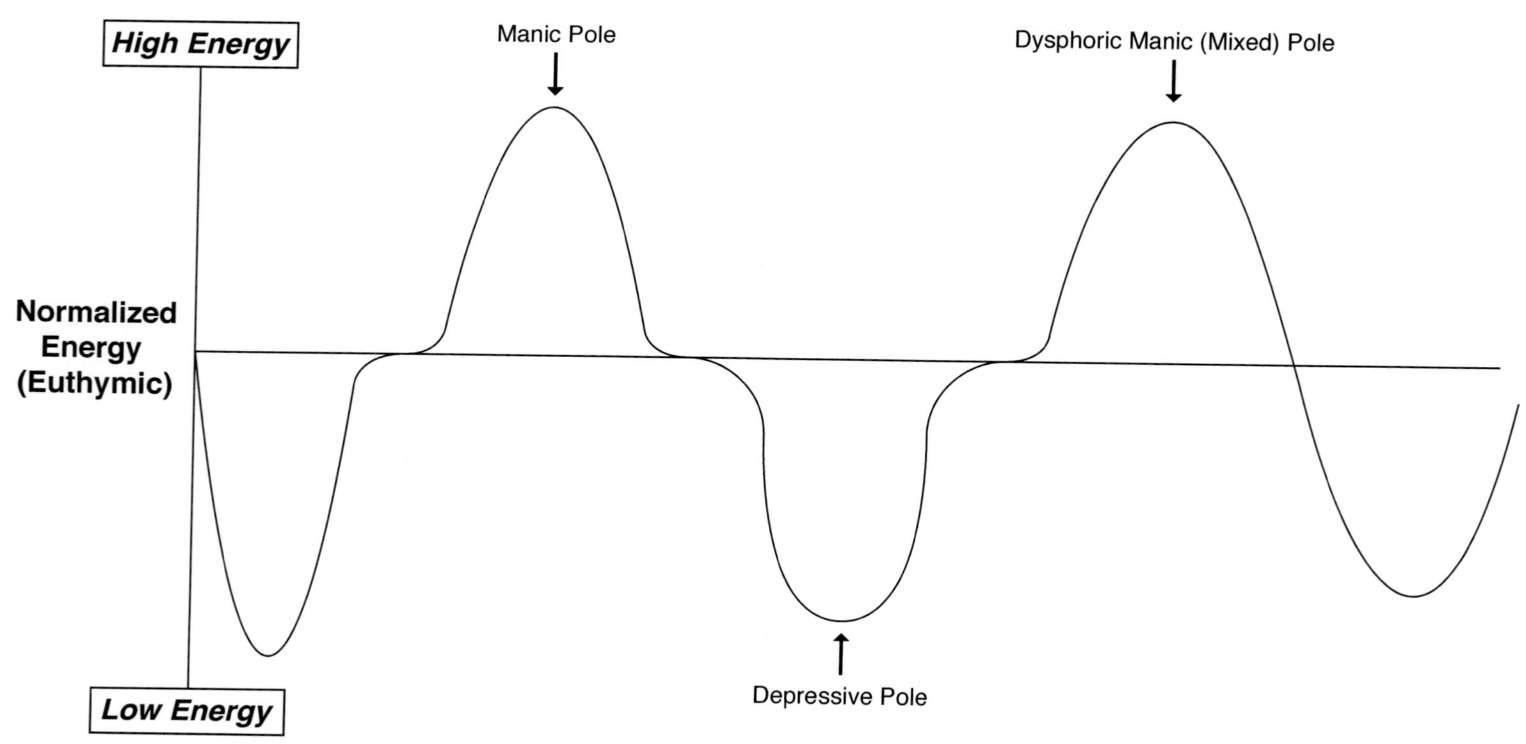
Bipolar Poles (Tripolar?)
High Energy
Manic Pole
Dysphoric Manic (Mixed) Pole
Normalized Energy (Euthymic)
Depressive Pole
Low Energy

Chart 5

DSM-IV & DSM-IV-TR: Manic Episode

When an individual experiences a discrete period of persistent and pervasive manic (elated, irritable or euphoric) mood, this term may be applied. The individual may be diagnosed with one of the bipolar disorders.

Criteria for Manic Episode
(cautionary statement)

A. A distinct period of abnormally and persistently elevated, expansive, or irritable mood, lasting at least 1 week (or any duration if hospitalization is necessary).

B. During the period of mood disturbance, three (or more) of the following symptoms have persisted (four if the mood is only irritable) and have been present to a significant degree:

(1) inflated self-esteem or grandiosity
(2) decreased need for sleep (e.g., feels rested after only 3 hours of sleep)
(3) more talkative than usual or pressure to keep talking
(4) flight of ideas or subjective experience that thoughts are racing
(5) distractibility (i.e., attention too easily drawn to unimportant or irrelevant external stimuli)
(6) increase in goal-directed activity (either socially, at work or school, or sexually) or psychomotor agitation
(7) excessive involvement in pleasurable activities that have a high potential for painful consequences (e.g., engaging in unrestrained buying sprees, sexual indiscretions, or foolish business investments)

C. The symptoms do not meet criteria for a Mixed Episode.

D. The mood disturbance is sufficiently severe to cause marked impairment in occupational functioning or in usual social activities or relationships with others, or to necessitate hospitalization to prevent harm to self or others, or there are psychotic features.

E. The symptoms are not due to the direct physiological effects of a substance (e.g., a drug of abuse, a medication, or other treatment) or a general medical condition (e.g., hyperthyroidism).

Chart 6

DSM-IV & DSM-IV-TR: Mixed Episode

When an individual experiences a discrete period during which characteristics of both major depressive and manic episodes are evident, it is classified as a **mixed** episode. The individual may be diagnosed with one of the bipolar disorders.

Criteria for Mixed Episode
(cautionary statement)

A. The criteria are met both for a Manic Episode and for a Major Depressive Episode (except for duration) nearly every day during at least a 1-week period.

B. The mood disturbance is sufficiently severe to cause marked impairment in occupational functioning or in usual social activities or relationships with others, or to necessitate hospitalization to prevent harm to self or others, or there are psychotic features.

C. The symptoms are not due to the direct physiological effects of a substance (e.g., a drug of abuse, a medication, or other treatment) or a general medical condition (e.g., hyperthyroidism).
Note: Mixed-like episodes that are clearly caused by somatic antidepressant treatment (e.g., medication, electroconvulsive therapy, light therapy) should not count toward a diagnosis of Bipolar I Disorder.

Criteria for Severity/Psychotic/Remission Specifiers for current (or most recent) Mixed Episode

Note: Code in fifth digit. Can be applied to a Mixed Episode in Bipolar I Disorder only if it is the most recent type of mood episode.

.x1--Mild: No more than minimum symptom criteria are met for both a Manic Episode and a Major Depressive Episode.

.x2--Moderate: Symptoms or functional impairment between "mild" and "severe."

.x3--Severe Without Psychotic Features: Almost continual supervision required to prevent physical harm to self or others.

Chart 7

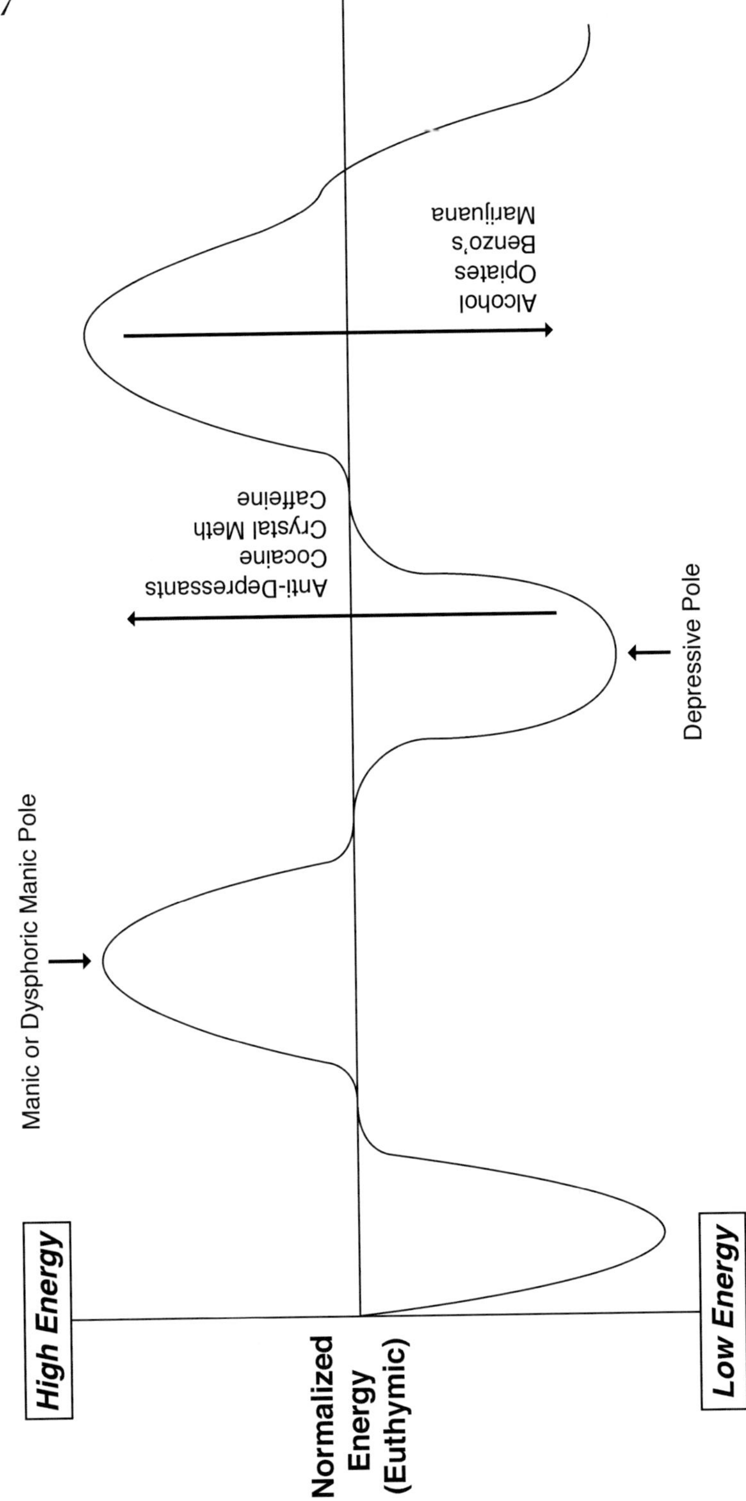

High Energy
Normalized Energy (Euthymic)
Low Energy
Manic or Dysphoric Manic Pole
Depressive Pole
Anti-Depressants
Cocaine
Crystal Meth
Caffeine
Alcohol
Opiates
Benzo's
Marijuana

Chart 8

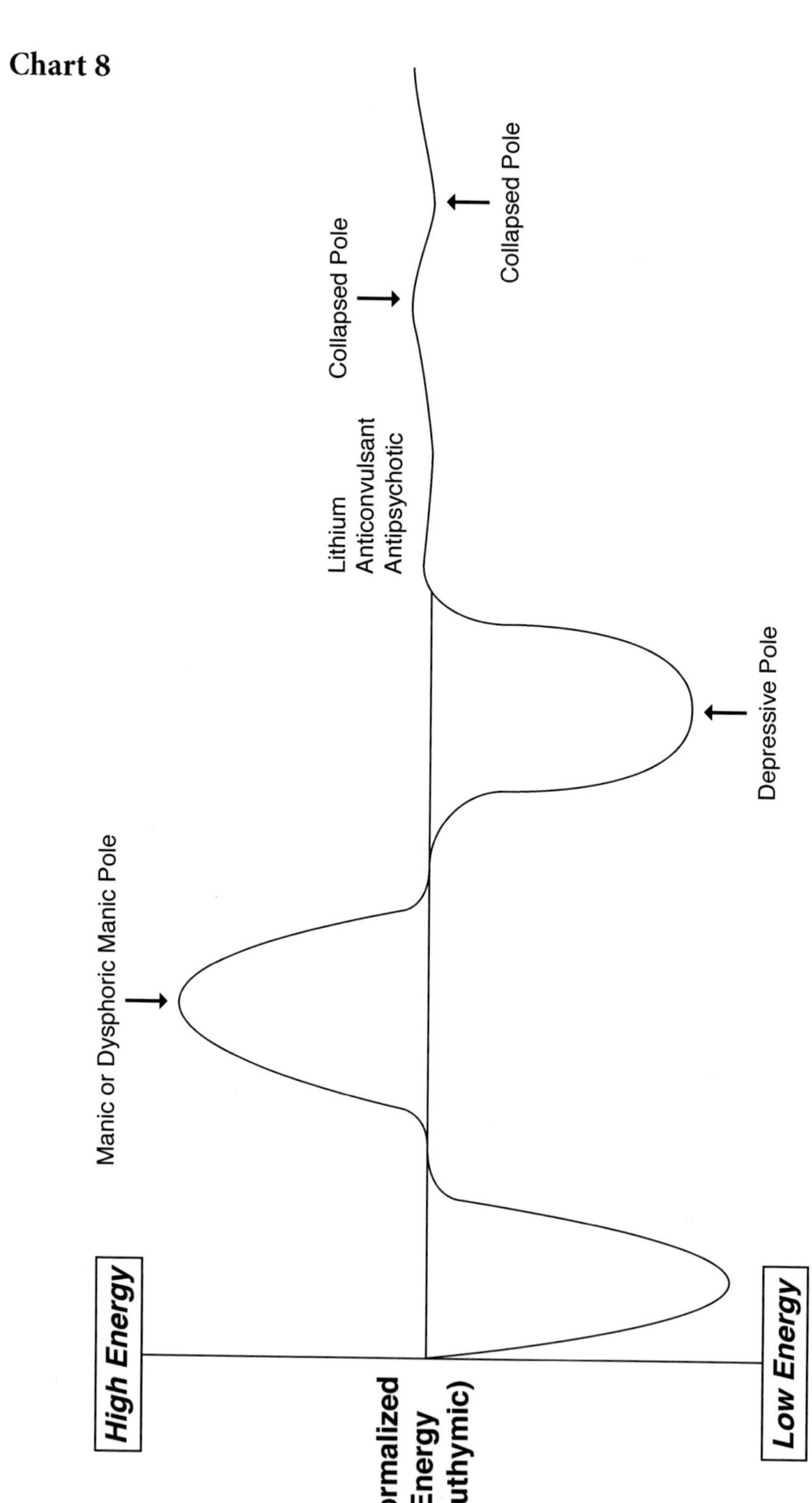

High Energy
Normalized Energy (Euthymic)
Low Energy
Manic or Dysphoric Manic Pole
Depressive Pole
Lithium
Anticonvulsant
Antipsychotic
Collapsed Pole
Collapsed Pole

Chapter 5

JOHN'S NEW REVELATION: THE SUN OF GOD

There truly is a wonderfully predictable and interdependent relationship between mood, sleep and sunlight. It shouldn't be news to anyone that sunlight has a profound behavioral effect on the animal kingdom as manifested by migratory patterns of birds and butterflies. The Sun also seems to dictate an animal's sleep/wake pattern (hibernation in winter) and reproduction (mating season in the spring). These changes in physiology should sound a bit familiar by now. It should undoubtedly remind us of the cycles of energy and hyper-sexuality seen in certain phases of bipolarity. In fact, we could possibly make the contention that "bipolarity" is the natural order of things in the animal kingdom and possibly humanity too. Further evidence of the coupled relationship between Sun, mood and sleep can be seen with the notable facts that light therapy helps treat depression, dark therapy helps treat mania, mood usually worsens with a bad night's sleep, and sleep usually worsens when we are in a bad mood.

I think humans, just like animals, are affected by the forces of nature... especially the ultimate force, The Sun. The fact that light affects human emotion/behavior shouldn't surprise physicians/nurses reading this text, we routinely see this phenomenon in the form of "sundowning" (changes in mental status in the elderly during the late afternoon) . Those however who suffer from a mood disorder are ESPECIALLY vulnerable to The Sun's effects because of the indomitable triad of mood, sleep and sunlight. Major depression appears to have a seasonal variation popularly known as seasonal affective disorder. This is a depressive condition that tends to exacerbate with darkness. It is the true state of "hibernation" as patients tend to become tired and load up on carbohydrates during dark winter months (like a bear). Other aggravators of depression in general do exist however and some of them are stress (stress worsens all Psychiatric conditions), changes in hormones (PMS and perimenopause) and substance use (prescription drugs like anti-hypertensive beta blockers or illicit drugs like heroin) just to name a few.

Symptoms of unipolar major depression can certainly show this previously mentioned susceptibility to changes in light, but manic depression in my opinion is the true poster child for this solar sensitivity. The reason being of course is that bipolar-like behavior is NORMAL in much of the animal kingdom, and last time I checked we as humans are still considered part of that kingdom. Due to this potential normalcy in the wild, it's quite possible that bipolar disorder MAY actually even be MORE prevalent than garden variety unipolar depression in humans contrary to the literature and conventional thinking. It's also not out of reason to speculate that unipolar depressives are possibly just manic depressives who simply spend most of their time in the depressed phase of bipolarity. That's why pharmaceutical companies will be pushing their antipsychotic medications for treatment of depression (Abilify, Zyprexa, Seroquel XR, Rexulti, Vraylar, Latuda). These medications are probably just treating the depressed patients who might have latent bipolarity.

Manic depression normally is defined by having less than 4 manic/ depressive cycles in a calendar year. Anything more than that is considered a "rapid cycler". How interesting that Psychiatry for years has used this seemingly "arbitrary" number (4) as criteria. We actually have 4 solstices in our 365-day calendar. We have a summer solstice June 21st (longest daylight of the year), fall solstice Sept 21st (length of the day equals the length of the night), winter solstice Dec 21st (shortest daylight of the year) and spring solstice March 21st (length of the day equals the length of the night) (Chart 1). Philosophically speaking, think of a solstice as an on/off switch for The Sun. It represents a time of the year with the greatest fluctuation of sunlight on a day to day basis. It's no different than a strobe light. The later changes brain chemistry via light gyrations and can induce seizures (interestingly but probably not coincidently, bipolar disorder and seizures are treated the exact same way....with anticonvulsants).

Now, where I live and practice Psychiatry in the desert of Southern California, we have very little cloud cover and presumably any Sun arching in the sky is the amount of Sun detected in our brains. Undeniably, I've observed an increase in bipolar patient emotionality during these particular times of year (from here on out, I'll define a solstice related event as an event that occurs from about 2 weeks before the day of the solstice to about 4 weeks after the solstice). I'm pretty much at the point that if a new patient sees me around these elapsed dates, they are usually bipolar. It is important to mention that since I live on a southern latitude, it is not unusual that bipolars here in the Desert start having problems a month BEFORE the Spring solstice, whereas bipolars in more northern regions experience difficulties sometimes after. In global aggregate however, my hopes are that I will prove (by charting) that the solar reactivity IN SUMMATION falls around the solstice or just after. Each global bipolar patient reacts differently to sunlight, and this is not just a function of differing latitudes, but also of differing individual biochemical sensitivities to light and darkness as well.

Before I can get into these details though, I probably should review some basic physiology of this process. Darkness is detected by the retina in the back of our eyes, and this information is passed onto the suprachiasmatic nuclei in the hypothalamus (our master hormonal controller in our brain). The hypothalamus then stimulates the pineal gland to produce melatonin from L-tryptophan (Chart 2). Melatonin then goes on to induce sleep and also has an influence on animal breeding behavior (Chart 3). From my observations, these solstices must be causing disruptions in melatonin secondary to the absolute amount of darkness (June 21 and Dec 21) and the accelerating fluctuations of darkness (Mar 21 and Sept 21) detected on the retina. The perception of this darkness however might take some time to translate into behavior…a sort of lag period for the process to take place. Emotionality IN SUMMATION (but not necessarily individually) tends to as mentioned start about 2 weeks before the day of the solstice, and it continues through a good portion of the following month. But don't forget, since equatorial latitudes are sunnier compared to northern latitudes (for instance in springtime), they in theory should be slightly out of sync compared to each other as mentioned.

Contrary to the animal kingdom, ANY energy phase of the human bipolar condition can occur at any of the 4 solstices in humans. I've seen fatigued patients in July and manic patients in December. I've even seen radical changes of energy all within the same day at any particular solstice. Unlike the sensible energy variations in the animal world, there is no logical explanation in humans. What is consistent though, is that each patient tends to have that unique "seasonal fingerprint" (or times of year) that is fairly predictable for emotional symptom worsening. This worsening of bipolarity can be retroactively reconstructed and time lined. Problematic events such as job firings (because of a fatigued phase), arrests/Psych hospitalizations/ drug use and rehabs/suicide attempts (in a dysphoric manic phase) or affairs/irrational purchases (manic phase) that cluster in and around these solstice dates, give a high probability of bipolar disorder as causality. One may see patterns in NON-solstice related months too, as some people simply have different sensitivities to light and darkness. Solstice related events are important, but a regular "monthly" pattern is probably more important as far as any individual bipolar patient is concerned. Clearly, a lot of very bad behavior occurs during these solstices and it's not courtesy of "The Prince of Darkness"...but rather The Sun of God.

To prove the relationship that the time of year influences human behavior, I took some time to timeline suicides and murder/ suicides (shooting sprees). Suicides would be an excellent proxy for emotionality and murder/ suicides as well. Murders were not included as many murders could simply be perpetrated for some type of secondary gain (like money) where as any event ending in a suicide is most of the time a result of personal emotional pain. I chose to use Wikipedia 's database of "famous suicides" and famous "killing sprees (with resulting suicide)" as my source of record. Immediately, one might say that the database is flawed as it represented "famous" people and maybe this group is not representative of the population. My only response to this is that it's very difficult to access any other broad representation of suicides that are equally distributed across the various geographical latitudes of the world (in order to make ONE graph). A good study in the future might also include suicides at only ONE latitude or perhaps graphing and comparing suicides in SMALL countries that share similar latitudes. In addition, actually ACQUIRING this suicide information is difficult and Wikipedia also includes vital BIOGRAPGHICAL information which assisted in my "Psychiatric Autopsy". A "Psychiatric Autopsy" was critical in determining who potentially suffered from a Psychiatric condition prior to the suicide. My contention being Psychiatric patients (especially mood disorders) are more affected by The Sun than non-Psychiatric. I would also mention that some of the suicides were not ultimately perpetrated by famous people, but often a relative of a famous person or the suicide itself became famous because it somehow became a news story (like Columbine). All the "killing sprees" however were perpetrated by non-famous people as one might expect, so fame flaming this bad behavior is less of an issue.

Some have already suspected that sunlight might confer suicidality in general based on statistics and graphing (Chart 4). This 1999-2004 monthly suicide chart found on Wiki is definitely not a straight line and appears to show a greater amount of suicides as the days get longer and brighter. Note though in Chart 5 how the SOUTHERN HEMISPHERE has a peak suicide rate in and around Dec (their summer) and THE NORTHERN HEMI-

SPHERE has a peak in and around June (their summer). This shows that The Sun probably plays a role as The Southern Hemisphere experiences less intense daylight when the Northern Hemisphere experiences more intense daylight and visa versa. When I constructed my own graphs, my hopes were that that the solstices would show more volatility because that's what I've been seeing in my office for 23 years now.

I think that The Sun probably effects EVERYBODY'S behavior, but more so for mood disordered patients (especially bipolars). The first graph I constructed (Chart 6) was therefore all famous suicides vs. time to get an idea of what a general population suicide chart would look like (all of my chart's data and subsequent graphs included both hemispheres and all latitudes so the reader should expect some muddiness). MY initial chart of ALL suicides vs. time shows a higher weighted suicide rate in early summer compared to winter time. We might have anticipated this given what we saw on Chart 4 (a previously made graph I found on Wiki). I see some "solstice activity" but nothing to get too excited over. At least I knew I was heading in the right direction. I suspect most of the 666 suicides investigated (not to insult the intelligence of my reader …but I swear that number wasn't engineered…I always thought it was 665 until I looked at my data again just before publication) on Wikipedia were located in The Northern Hemisphere as this looks more like a Northern Hemisphere distribution like we saw in Chart 4.

When researching all of the suicides, many of them occurred years ago and Psychiatric illness was not even well understood. So therefore, for my second graph, I performed a "Psychiatric Autopsy" and tried to identify those amongst this overall group who had a good chance of being PSYCHIATRIC in general. This was an attempt to see how sunlight effected the whole Psychiatric group which I suspect has a high but not inclusive representation of mood disorders…but it's impossible to know for sure who had a mood disorder and who didn't. It was a judgment call on my part to decide who, in retrospect, appeared to have a Psychiatric condition given the biographical data provided. If a biography included details such as substance abuse or "melancholy" for example…they were added to my list as being probably "Psychiatric". I needed a website with extensive biographical information for each suicide to help with this, which is why Wikipedia was so helpful. My Psychiatric autopsy ONLY determined if the patient had a probability of a mental illness and nothing more.

So, in trying to tease out AN EVEN BETTER solstice related effect as seen in my office, I needed to also figure out who amongst this previously mentioned "Psychiatric" group had a likelihood of having a mood disorder (recall, I hypothesize that mood disorders are most sensitive to The Sun). Based on these biographies however, it was very difficult to figure out who had a mood disorder. If a biography stated the patient was "Psychiatrically hospitalized", I knew that he/she was "Psychiatric"...but I could not necessarily confirm it as a mood disorder. That's why I thought it would be interesting to determine who amongst the group were EMPLOYED as "artists". This might be a sensitive proxy for this mood disorder group as we discussed in the last chapter. Plotting artist suicide versus time might show the most accurate solstice related fluctuation in suicides. These are the real deal mood disordered people who I might see in my office.

I plotted 3 groups of suicides against time: 1) as mentioned ALL suicides against time, 2) a group that overall appeared to have a high suspicion of a Psychiatric Axis 1 condition (Chart 7) based on my interpretation of that person's life (my Psychiatric Autopsy data). Axis II disorders (personality disorders) were not included in this "Psychiatric" grouping as I contend Axis II personality Disorders are not biologically based (another chapter) and therefore should not respond vigorously to biological cues. And 3) People whose primary jobs were artistic (writers, poets, actors, painters, designers etc...this identifies possible mood disorders, especially bipolar) (Chart 8).

In visual analysis of our "Psychiatric Autopsy" chart (Chart 7), we don't see an exact distribution of solstice oriented suicides as hoped , but we clearly don't see a straight line either. We do see relative over-representations seen in Dec (predictable), late Feb (not predicted), April (predictable), late June (predictable) and early Oct (predictable). Remember, my sample population only numbered 666 (I honestly don't blame you if you don't believe me) (Chart 9) and might be too small to notice any true trends. In addition, both hemispheres and all latitudes were included. Sampling date ends with suicides up to April of 2009 (when thanks to the recession, I had a lot more time on my hands, and I started writing this book). Suicides where the victim disappeared and was later found dead were NOT included, as the true date of the suicide could not be ascertained (Chart 10...omitted group).

The third chart (Chart 8) was "artists" against time. Again, my contention is that everyone responds to The Sun but it is the people with mood disorders who are most exquisitely sensitive. I don't know who had a mood disorder from Wikipedia's biographical data, but I did know whose primary occupation was artistry. This graph again isn't perfect, but it does show over-representation in and around all four solstices. Just like the "Psychiatric Autopsy" chart however, we do see a bump in Feb which is clearly not expected. However, you will soon learn the possible cause of this bump later in the chapter. I call it "The Britney Effect". If the reader still is in question of this solstice effect…I will once again refer to "Google Trends". "Google Trends" is an application of Google that allows investigation of frequency and location of any Googled term. If one "Google Trends" the words "assisted suicide"…each year the EXACT SAME GRAPH is formed (Chart 11). It is a true "sinusoidal wave" with peaks at the first solstice (March 21st) and third solstice (Sept 21st). It is in my opinion the 1st and 3rd solstices (transition solstices) are the most powerfully influential on mood. At these emotionally sensitive times of year, the unstable are clearly searching for solutions to their emotional instability and this is proof of it.

Although early summer in the United States is considered to have the most suicides traditionally, I maintain the spring solstice is the most deadly (I call it "Bipolar Alley"). This is based on the density of suicides on my chart, my Psychiatric practice, and the types of offenses that are committed. The day of the Spring solstice is March 21st. Bipolar patients (and maybe unipolar patients) tend to decompensate in mid-March through the end of April. Don't forget, even though the animal kingdom is becoming manic at this time (energized and hyper sexual…aka mating season), humans are simply becoming emotional…whether it be a fatigued state, a manic state, or an irritable dysphoric manic state. Many people can be manic this time of year, and the term "spring cleaning" is probably just a euphemism for "I'm feeling manicy and getting stuff done". But on the other hand, as I mentioned, many of the problems that occur at this time of year tend to revolve around the dysphoric manic IRRITABLE state. As a result, numerous profoundly "evil" violent acts have occurred in the spring: Heaven's Gate (3/26/1997), Boston Marathon Bombings (4/15/2013), Virginia Tech (4/16/2007), Waco Texas (4/19/1993), Oklahoma City Bombing (4/19/1995) and Columbine (4/20/1999). Of these, The Oklahoma and Boston marathon bombing smell the least like bipolar but many of the others are marinating in it. Marshall Applewhite (Heaven's Gate Cult leader) had a Psychiatric hospitalization history and clearly was manic, most likely flagrantly psychotic (he believed he was Jesus Christ incarnate). David

Koresh (Branch Davidian cult leader…Waco TX) in all likelihood also had bipolar disorder as manifested by his hyper-sexuality (polygamy, child sexual abuse?) and delusions that he too was "The Son of God". Seungui Cho (Virginia Tech) also had a very high probability of bipolar as he was a writer, and these writings usually revolved around violence. And lastly, there was Columbine. Dylan Klebold, based upon his biography had very little mental pathology. Eric Harris on the other hand, was being treated for depression with Luvox (an antidepressant). As we have hopefully learned, bad things happen when undiagnosed bipolars receive antidepressant treatment WITHOUT a mood stabilizer.

A notable suicide that occurred during this time period was the author John O'Brien (4/10/1994). His book "Leaving Las Vegas", later adapted to film, was a loose autobiography about a man with chronic alcoholism. He was probably bipolar and this illustrates to us several important points: Bipolars tend to be writers AND they frequently are intractable alcoholics AND they kill themselves around a solstice. Please keep in mind that pure-play unipolar depressives are already depressed and tired, and based on my theory….would have very little use for alcohol. It's the irritable bipolar patient who needs the anxiety relief that a substance like alcohol provides. Hence my conjecture that O'Brien was bipolar and not just "depressed".

With regards to suicides in particular at this solstice, there are too many to list in this paragraph, but please refer to my master suicide list for specifics. Many famous actors and musicians have killed themselves in this period including: Brad Delp 3/9/2007 (lead singer for Boston), Richard Jeni 3/10/2007 (comedian with "depression and psychosis" which is typically code for bipolar), Kurt Cobain 4/5/1994 (lead singer for Nirvana) , David Strickland 3/22/99 (extensive addiction to cocaine/ alcohol and starred in "Suddenly Susan") and Prince on April 21,2016 (unintentional Fentanyl overdose) . Layne Staley…the lead singer for "Alice in Chains"….was found dead on April 19th as a result of suicide or an overdose of cocaine and heroin (aka Speedball). The date of his death was hypothesized to be about April 5, 2002. Although Layne is an obscure reference to most, I add this example not only because he was my favorite male vocalist of all time, but also because Layne formed a rock group after his days with "Alice in Chains" called "Mad Season". It is quite obvious to me he chose this name as I'm sure he experienced numerous "mad seasons" being potentially bipolar.

I don't really like including homicides (unless it's a murder/suicide) as evidence of violent bipolar behavior. Sometimes there is "logical" secondary gain involved with murder but I'd like to mention a few significant events. Mid-April is the time of The Crucifixion of Jesus. It hangs dead in the cross hairs of "Bipolar Alley". This date could represent two possible bipolar events. Either Jesus was in fact bipolar (aggressively turning over tables and psychotically stating He was the Son of God) and as a result he was crucified for heresy. Or, He was the Son of God, and mass solstice related hysteria led to His Death. But there is also the possibility that Jesus was The Son of God AND He was Bipolar. In which case, He would have been the first person in history to have the delusion that He was in fact Himself (haha.., a little light hearted humor to ease the pain of a sensitive topic). In another example, "The Craigslist Killer" Philip Markoff robbed 3 women and killed one in the middle of Bipolar Alley as well…April 10,14,16. He was thought to be quite bright, but also a violent, hyper sexual substance abuser. He went onto commit suicide in a non-solstice month (August). I'd also like to mention the famous term "Beware of the Ides of March". March 15th is the infamous day of Julius Caesar's murder.

The Germanwings plane crash that occurred on March 24th 2015 should also be considered a bipolar event. Andreas Lubitz had sought Psychiatric care for some time prior to this solstice related tragedy. This event clearly was a murder/suicide no different than a shooting spree. I can't help but think that Malaysia flight 370 that was lost on March 8th 2014 was not only a similar solstice suicide mission, but was also the inspiration for the Germanwing's tragedy.

By the time this chapter is finished, I would have given compelling evidence that The Sun affects our behavior which in turn also effects financial markets as well. With regards to the March solstice, please note the highly emotional March 9th mega low that occurred in 2009 in the Dow, S and P, and Nasdaq. Clearly "Apocalyptic" events come in many packages such as war, financial turmoil and generalized mayhem. The early astrologists must have really known what they were doing when they assigned April as Aries (Mars)…he truly is The God of War (and chaos!).

If one looks at the statistics, "summer" has a very high number of suicides in the Northern Hemisphere due to its proximity to the June 21st solstice. This fact alone should tell us that either sunlight (or less likely heat) is somehow involved in our mood and behavior. I found numerous familiar names who have taken their lives in this time period. In addition, there are numerous unsolved mysteries associated with many of them. Let's start with an easy one. Ernest Hemingway was a writer and had a prolific alcohol history. In addition, his father, sister, brother and Grandfather all killed themselves. Clearly, this man was bipolar given his profile, family history and the date of his suicide as 7/2/1961. Bipolarity is genetic and was probably involved with his daughter Margaux's death as well… she killed herself 7/1/1996. They apparently had the same light sensitivity given the almost identical day of death. Another interesting story is the unknown circumstances around George Reeves (Superman). He was found shot in the head on 6/16/1959 and the story was chronicled in the 2006 movie "Hollywoodland". The facts that had me thinking bipolar were his profession (actor), his use of pain killers (supposedly from a car accident), he was intoxicated with alcohol at the time (was this happening frequently?) and he was suffering from "depression" according to some (Wikipedia). Another notable suicide in July was Shannon Wilsey on 7/11/1994 (pornography actress aka "Savanna"). This should illustrate that pornography often attracts those who are "hyper sexual" and possibly bipolar (look for the tattoos!). Vince Foster (former Clinton Administration) was being treated with the antidepressant Trazodone which very easily could have conspired with "The Sun" to induce his possible bipolarity into a suicidal dysphoric manic state which resulted in completed suicide on 7/20/1993. Chris Benoit, the famous wrestler had a few risk factors that may have influenced his behavior in killing of his wife, child and then himself. Professional wrestling actually IS ACTING and is also violent (both bipolar qualities). Add the summer solstice sun of 6/24/2007 and probable anabolic steroid abuse, and familicide is the unfortunate result. Although the massacre in Aurora Colorado at a movie theatre did not include a suicide, I'm wondering if the shooter James Holmes wasn't also bipolar. As a Psychiatrist, I'm in many ways an investigator of clues. The evidence is as follows: this case involves a date just barely within the solstice influence (July 20,2012), hyper sexuality (accused shooter was on a sex web site), high intelligence (pursuing a PhD in Neuroscience), sleep issues (he should have been sleeping at the time of the assault), he had Zoloft (an antidepressant) in his system, aggression, and he dyed his hair orange (similar concept as having a tattoo) (Chart 12). He was probably bipolar but given the extent of his extreme shyness, the diagnosis might be somewhat towards the schizophrenic end of the bipolar continuum. And finally, in my opinion, it's only a matter of time before it is considered that Dylann Roof, notoriously known as the Charleston South Carolina church shooter (6/17/15), is possibly diagnosed bipolar as well (OCD symptoms, Suboxone [Opiate like] abuser).

Completed suicides most of the time represent the end result of the extreme discomfort that some bipolars feel when their condition worsens (usually dysphoric mania). As mentioned, one other way they deal with this discomfort is self-medication with drugs and alcohol (like Prince as previously mentioned). When substances are used and abused to self-medicate said symptoms, quite often a dose that was supposed to make them feel better actually causes a miscalculated death. This is termed an unintentional overdose. Jim Morrison, the lead singer and lyricist for The Doors, died on 7/3/1971 of not surprisingly a heroin overdose. Once again, in my opinion, heroin abusers are considered bipolar until proven otherwise. The official cause of death for Michael Jackson is Propofol (an anesthetic). He also had other central nervous system depressants in his system including Valium, Lorazepam and Midazolam. This tells me he was highly irritable and not sleeping…quite indicative of a dysphoric manic state. Given the date of death 6/25/2009, his musical genius, rumors of a spending addiction…everyone should be thinking he might have been bipolar as well. Unfortunately, inappropriate treatment of this condition with pure play CNS depressants to calm his anxiety resulted in death secondary to cardiac and pulmonary failure. Later in this book I'll hint that he may have had a personality disorder as well. I never examined him but I think he may have had both conditions. The reality is, for as much as The Universe gave him (fame, wealth, talent), The Universe took in return in the form of mental illness. I call it The Universe's "balancing act" (keeps us all humble and equal). Another way of looking at this balancing act is "the nicer the meal, the greater the tab". The whole idea of net zero balance is a recurrent theme in The Cosmos (matter balancing out all anti-matter/ for every motion there is an equal and opposite motion etc.). I wonder the same thing about OJ Simpson's balancing act. Although this once shining star is described as having personality characteristics akin to a sociopath, I also ponder the diagnosis of bipolarity given the dates of the Las Vegas Robbery (9/13/2007) and the unproven homicide of Nicole Brown and Ron Goldman (6/13/1994).

As long as we are discussing murders, Jody Arias was found guilty by a jury of her peers in the June 4, 2008 murder of Travis Alexander. Many factors here clinch a possible bipolar diagnosis as well. The murder was chaotic, it was roughly 2 weeks before the solstice, she hadn't been sleeping for several nights prior to the murder, she apparently was hyper sexual, and was an accomplished artist (painter, singer). She also appears to demonstrate elements of sociopathy just like OJ but that's a different story. Aaron Hernandez, the former New England Patriot, also showed characteristics of possible bipolarity. He was convicted of murder that occurred at a solstice (6/17/2013), and had numerous solstice related infractions (9/30/2007 "shots fired", 7/16/2012 double murder suspect). He was well known to be a marijuana abuser (self-medication), and had copious tattoos. He went on to commit suicide during Bipolar Alley (04/19/2017). Omar Mateen, the perpetrator of the second most deadly US shooting spree in history on June 12, 2016 also fits the profile of possible bipolar. In the third grade, he was already preoccupied with "violence and sex" (wiki) and as he got older instigated numerous fights and had been arrested for battery. His ex-wife even characterized him as "bipolar" (wiki).

And then there is the Sept 21st Solstice. Is The FALL-en Angel responsible for this one? This solstice will be appreciated by anyone who has interest in financial market psychology. I like to think of the stock market as a giant Ouija board which measures the collective emotional unconsciousness of the species as a whole. Traditionally, September and October show extreme volatility in the stock market…and now we know why. As The Sun starts to arc downwards in late Sept, the length of the days relative to the nights is in greatest flux and the intensity of The Sun is weakening (just like "sundowning" in elderly patients). Another way we can conceptualize this loss in Sun intensity is that this date often represents the date after which most people are unable to tan (lessened sun intensity compared to the summer). The same holds true for March 21st where the sun's intensity after this date improves successful tanning for most.

There are three ways to historically view fluctuations in the market. First is to monitor your monthly 401k statement. Second is to actually look at a retroactive chart of The Dow, Standard and Poor's, and Nasdaq composites to visually see fluctuations in daily value. If we did this we would see Apocalyptic lows on the week of Oct 6th 2008 and on March 9th 2009. The later resulted in a Standard and Poors absolute low of 666 points (yikes, kinda spooky and both uncomfortably close to solstices too) (Chart 13). The other way to monitor the market "emotionality" is to observe "The VIX". This is the CBOE volatility index which measures the emotionality (fear or greed) in the market through the buying of options to protect existing stock holdings (put /call options ratio). For example, let's say you own shares of a fictitious company ESQ123. If you felt that the price was going down, you would buy "puts" (a bet that the price of each ESQ123 share is going down) which would increase in monetary value as your original shares decreased in monetary value. The end result would be a diminished loss of your original investment. A high number on the VIX implies an increased frequency of purchased "put options" (because of fear in the market) and it is usually associated with a market drop. A low value in the VIX implies relatively high purchasing of "call options" implying "mania" and the market moving upwards. VIX measurements have only been monitored since 1990, but observing the VIX over the last 20 years shows a consistency that most fearful spikes upwards occur during these solstices…especially Sept and Oct in general, and profoundly during Sept/Oct 2008 (Chart 14). Solstices probably played a substantial part in the market crash of 1929 as it occurred Oct 24th-29th (23% market drop) and the 1987 crash which was Oct 14th-19th (28% drop). Unfortunately, The VIX was not available during these times thus the plunges can't be seen on any VIX charting. Now that I have identified emotional times of the year, later in the chapter we will figure out the most financially "emotional" years of the century…and it's all dictated by sunlight. But I digress…back to the Sept solstice.

There are numerous suicides and overdoses at this solstice and the former can be viewed on the master suicide list. One suicide in particular that should be addressed is that of Sigmund Freud….a founding father of Psychiatric Psychoanalytic Theory. It's always been joked about that Psychiatrists have as many issues as their patients and this might be true based on these observations. Firstly, he spent most of his years constructing the "Psychosexual Development" of humans. Not a big deal, but in researching suicides, I found that he had a "ménage a troi" (three-way sex) with one male Psychiatrist named Victor Tausk and another female Psychiatrist named Lou Salome. The former went on to kill himself after the encounter. After discovering his personal history and professional preoccupations…I'm kind of thinking Freud had an unhealthy preoccupation with sex (hyper sexuality). Freud killed himself near the solstice (9/23/39) and with (you guessed it) Morphine (a pain killer). Clearly, the greats tend to be bipolar.

I would also like to mention three unintentional overdoses of importance. Jimi Hendrix, the famed musician ironically sang a song called "Manic Depression"…that in of itself is a clue as to how he felt. There has been a controversy that he was murdered, but given the day of his sleeping pill overdose (9/18/1970)…I'm betting on an unintentional OD secondary to seasonal worsening of his possible bipolarity and the insomnia that goes with it. Janis Joplin was also a musical legend and the possibility of bipolarity is quite high with her as well given the date (10/4/1970) and drug choices (heroin, alcohol).

September of 2010 brought a rash of unusually clumped and highly publicized suicides in the gay community as well. There was a string of 9 suicides in all. They began Sept 9th (Billy Lukas, Indiana), and stretched right through the solstice until Sept 30th (Caleb Nolt, Indiana). Tyler Clemente's case was the most famous of the suicides. As you recall, a streaming video of he and another man was clandestinely broadcast on the net and he subsequently jumped from a bridge on September 22nd. I'm guessing all of these unfortunate cases COULD have been suffering from an underlying bipolar condition which exacerbated with stress and changes in sunlight. I hope this illustration not only contributes to the recognition and eradication of bullying on any minority group, but also highlight the need for recognition and management of mental illness. The other suicides were as follows: Cody Barker-Sept 13th –Wisconsin, Seth Walsh-Sept 19th-California, Asher Brown-Sept 23rd-Texas, Harrison Brown- Sept 25th-Colorado, Raymond Chase-Sept 29th-Rhode Island, and Felix Sacco-Sept 29th-Massachusetts.

I would be remiss if I didn't mention the events surrounding 9/11. It would be tempting to add this to the list of solstice related tragedies, but it wouldn't be appropriate. Solstice related "bipolar" events tend to be frenzied and relatively spontaneous. 9/11 was obviously a carefully planned event that perhaps was years in the making. Having said that, the hijackers on the day of reckoning could have been in a solstice related hyper religious suicidal bipolar state, simply by coincidence of the pre-chosen date. The mass shooting at the Mandalay Bay in Las Vegas on October 1, 2017 was, however, in my opinion a classic solstice related tragedy.

From my observation, The Dec 21st solstice probably has the weakest effect on mood disorders (although this may be refuted by the enormity of the January 8th, 2011 shooting spree involving Rep. Gabrielle Giffords at a town hall meeting in Tucson, AZ). Residents of Newtown, Connecticut might also beg to differ (school shooting Dec 12th, 2012). But despite its relative weakness, according to Mayan prophecy, this solstice was to usher in "the Apocalypse" in 2012 (12/21/2012). If people refer to "The Holiday

Blues"...they are unintentionally referring to this particular solstice effect. I have a friend who owns a wine shop and he contends alcohol sales go through the roof at this time of year. He postulates that alcohol intoxication is the best way to deal with difficult family members during the Holidays. I retort back that it's probably a solstice issue, but in teasing it out, we both are probably speaking the same language.

Unfortunately, numerous suicides have manifested in this time period but one in particular interests me. Frederick Fleet was the look-out for The Titanic. Frederick hung himself during this solstice (1/10/1965)...more than 50 years AFTER the ill-fated behemoth struck an iceberg on 4/14/1912. Clearly his suicide was NOT an impulsive post-sinking event as it occurred many years after the fact. But, how interesting is it that The Titanic went down in the thick of "Bipolar Alley"? Maybe somewhere along the chain of command bipolarity played a role in the Titanic's fate? Frederick Fleet, as evidenced by a violent suicide at the fourth solstice, very well may have had the condition and was unstable during that voyage. It's possible his sense of judgment and perception was impaired that April evening which in turn increased the chance of an accident. It's also quite possible that the unreasonably "manic" speed allegedly demanded by J. Bruce Ismay (Managing Director of White Star Lines) was also a result of mania. After the sinking, Ismay and the other survivors were saved by The Carpathia. He was said to be emotionally inconsolable at the time and placed under opiate treatment for the balance of the trip. I also wonder if the Costa Concordia wreck on January 13, 2012 had a similar bipolar causality but at a different solstice. All my allegations of bipolarity based on human illustrations are pure speculation of course.

Two notable unintentional overdoses occurred at this solstice as well. Chris Farley, one of my favorite comics, died on 12/18/1997 after binging on the oppositely acting cocaine and morphine. Recall that these drugs are often used simultaneously by bipolars to treat the rapidly occurring poles worsened by the other drug. Chris Farley was a comedic giant, and bipolarity is quite common in this particular profession as it requires supreme intelligence, creativity and animation. He allegedly had profound bouts of depression towards the end of his life, so the possibility of bipolarity certainly exists. Many would concede that he simply had depression, but anybody who chooses to abuse drugs that are CNS depressants (like opiates and alcohol) are clearly battling irritability. In addition, I think his excessive eating was probably self-medication. Some bipolars have excessive and otherwise unexplainable weight gain as food consumption seems to be their "drug" of choice to treat their irritability (think Elvis). Once again, depression+ IRRITABILITY= bipolar disorder most of the time. Another virtuoso was Heath Ledger, an academy award winning actor who died on 1/22/2008. Not surprisingly, opiate based pain killers were involved (Oxycodone, Hydrocodone) as were central nervous system depressants like Valium, Restoril, and Xanax. People who overdose on CNS depressants usually die from the respiratory depression associated with these chemicals effects on the brain stem.

The 4th Solstice (Dec 21st) may also trigger other unusual human behaviors (especially in light sensitive bipolar patients). Recall that "mania" in the animal world is characterized by hyper sexuality and arousal. This behavior in the animal kingdom most often occurs around the 1st solstice (March 21st) or shortly thereafter (aka: mating season). However, mania in humans may be triggered by any of the solstices. The 4th solstice (absolute darkness) may be a profound time of mania (hyper sexuality) as evidenced by the month of September being the most common birth month. September of course is the 9th gestational month after the 4th solstice. Some might argue that it is simply a reflection of the cold weather fostering the need for thermal closeness…but "Google Trends" proves otherwise. If we Google trend the word "sex"...we notice a repeating spike at the fourth solstice year after year (Chart 15a). This tells me that manic people have sex on the brain at this solstice which results in high Google inquiries and the increased performance of sex itself. I also believe "mania" at this solstice could be the cause of the heavy buying often seen in the stock market in December (aka A Santa Clause Rally). For example, Bitcoin prices doubled during December 2017, but then predictably crashed 30% (mood change) at the exact timing of the winter solstice (Dec 19-22) (Chart 15b). In addition, I think "buying" at the holidays (holiday shopping) is also a collective manifestation of mania in general. Funny how The Universe chemically prepared everybody for Holiday shopping......there are no coincidences in my opinion.

It's been highly publicized that Britney Spears also has a Psychiatric condition, possibly bipolar. Her drugs of choice are unknown but alcohol seems to be involved. I mention her case not to disparage her, but only to illustrate that many bipolar patients may not follow the EXACT umbrella of the solstice, but they do, as mentioned, tend to have predictably vulnerable PATTERNS of the year when they worsen. Britney seemed to have difficulty in early Jan but most notably in February (clearly NOT associated with a solstice). February 6th, 2006 she was photographed with her son in her lap as she drove her car implying poor judgment. February 14th, 2007 she was admitted to Crossroads drug rehab and then she shaved her head on February 16th. On February 20th, she attended another drug rehab called Promises in Malibu CA. To review, a drug rehab visit implies that the patient's Psychiatric condition is in the process of exacerbation, and the patient is frantically trying to "self-medicate" with substances. The following year she had an episode of 4-day insomnia in Jan 2008 resulting in a Cedar Sinai Hospitalization from which she was discharged Feb 6th. From my experience as I have mentioned, some of my bipolar patients (in the desert southwest) begin their March 21st solstice VERY EARLY due to the sunny nature here in Southern Cal. It becomes sunnier earlier. Now we know why my suicide charts 1, 2 and 3 had bumps in Feb! My data source is probably flawed. "Famous Suicides" include famous people. Many of these famous people are famous because they are in the entertainment industry which is located in sunny Southern California. Sunny Southern California has its own distribution of suicides because of its southern latitude. Therefore, this is why I call my Feb bump "The Britney Effect".

At this point I would like to again work backwards in an attempt to understand some related concepts. I began the chapter discussing how "bipolarity" is actually the norm in the animal kingdom. I then went on to hopefully give a good argument that "bipolarity" might even be normal in humans...or at the very least EXTREMELY common. Human symptoms of this condition in many ways mimic those of the animal kingdom. Now peering back at the animal kingdom...we can make sense of many animal related tragedies. Tilikum, the killer whale, killed his trainer Katie Byrne, after she inadvertently fell in a holding tank at Orlando's SeaWorld. Note the date Feb 24th, 2010. This is approaching the first solstice (March 21st) but with the "The Britney Effect" timeline. The interesting part is that Tilikum killed another human at almost the same date (Feb 21st) in 1991. Clearly this animal's behavioral "fingerprint" shows a vulnerability in Feb (just like Britney). A third victim of this whale is also noted. But unlike the other deaths, this one occurred on July 2nd, 1999 (very close to the second solstice, June 21st). The circumstances around this death are as follows. A park visitor hid in the zoo complex afterhours and somehow during the night found his way into Tilikum's pool. The visitor was found dead the next morning. Given the bizarre nature of this event, I would bet that it was the GUEST who was in fact manically psychotic at that solstice, and the animal simply did what came naturally (given the fact there was a persistent presence in his environment). Another animal related tragedy that took place in Feb was that of the Connecticut Chimpanzee that inexplicably mauled Charla Nash on Feb 16th, 2009. I'm guessing this close to springtime volatility is a manifestation of "mating season". One last example of a solstice related tragedy occurred at close to the 3rd solstice. Siegfried and Roy's 7-year-old White Tiger "Montecore" spontaneously attacked his trainer Roy Horn during one of the shows held in Las Vegas. The date: October 3rd 2003, a date that on my timeline shows profound behavioral volatility in humans. Given the common effect of The Sun....it would be interesting to see if there is any temporal relationship in frequency of random animal attacks (like dogs, whales, primates and bears etc.) and increased volatility in human behavior such as shooting sprees/ suicides and stock market swoons. I'll be watching for these associative tragedies to occur in the upcoming years of the so-called "Apocalypse".

Now, back to humans. If a patient does not have a "sensitive" solstice related worsening (like we saw with Britney Spears February vulnerability), it's always useful to at least look for some type of repetitive seasonal pattern or certain predictably problematic month that serve as their disease's solar "fingerprint". For one reason or another, these "off solstice" bipolar patients are just a little more OR less sensitive to light and dark (and of course latitude plays a part as well). By paying attention to these vulnerable times of year for any particular human bipolar patient (and maybe animal too!), future problems can be avoided by medicinal prophylaxis or stress avoidance.

Like I've mentioned, the emotionality seen at the time of the solstices isn't a fool-proof tool for predictability. Even my graph of allegedly "Psychiatrically vulnerable" patients showed activity during the supposedly quiescent months of Feb, May, Aug and Nov. In these cases, its' possible patients are following a cycle, but they are inherently either a little more or less sensitive to the effect of light (or darkness). Then there is the issue of latitude which thus far I've regrettably mentioned about 10 times. A person located in an equatorial latitude will clearly be exposed to more intense light at any given time relative to a northern latitude. This would mean they would respond earlier in the case of the spring solstice for example. Having said that, there are several notable examples of possible bipolars who did not die near a solstice. The King, Elvis Presley, who has long been suspected as being bipolar (hyper sexual, eating disordered weight gain, and chronic depression) died of an unintentional overdose (14 different types of pills were found in his system) on 8/16/1977. Marilyn Monroe, had a personal history of Psychiatric illness and a mother who was Psychiatrically hospitalized for a mental breakdown (genetics!). Marilyn was found on 8/5/1962. She overdosed on Chloral hydrate (a sleeper) and Nembutal (Pentobarbitol). And Finally, Anna Nicole Smith seems to also possibly fit criteria for bipolarity…bouts of depression, worked in the sex industry, and she was an artist (painter). She died on 2/2/2007 secondary to toxicity from opiates. However, even though her death didn't correspond to a solstice… her son's did. Her son died on Sept 10 2006 with Lexapro and Zoloft (both antidepressants) in his system. Undoubtedly, he was feeling depressed, he consumed two separate antidepressants which helped the depression, but probably induced a dysphoric manic state. This irritability was probably self-medicated with opiates (and subsequently Methodone to treat the opiate abuse) which in turn killed him by respiratory depression. Genetically, I think his Psychiatric condition was identical to his mom's. In a similar case of antidepressant induction of a possible irritable dysphoric mania, Brynn Hartman killed her husband, legendary Comic Phil Hartman, then herself on a non-solstice date of 5/27/1998. She was being treated with Zoloft at the time for depression. If the reader can remember anything from this impossibly long chapter…please remember that antidepressants on their own are frequently bad news for bipolars. Finally, there was "Jonestown" in Guyana South America. The mass suicide that killed 918 people occurred on the non-solstice date of 11/18/78. However, in the southern hemisphere...November is Springtime so MAYBE this is a quasi "Bipolar Alley" effect but in reverse.

Just as The Sun has a cycle during the day, and a cycle during the year, it also has a much larger cycle which spans every 11.1 years or so. This is the sunspot cycle. As the gaseous Sun rotates on itself, its equatorial regions rotate faster than the regions that are closest to the poles. As a result, there is a twisting of the lines of force within The Sun's overall magnetic field. As these lines of force become more twisted and unstable, large arcs of energy form and avulse in an attempt to stabilize this magnetic mess. Sunspots are cooler dark areas on The Sun that serve as origins of these arcs. Although sunspots are dark and cool, they are the progenitors of the large arcs which eventually cause enormous solar flares and coronal mass ejections (CME's) that at their largest, experience the energy of upwards to 100 Billion Hiroshima type nuclear bombs. Loosely translated, when there are more sunspots…The Sun produces more generic energy, extreme ultra violet light radiation, irradiance, magnetism and visible sunlight.

If we plot sunspots against time (Chart 16), we observe a sinusoidal wave pattern that typically lasts from trough to trough about 11.1 years. This cycle represents a cyclical nature of white light brightness, magnetism and extreme ultra-violet light (and other energy wavelengths) intensity as detected on and around Earth. A trough has the lowest intensity and a peak has the highest. This in many ways mimics the fluctuation in intensity of light that we see on Earth during the seasons. Of course, seasonal fluctuation is purely based on the Earth's axis of rotation relative to The Sun and is independent of what is occurring on The Sun's surface. I contend that sunspots effect our collective behavior (but especially effects those with mood disorders) just as the seasons do.

Since these cycles are so long, it's quite difficult to accurately assess suicide completions as we did with seasonality. The reason being, the suicides I accessed on Wikipedia were heavily weighted towards modern day (the last 40 years or so). "Modern day" would have encompassed numerous elapsed seasonal changes, but would have only represented a few sunspot cycles and it would be difficult to establish any trend. Furthermore, a "psychiatric autopsy" would be more difficult to formulate given the fact that the more detailed biographies are usually associated with more recent suicides (which unevenly weights more recent sunspot cycles). However, a different proxy can be used and it relates to the overall "buying and selling" trends that we see in business. "Buying and selling" activity can approximate either the greed (spending sprees) as seen in mania or the irritability (fear of losing money) as seen in dysphoric mania. The "depressed" phase of bipolarity confers neither buying nor selling…depressed people are apathetic and don't do anything. Fair warning to the reader, this next section is highly technical as far as stock market philosophy (our collective unconsciousness) is concerned. If you don't want the feeling of putting your head in a vice-grip….you can easily advance to the second to last paragraph of this chapter. In reality, it was a trial to write, so it may be a trial to read.

I'm not the first to correlate sunspots with business market psychology (JS Jevon, Michael Mandeville, Charles Nenner). However, I do believe my seasonal cycle data in conjunction with sunspot cycle data confer a novel and powerful tool to understanding our collective behavior as humans. If we look at a chart of 260 years of recorded sunspots, we can easily see a correlation between peaks and troughs correlating with financial market instability (Chart 17). Peaks (intense brightness) seem to be the most powerful predictor of our fearful behavior as manifested by the numerous examples of market panics/recessions relative to the cycle troughs. Troughs however are associated with "all out" market crashes and are rare but deadly (1987, 2008).

Most of the sunspot cycle peak instability occurs SLIGHTLY AFTER that peak. A good debate could be made that this point in time could be the analogue of the summer solstice. Sunspot troughs are less frequently problematic to financial markets, but when they occur they are leviathans as seen in 2008 and 2009 (more to come). The next trough will occur somewhere around 2018 to 2020. Great care should be taken with one's assets during this time especially after this most unusual nine-year market bubble (2009-2017 and beyond?). Market "booms" usually occur during sunspot "upswings" as manifested by the "roaring 20's," the technology boom of the late 1990's and believe or not, the CURRENT sunspot cycle 24 (beginning 2009 (Chart 18)). Perhaps the slowly increasing amounts of sunspots are methodically whipping the collective unconsciousness into a mania as similarly seen in the springtime. Increased brightness of The Sun either by Earthly season or sunspot cycle seems to improve the human tendency to buy whether it be merchandise or equity. It would therefore follow that solar cycle peaks begin recessions as there is no more acceleration of sunspot formation, and ipso facto humanity is no longer manicy and compelled to shop. However, for unknown reasons, the market continued to expand after the peak in 2014, which makes me quite worried for the impending trough around 2019-2020.

I believe that any buying/selling trends in the stock market are almost totally a fait accompli. That is, the news of the day is somewhat irrelevant, the market will mostly follow a pre-ordained pattern that's dictated by The Sun. Pundits seem to believe that economic news drives markets, which occasionally might be true. However, in general, we buy or sell based upon what mood we are in first, but then pick and choose the news story that correlates with the direction of the market that day. In a MANIC market (like from Dec 2008 until mid 2014), "bad news" is considered "good news" and we buy regardless of what the fish wrap says. An excellent example is a publically traded company that reports a good quarter. If we are manic, people buy the equity on that announcement. But If we are dysphoric manic (a bad irritable mood)....we "sell on the news" as they say in the business. Another basic example would be the timing of asking for a raise. If your boss is in a bad mood, stay away until he/she seems happier. What

I'm trying to say is that the concept of "free will" may be over-rated.

We also see volatility at sunspot peaks with regards to Human conflict. World War I occurred in 1917, World War II in 1939, Vietnam 1968-1970, Iran War 1979, First Gulf War 1990-1991, Kosovo Conflict 1999, and the events surrounding 9/11/2001. All these wars occurred at a peak in the sunspot cycle. As previously mentioned when discussing the Sept 21st solstice as it relates to 9/11, I don't believe the solstice itself was responsible as the preparation for it probably took years. However, the conception and preparation for 9/11 seems to be more related to the sunspot number (a maximum "peak" in sunspots around 1999-2001).

A point of peak sunspots is known as a "solar maximum" and the point of trough sunspots is known as the "solar minimum". Apocalyptic events seemingly started at our Cycle 23 solar maximum with the bursting of the tech bubble March 2000, the events of 9/11, and the beginning of the War in Iraq (slightly late: March 2003) (Chart 19). Our solar minimum began somewhere in 2007 which ushered in the bursting of the housing bubble, a subsequent worldwide credit crisis, massive unemployment, unprecedented perturbations in gas prices and startling losses in the stock market. The most recent solar minimum (2007-2009) is considered the longest in a century. That is, the relative amount of light from The Sun was at its lowest in 100 years because for two years there were no sunspots. There should be no surprise that the "perfect storm" of darkness revolved around the date Dec 21st, 2008. This is the darkest time of year (winter solstice) overlapping with the darkest year in a century (Footnote 1). It therefore was theoretically speaking the darkest day in 100 years. This date would serve as a "fulcrum" between the stunning stock market volatility seen in and around the prior Sept 21st solstice of 2008 and again with Apocalyptic lows near the subsequent March 21st solstice on March 9, 2009.

Two graphs show the undisputed effects of a "solar minimum" and "solar maximum" on human behavior. First is a retail sales chart from 1999 and beyond (Chart 20). This chart shows impressive fluctuations in buying trends in 2001 (solar maximum) and again in 2008 (solar minimum). Also, if we look at a 20-year chart of the VIX (Volatility Index as previously described) (Chart 21), we see a gentle arc of volatility that goes upwards starting in 1995 (solar minimum) and peaking somewhere around 2000-2001 (solar maximum). The VIX then slowly comes down in sync with sunspot numbers then mightily flares upward again once the solar minimum is established. Once again, most solar minimums don't cause many problems but this perfect storm of seasonal and sunspot darkness sent emotions on Earth into a frenzy, and this is perfectly reflected in the VIX and related chaos. Unbelievably, The VIX during sunspot cycle 23 seemed to be an exact proxy for sunspot numbers! But since VIX data hasn't been around that long, it will take many more sunspot cycles to elucidate a typical and definitive cause and effect relationship.

As another example, I'd like to dissect the events of May 6, 2010. This day brought about an infamous day in the US Stock market known as "The Flash Crash". To recap "The Flash Crash", The DOW had a slow and steady market gain since the beginning of 2010 (Chart 22). Note that the springtime (Bipolar Alley) is in my opinion the most powerful of all the solstices. In saying this, please keep in mind that any of the phases of bipolar disorder can be represented. Many people can present irritable (dysphoric manic) as exemplified by the numerous suicides and homicides that I hopefully have delineated. But also, recall that while some are irritable, THE MAJORITY are manic at this time of year (ascending sun). This is manifested in the stock market by buying. We saw "mania" in the beginning of 2010 (roughly Feb through May) and the year before (2009) starting at the March 9th Standard and Poor low of "666". In fact, for at least the following 6 years, we can see that springtime (ascending Sun) is predominantly "manicy" in the stock market (Chart 23). This springtime buying mania usually ends around the first week of May according to this chart. This is why the term "sell in May and go away" exists. The implication being the years gains have been established seemingly because the "ascending sun" is now starting to level out and soon become "descending" come June.

[Author's ill-advised opinion: Generally speaking, if you plan to SELL something, do it anytime from late December to late April. Other people's mania during an ascending Sun will confer their impulse buying. Conversely, if you want to BUY something, the best time is late July to late November. Other people's dysphoric mania occurring as The Sun descends will confer their impulse selling.]

Now back to "The Flash Crash". Just three weeks prior to this event on May 6th, in addition to the termination of the "manic buying" associated with springtime ("sell in May and go away"), the ever-increasing number of sunspots for the new 24th sunspot cycle inexplicably dropped off to zero. This lasted for several weeks up until the end of April. At this time, an unusually powerful resurgence of sunspots appeared all at once (77 in all…Chart 24) and subsequently "short circuited" our brains, thus ushering in the drop in the market starting May 4th and ending May 7th. Note how this fluctuation in sunspots almost exactly mirrors The VIX (The Volatility Index… Chart 25). Now, here are a few "Satanic" hooks you might have missed. Just as the previous year saw an S and P low of 666…on this day of "The Flash Crash", the DOW dropped 999 points (upside down 6's). In addition, a botched trade at the New York Stock Exchange for Proctor and Gamble, started the tumble. Recall, P and G in the 80's was banned by many consumers for having a logo which resembled the number 666 (Chart 26). Many believed the market was reacting to riots in Greece as a result of the Greek Debt crisis…but I contend those riots may also have been as a result of the dramatic change in sunspots.

We saw a similar sunspot effect on July 17, 2014. In retrospect, sunspot cycle 24 (the current sunspot cycle) was peaking at around this time in 2014. However, sunspots abruptly and inexplicably went to zero on this ONE DAY in July (Chart 27). On that day, we saw Malaysia Flight #17 shot down over The Ukraine, Israeli troops invade Gaza and The Dow drop 161 points.

In addition to solstices and sunspots, another force of nature may also be affecting our brains......and that's magnetism. An excellent example of this correlation of geomagnetism and human emotion is seen in early 2010. On January 20th and Feb 4th , there were two minor surges of geomagnetism detected on earth during an otherwise quiescence of sunspot fluctuation, magnetism or news stories (Chart 28). Over the next several days after each event, there were correspondingly substantial random drops in the stock market and the VIX rose in accordance (Chart 29). There should be no surprise that geomagnetism could possibly alter the human brain. Geomagnetically induced currents (GIC's) originating from a coronal mass ejection (CME) on The Sun are well known to cause disruptions on many components of an electrically based gridding such as circuit breakers and the windings on transformers. The brain is in many ways functions as a battery (from the plethora of chemical and electrical synapses) and theoretically could also demonstrate "antennae" like qualities. Thus, it is not far-fetched to imagine the brain could be altered by similar solar disturbances. In fact, who's to say our battery like brains are not in turn all interconnected by the Earth's magnetic field thus producing a collective unconsciousness or maybe even so-called psychicism. In conclusion, navigating both near and long term predictability of the market requires understanding of solstices, sunspots and geomagnetism.

This current sunspot cycle is the weakest since The Great Depression (aka Solar Cycle 16) (Chart 30). Sunspot Cycle 16 was unique in that the damage it imposed on the Earth not only involved a waning peak (roughly 1929...."The Crash") and a trough (roughly 1933), but the carnage lasted THE WHOLE DESCENDING ARM IN BETWEEN. Startlingly, our current similarly weak Solar Cycle 24 visually LOOKS almost exactly like that Great Depression Solar Cycle 16 (current=black, Great Depression= purple) (Chart 31). This is possibly not a good sign if solar history has any valence on predicting the future and I certainly hope I'm wrong. If we search the word "happy" on Google Trends (Chart 32a), look how the search word "happy" started to increase in 2008 (beginning of Solar Cycle 24) . It then peaked when Solar Cycle 24 peaked (2014), and now it's starting to descend with sunspot number. People RIGHT NOW are apparently becoming "less happy". In addition, the opiate crisis took a logarithmic turn for the worse in 2009, the beginning of our apocalyptically unstable sunspot cycle 24 (Chart 32b....Heroin deaths).

I contend weak sunspot cycles (like the one we are in now and The Great Depression) cause The Sun to have frequent bouts of premature "flickering" (sunspots randomly dropping to zero) thus causing a strobe-like "on/off" effect during the descending phase of the cycle. We saw the result of this effect during the June solstice of 2016. At the very same time as a traditionally unstable solstice, sunspots unexpectedly and PREMATURELY (relative to more normal/stronger solar cycles) dropped to zero for several weeks. This had not happened since Dec 2010. As a result of these combined extreme fluctuations in solar energy (solstice/sunspot), we saw a series of unimaginable Apocalyptic events that left most of us apoplectic (Orlando FL shooting spree 6/12, Istanbul Airport suicide bombings 6/29, Dallas Police murders 7/7, Nice France truck attack 7/14, failed Turkish military insurrection 7/15 and Baton Rouge Police shooting 7/17 (Chart 33). There were more (Munich, Japan stabbings), but I ran out of room on my chart! We might expect more chaos during the coming years unfortunately. Homicides (and suicides) ran rampant during the 4-year descending phase of The Great Depression Solar Cycle 16 (1929-1933) (Chart 34) and as mentioned our current cycle appears almost identical. It regretfully may be one long solar sunspot disturbance (in the form of "flickering") causing erratic human (and animal!!) behavior especially at solstices. I will also be looking for odd gyrations in the "normally" sinusoidal VIX (Chart 35) and the stock market. During this very weak solar cycle, highlighted by a fickle undulating Sun, investments in Pharmaceutical companies that manufacture bipolar medications and sleep aids might be an interesting investment in the event the market doesn't drop.

The solar maximum of Cycle 24 occurred somewhere in mid 2014. This was a little more than a year after the commencement of the so called Mayan Day of The Apocalypse…Dec 21, 2012. Ironically, on a macro scale, this timing is fairly prescient. During the time after this day of The Apocalypse, which just HAPPENS to include the peak AND decent of Solar Cycle 24 sunspots (much like the descending phase of Solar Cycle 16....aka The Great Depression), we should watch for God's Sun to once again contribute to our unreasonable fears, painful depressions, and hedonistic manias. With BRIGHT natural powerful forces like this...I ask who needs Lucipher (Lucipher = "bright light" in Latin)?

Chart 1

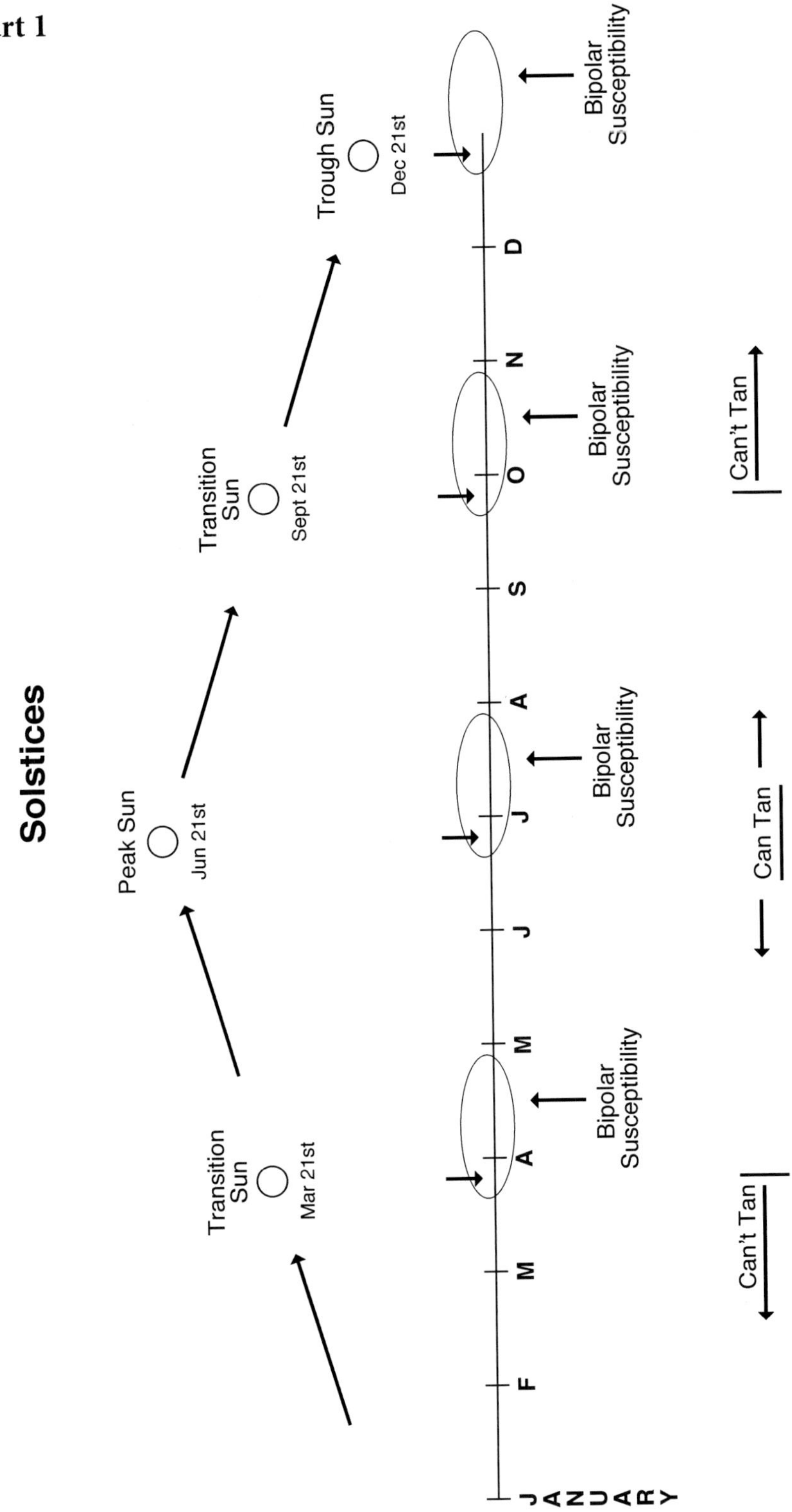

Solstices

Transition Sun
Mar 21st

Peak Sun
Jun 21st

Transition Sun
Sept 21st

Trough Sun
Dec 21st

JANUARY F M A M J J A S O N D

Bipolar Susceptibility

Bipolar Susceptibility

Bipolar Susceptibility

Bipolar Susceptibility

Can't Tan

Can Tan

Can't Tan

Chart 2

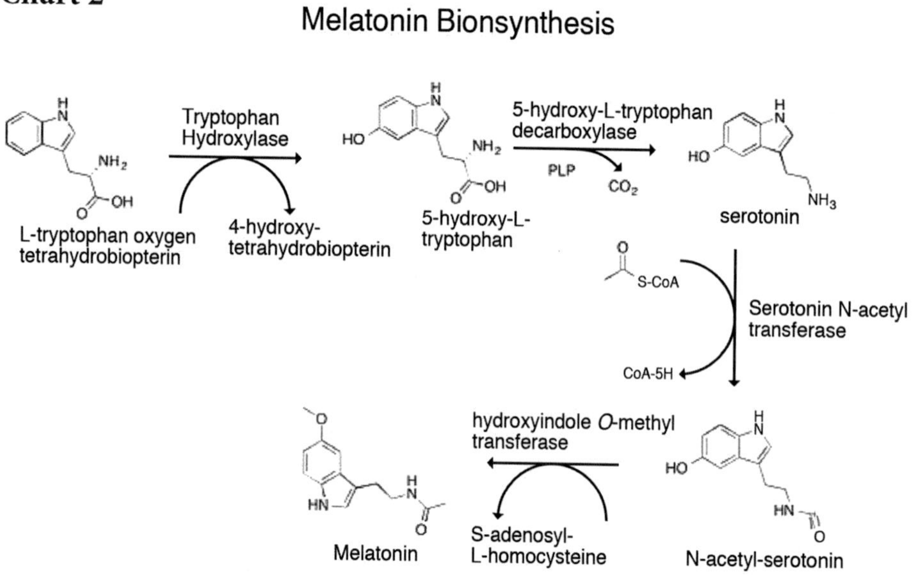

Melatonin Bionsynthesis

L-tryptophan oxygen tetrahydrobiopterin

Tryptophan Hydroxylase

4-hydroxy-tetrahydrobiopterin

5-hydroxy-L-tryptophan

5-hydroxy-L-tryptophan decarboxylase

PLP

CO_2

serotonin

S-CoA

Serotonin N-acetyl transferase

CoA-5H

N-acetyl-serotonin

hydroxyindole O-methyl transferase

S-adenosyl-L-homocysteine

Melatonin

Chart 3

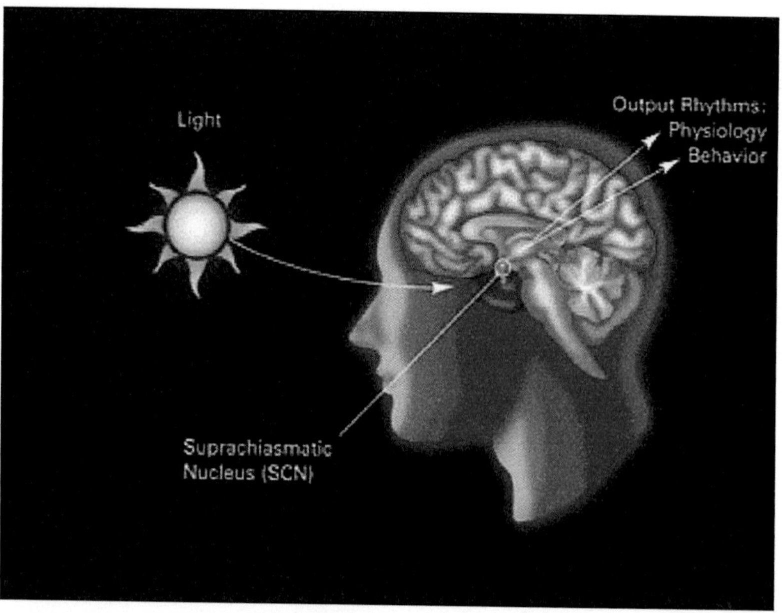

A variation of an eskinogram showing the influence of light and darkness on circadian rhythms

National Institute of General Medical Sciences - Circadian Rhythms

Diagram illustrating the influence of dark-light rythms on circadian rythms and related physiology and behavior.

Chart 4

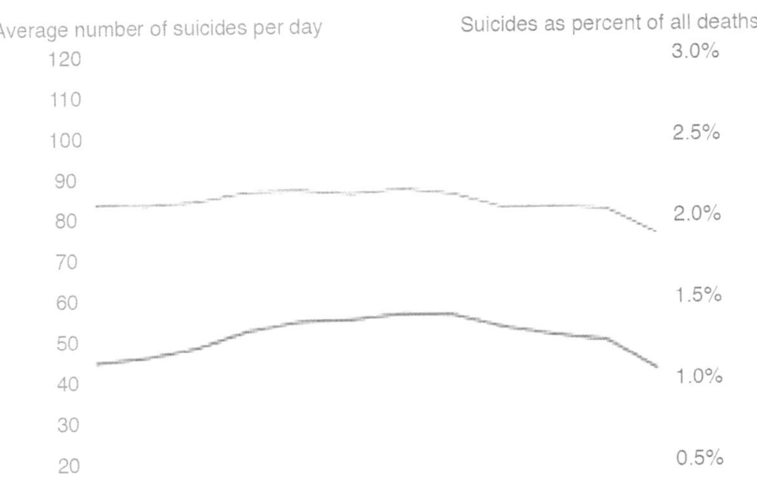

Chart 5

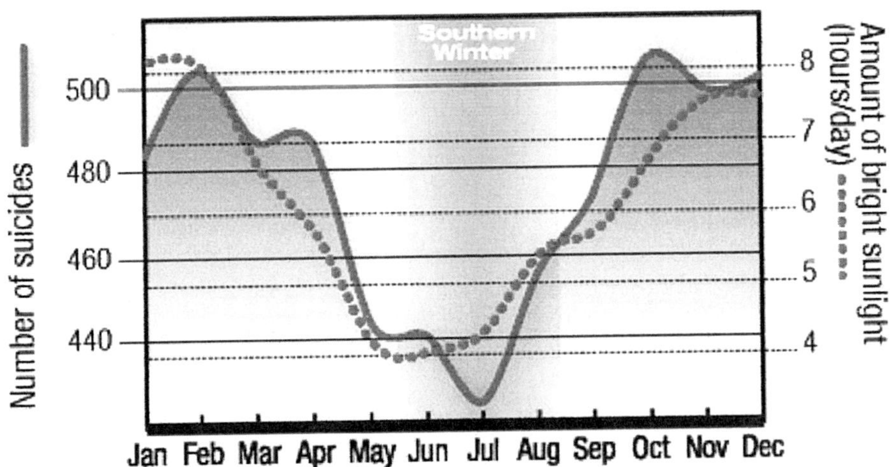

*Monthly values encompass consecutive three-month periods. For example, values for July were derived from the mean of values for June, July, and August, and values for August were derived from the mean of values for July, August, and September.

Source: *American Journal of Psychiatry*, April 2003

Chart 6

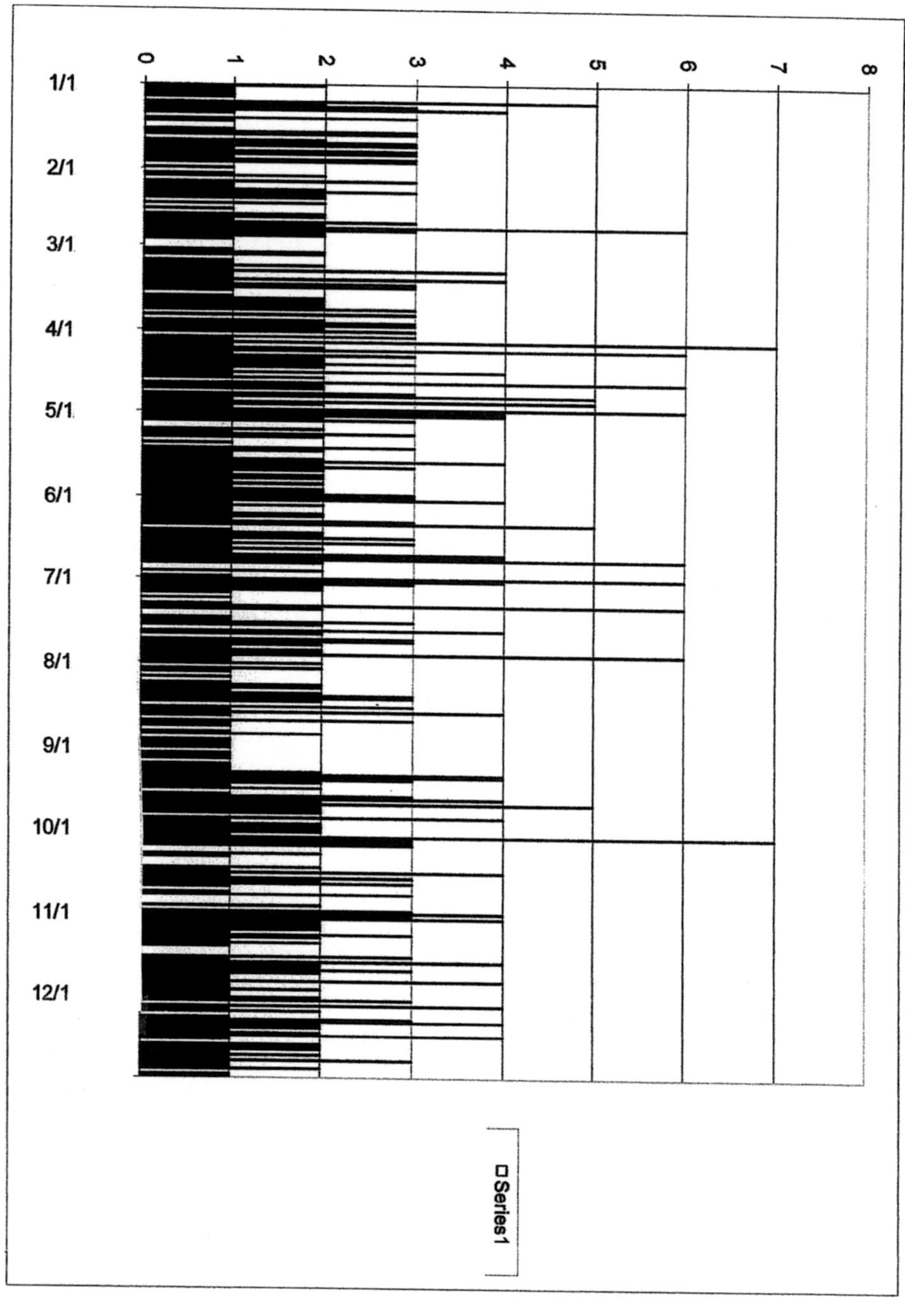
All deaths vs. month
0
1
2
3
4
5
6
7
8
1/1
2/1
3/1
4/1
5/1
6/1
7/1
8/1
9/1
10/1
11/1
12/1
Series1

Chart 7

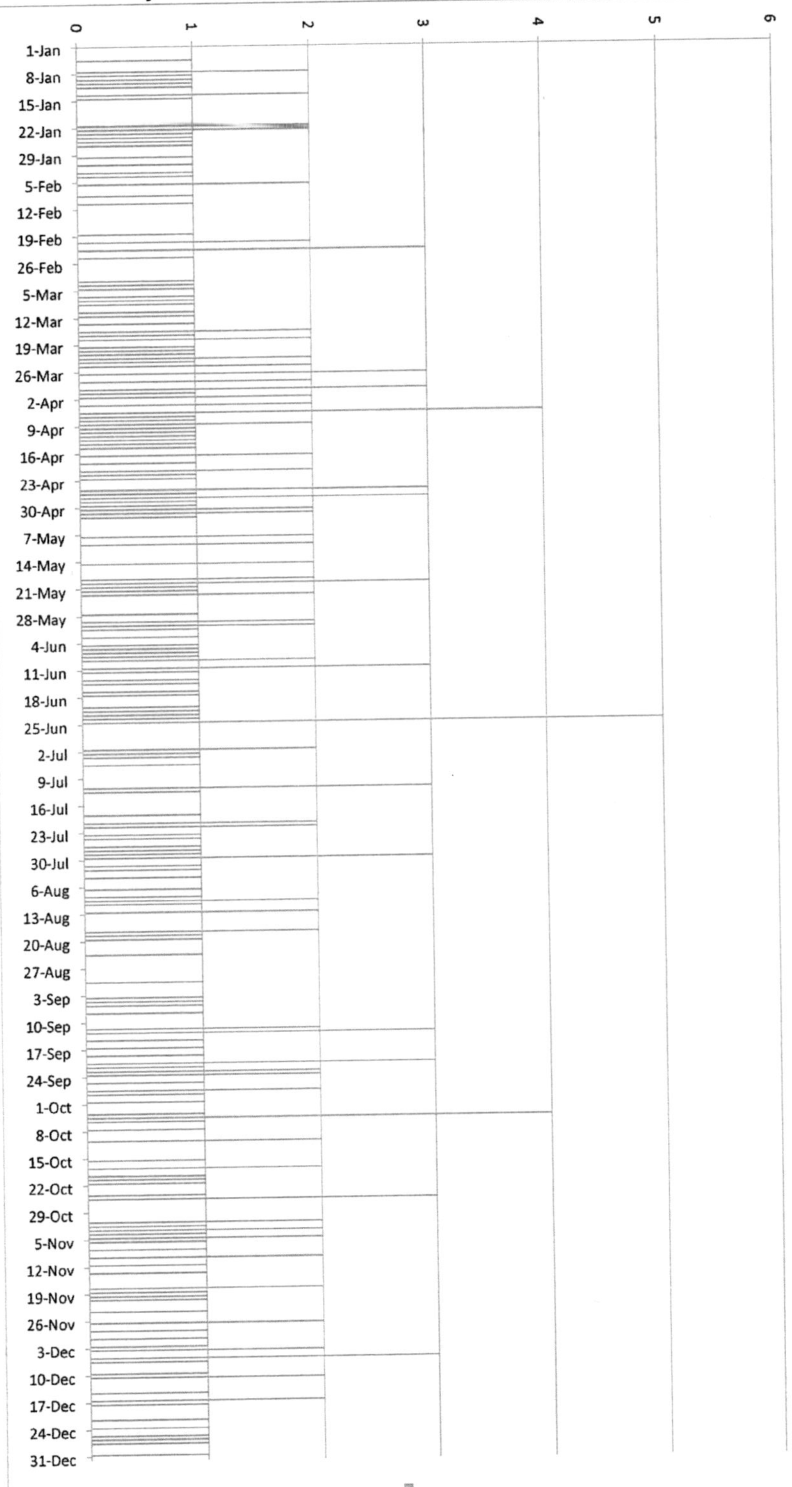
All Psych Cases (Psychiatric Autopsy) vs. month
0
1
2
3
4
5
6
1-Jan
8-Jan
15-Jan
22-Jan
29-Jan
5-Feb
12-Feb
19-Feb
26-Feb
5-Mar
12-Mar
19-Mar
26-Mar
2-Apr
9-Apr
16-Apr
23-Apr
30-Apr
7-May
14-May
21-May
28-May
4-Jun
11-Jun
18-Jun
25-Jun
2-Jul
9-Jul
16-Jul
23-Jul
30-Jul
6-Aug
13-Aug
20-Aug
27-Aug
3-Sep
10-Sep
17-Sep
24-Sep
1-Oct
8-Oct
15-Oct
22-Oct
29-Oct
5-Nov
12-Nov
19-Nov
26-Nov
3-Dec
10-Dec
17-Dec
24-Dec
31-Dec
Series1

Chart 8

Artists (Mood Disorder) vs. month

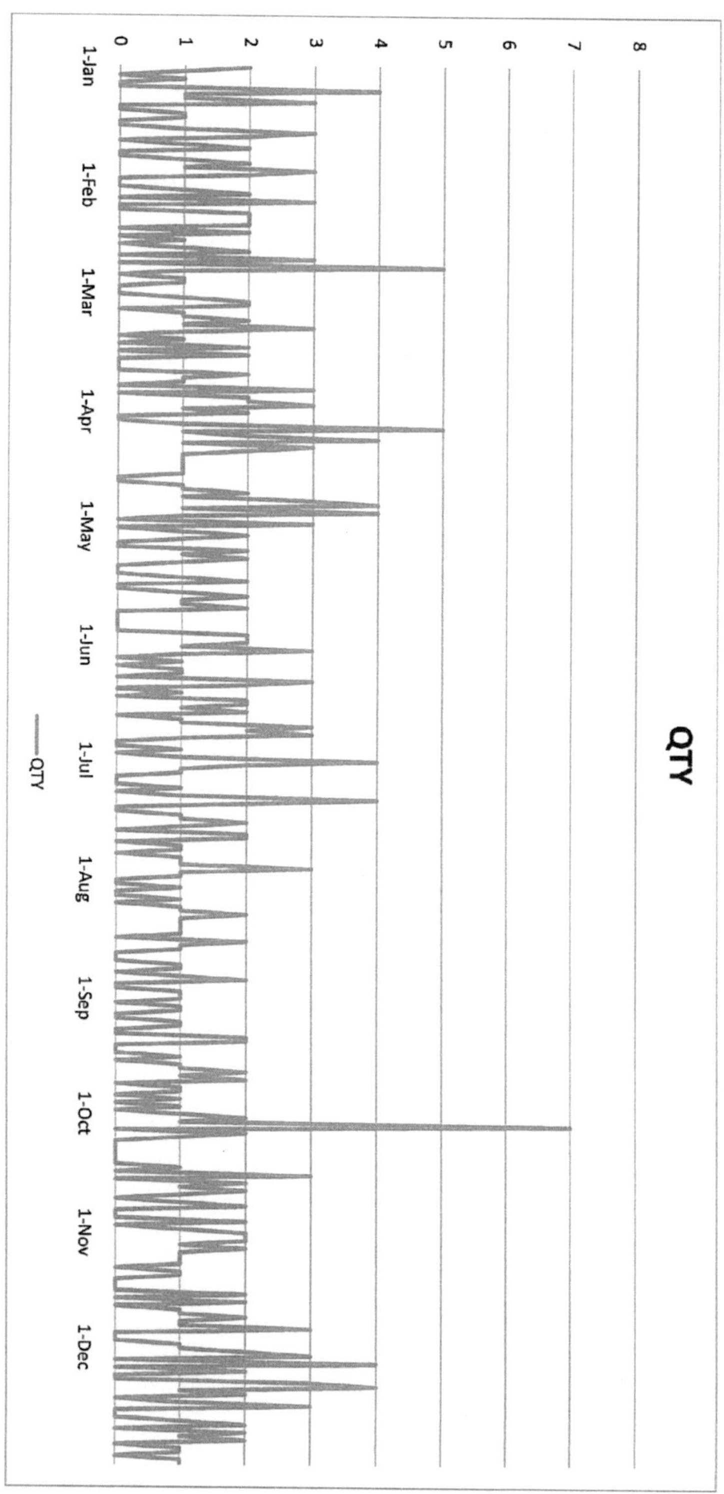

Chart 9

FIRST NAME	LAST NAME	OCCUPATION	ARTIST OR NON-ARTIST	SUICIDE OR MURDER/SUICIDE	METHOD	VIOLENT OR NONVIOLENT DEATH	MONTH	DAY	YEAR	DESCRIPTION (ETOH=ALCOHOL)	LOCATION	PSYCHIATRIC AUTOPSY DETERMINATION: M=MENTALLY ILL OR U=UNKNOWN
JOHNNY	ACE	SINGER	A	S	GUNSHOT	V	12	25	1954	ETOH	TEXAS	M
CHRIS	ACLAND	MUSICIAN	A	S	HANGING	V	10	17	1996		ENGLAND	U
HATAZO	ADACHI	GENERAL	NA	S	SEPPUKU	V	9	10	1947		SOL ISLE	U
ROBERT	ADAMS JR	CONGRESS-MAN	NA	S	GUNSHOT	V	6	1	1906		WASH DC	U
STUART	ADAMSON	MUSICIAN	A	S	STRANGULA-TION	V	12	16	2001	ETOH NERVOUS BREAKDOWN		M
AHN	JAE-HUAN	ACTOR	A	S	CO POISONING	NV	9	8	2008		S KOREA	U
RYUNOSUKE	AKUTAGAWA	WRITER	A	S	BARBITURATE	NV	7	24	1927	MENTAL ILLNESS HALLUCINA-TIONS	JAPAN	M
ROSS	ALEXANDER	ACTOR	A	S	GUNSHOT	V	1	2	1937		SO CAL	U
MIKE	AWESOME	WRESTLER	A	S	HANGING	V	2	17	1907		FLA	U
ALFRED OF	EDINBURGH	PRINCE	NA	S	GUNSHOT	V	2	6	1899		ENGLAND	U
LEANDRO	ALEM	POLITICIAN	NA	S	GUNSHOT	V	7	1	1996		ARGENTINA	U
SALVADOR	GOSSENS	POLITICIAN	NA	S	GUNSHOT	V	9	11	1973		CHILE	U
JEFF	ALM	FOOTBALL	NA	S	GUNSHOT	V	12	14	1993	ETOH BARBITURATE FIORINAL		M
JEAN	AMERY	WRITER	A	S	SLEEPING PILLS	NV	10	17	1978			U
KORECHIKA	ANAMI	GENERAL	NA	S	SEPPUKU	V	8	15	1945			U
FORREST	ANDERSON	GOVERNOR	NA	S	GUNSHOT	V	7	20	1989			U
FRIDOLIN	ANDERWERT	POLITICIAN	NA	S	?	V	12	25	1980			U
GWILE	ANDRE	ACTOR	A	S	IMMOLATION	V	2	5	1959	ETOH	CAL	M
ROGER	ANGLETON	MURDERER	?	S	HANGING	V	2	7	1998		TX	U
MARCUS	ANTONIUS	GENERAL	NA	S	STABBING	V	8	1	30 BC			U
MARSHALL	APPLEWHITE	MUSICIAN	A	SM	CYANIDE/ ARSENIC	NV	3	26	1997	HEAVANSGATE PSYCH HOSP "REINCARNA-TION OF JC" SO CAL	CAL	M
HUBERT	AQUIN	WRITER	A	S	GUNSHOT	V	3	15	1977	PSYCH HOSP	MONTREAL	M
DIANE	ARBUS	PHOTOGRA-GHER	A	S	SLIT WRISTS/ BARB	NV	7	26	1971	DEPRESSION	NY	M
REINALDO	ARENAS	WRITER	A	S	ETOH/DRUGS	NV	12	7	1990		NY	U
PEDRO	ARMENDARIZ	ACTOR	A	S	GUNSHOT	V	6	18	1963		LA, CAL	U
EDWIN	ARMSTRONG	INVENTOR	NA	S	JUMP	V	1	31	1954	DEPRESSED	NY	M
NIKOLAS	ASIMOS	MUSICIAN	A	S	HANGING	V	3	17	1988	MENTAL INSTITUTION	GREECE	M
DAVID	ATCHISON	LAWYER	NA	S	HANGING	V	10	5	2007	CHILD MOLESTOR	FLA	U
GEORGE	AULT	PAINTER	A	S	DROWNING	NV	12	30	1948	MOM PSYCH HOSP 2 SYBS SUICIDE ETOH		M
PEKKA-ERIC	AUVINEN	STUDENT	NA	SM	GUNSHOT	V	11	7	2007	JOKELA SHOOL SHOOTING, 8 KILLED, ANTI-DEPRESSANTS	FINLAND	M

NIKKI	BACHARACH	MUSICIAN	A	S	SUFFICATION	NV	1	4	2007	BURT BACHARACH DAUGHTER PSYCH HOSP ASPERGERS?		M
CHET	BAKER	MUSICIAN	A	S	JUMP	V	12	23	1929	COCAINE HEROIN		M
JAMES	BAKER	WRITER	A	S	?	?	11	5	1997	ETOH POLY-SUBSTANCE	SO CAL	M
ALBERT	BALIN	BUSINESS-MAN	NA	S	SLEEPING PILLS	NV	11	9	1918		GERMANY	U
JOSE	FERNANDEZ	POLITICIAN	NA	S	GUNSHOT	V	9	19	1891			U
ROBERT	BARLOW	WRITER	A	S	BARBITUATE	NV	1	1	1951		MEXICO	U
ISOBEL	BARNETT	ACTOR	A	S	ELECTROCU-TION	V	10	20	1980		ENGLAND	U
DON "RED"	BARRY	ACTOR	A	S	GUNSHOT	V	7	17	1980		SO CAL	U
DIANNA	BARRYMORE	ACTOR	A	S	ETOH/SLEEP-ING PILLS	NV	1	25	1960	PSYCH HOSP DEPRESSION ETOH POLY-SUBSTANCE NY		M
GERT	BASTIAN	POLITICIAN	NA	S	GUNSHOT	V	10	19	1992		GERMANY	U
JOHN "CLIFF"	BAXTER	BUSINESS-MAN	NA	S	GUNSHOT	V	1	25	2002	ENRON CEO	TX	U
THOMAS	BAYNE	POLITICIAN	NA	S	GUNSHOT	V	6	16	1864		WASH DC	U
GERTRUDE	BELL	WRITER	A	S	SLEEPING PILLS	V	7	12	1926		ENGLAND	U
PETER	BELLAMY	MUSICIAN	A	S	?	?	9	24	1991		ENGLAND	U
JUAN	GARCIA	MATADOR	NA	S	GUNSHOT	V	4	8	1962			U
JAN	BENES	WRITER	A	S	GUNSHOT	V	6	1	2007		CZECH	U
BRENDA	NELSON	ACTOR	A	S	GUNSHOT	V	4	7	1982		LA,CAL	U
OTA	BENGA	ZOO AT-TRACTION	NA	S	GUNSHOT	V	3	20	1916	DEPRESSED		M
WALTER	BENJAMINE	WRITER	A	S	OPIATES	NV	9	27	1940		SPAIN	U
JILL	BENNETT	ACTRESS	A	S	?	?	10	4	1990	HX OF DEPRESSION	ENGLAND	M
CHRIS	BENOIT	WRESTLER	NA	SM	HANGING	V	6	24	2007	KILLED WIFE AND SON	GEORGIA	M
PIERRE	BEREGOVOY	POLITICIAN	NA	S	GUNSHOT	V	5	1	1993	DEPRESSED	PARIS	M
JOHN	BERG	ACTOR	A	S	CO POISONING	NV	12	15	2007		SO CAL	U
HANS	BERGER	PHYSICIAN	NA	S	HANGING	V	6	1	1941			U
MARY KAY	BERGMAN	ACTRESS	A	S	GUNSHOT	V	11	11	1999	DEPRESSION AND ANXIETY	SO CAL	M
RICKY	BERRY	BASKET-BALL	NA	S	GUNSHOT	V	8	14	1989		SO CAL	U
JOHN	BERRYMAN	WRITER	A	S	JUMP	V	1	7	1972	HX OF DEPRESSION AND ETOH DAD SUICIDE	MINN	M
BRUNO	BETTLEHEIM	PSYCHOLO-GIST	NA	S	?	?	3	13	1990	DEPRESSION	MD	M
JENS	BJORNEBOE	WRITER	A	S	HANGING	V	5	9	1976	HX OF DEPRESSION AND ETOH	NORWAY	M
JEREMY	BLAKE	PAINTER	A	S	DROWNING	NV	7	17	2007		NY	U
CLARA	BLANDICK	ACTRESS	A	S	SLEEPING PILLS	NV	4	15	1962	AUNTIE EM WIZARD OF OZ	LA CAL	U
KENNY	BLATCHFORD	POLITICIAN	NA	S	DROWNING	NV	4	20	1933	NERVOUS BREAKDOWN	CANADA	M
BARBARA	BLIDA	POLITICIAN	NA	S	GUNSHOT	V	4	25	2007		POLAND	U
ISABELLA	BLOW	WRITER	A	S	PARAQUAT POISONING	NV	5	7	2007	DEPRESSION SEVERAL SUICIDE ATTEMPTS	ENGLAND	M

LUDWIG	BOLTZMANN	PHYSICIST	NA	S	HANGING	V	9	5	1906	HX OF BIPOLAR		M
JEREMY	BOORDA	ADMIRAL	NA	S	GUNSHOT	V	5	16	1996			U
TADEUSZ	BOROWSKI	WRITER	A	S	ASPHYXIATION	NV	7	1	1951			U
GEORGES	BOULANGER	GENERAL	NA	S	GUNSHOT	V	9	30	1891			U
TOMMY	BOYCE	MUSICIAN	A	S	GUNSHOT	V	11	23	1994	COMPOSED FOR MONKEES HX OF DEPPRESSION		M
KARIN	BOYE	WRITER	A	S	SLEEPING PILLS	NV	4	24	1941			U
CHARLES	BOYER	ACTOR	A	S	SECONAL	NV	8	26	1978		AZ	U
CAMILO	BRANCO	WRITER	A	S	GUNSHOT	V	7	1	1890			U
JONATHON	BRANDIS	ACTOR	A	S	HANGING	V	11	12	2003			U
TARITA	BRANDO	MODEL	NA	S	HANGING	V	4	16	1995	SCHIZOPHRE-NIA? ETOH AND SLEEPING PILLS		M
MIKE	BRYANT	MUSICIAN	A	S	JUMP	V	4	25	1975	DEPRESSION	PARIS	M
EVA	BRAUN	HITLERS WIFE	NA	S	CYANIDE	NV	4	30	1945			U
RICHARD	BRAUTIGAN	WRITER	NA	S	GUNSHOT	V	9	14	1984	SCHIZOPHRE-NIA? DEPRESSION	CAL	M
HERMAN	BROOD	MUSICIAN	A	S	JUMP	V	7	11	2001	DEPRESSION SPEDD ETOH	AMSTER-DAM	M
BARRY	BROWN	WRITER	A	S	GUNSHOT	V	6	25	1978		CAL	U
OSKAR	BRUSEWITZ	CLERIC	NA	S	IMMOLATION	V	8	22	1976		E GERMANY	U
EUSTACE	BUDGELL	WRITER	A	S	DROWNING	NV	5	4	1737		LONDON	U
BERNARD	BUFFET	PAINTER	A	S	SUFFOCATION	NV	10	4	1999		FRANCE	U
REM-BRANDT	BUGATTI	SCULPTOR	A	S	GAS	NV	1	8	1916	MENTALLY ILL DEPRESSION		M
DAN	BURROS	KKK	NA	S	GUNSHOT	V	10	31	1965	MENTAL INSTABILITY		M
ANDREAS	CAICEDO	WRITER	A	S	SECOBARBITOL	NV	3	4	1977		COLUMBIA	U
JOSE	CALVA	WRITER	A	S	HANGING	V	12	11	2007	CANNABILISM	CAL	U
DONALD	CAMMELL	DIRECTOR	A	S	GUNSHOT	V	4	24	1996			U
GERMAINE	LEFEBVRE	ACTRESS	A	S	JUMP	V	3	17	1990	BIPOLAR	SWTZRLND	M
ARTHUR	CAREWE	ACTOR	A	S	GUNSHOT	V	4	22	1937		SO CAL	U
WALLACE	CAROTHERS	CHEMIST	NA	S	CYANIDE	NV	4	29	1937	DEPRESSION ETOH ANXIETY	PENN	M
DON	CARPENTER	WRITER	A	S	GUNSHOT	V	7	28	1995			U
DORA	CARRINGTON	PAINTER	A	S	GUNSHOT	V	3	11	1932	MULTIPLE ATTEMPTS		M
KEVIN	CARTER	PHOTOGRA-PHER	A	S	CO POISONING	NV	7	27	1994	DEPRESSED	S AFRICA	M
TIM	CARTER	RUGBY	NA	S	HANGING	V	6	19	2008		ENGLAND	U
HUGH	CASEY	BASEBALL	NA	S	GUNSHOT	V	7	3	1951		GEORGIA	U
ADOLPHE	CASSANDRE	PAINTER	A	S	?	?	6	17	1968	DEPRESSION	PARIS	M
LORD	CASTLERE-AGH	POLITICIAN	NA	S	SLIT THROAT	V	8	12	1822	NERVOUS BREAKDOWN DEPRESSION	ENGLAND	M
UGO	CAVALLERO	SOLDIER	NA	S	GUNSHOT	V	9	13	1943		ITALY	U
PAUL	CELAN	WRITER	A	S	DROWNING	NV	4	20	1970			U
ANA	CESAR	WRITER	A	S	JUMP	V	10	29	1983		RIO	U
VALERIE	CHACON	WIFE OF BOB	NA	S	GUNSHOT	V	3	16	1982		CAL	U
PAULINE	CHAN	PORN AC-TRESS	A	S	JUMP	V	7	31	2002	DEPRESSION POLY-SUBSTANCE	SHANGHAI	M
IRIS	CHANG	WRITER	A	S	GUNSHOT	V	11	9	2004	DEPRESSION	CAL	M
KATHY	CHANGE	ACTRESS	A	S	IMMOLITION	V	10	22	1996		PA	U
CLAUDE	CHAPPE	INVENTOR	NA	S	JUMP	V	1	23	1805		PARIS	U
THOMAS	CHATTERTON	WRITER	A	S	ARSENIC	NV	8	24	1770	IQ=170	ENGLAND	U

LESLIE	CHEUNG	ACTOR	A	S	JUMP	V	4	1	2003	DEPRESSION	HOMG KONG	M
VERE	CHILDE	WRITER	A	S	JUMP	V	10	19	1957			U
BRETT	CHIDESTER	STUDENT	NA	S	SALVIA DIVINO-RIUM	NV	1	23	2006	"BRETTS LAW"		M
ISAMU	CHO	GENERAL	NA	S	SEPPUKU	V	6	23	1945			U
SEUNGHUI	CHO	STUDENT	NA	SM	GUNSHOT	V	4	16	2007	VIRGINIA TECH SELECTIVE AUTISM? WRITER	VA	M
CHOI	JIN-SIL	ACTRESS	A	S	HANGING	V	10	2	2008		S KOREA	U
CHONG-ZHEN		EMPEROR	NA	SM	HANGING	V	4	25	1644		CHINA	U
EDWIN	CHRISTY	ACTOR	A	S	JUMP	V	5	21	1862		NY	U
CHRISTINE	CHUBBUCK	JOURNALIST	A	S	GUNSHOT	V	7	15	1974	LIVE TV 3 WK PREOCCUPA-TION	FLA	U
CHUNG	MONG-HUN	BUSINESS-MAN	NA	S	JUMP	V	8	4	2003		N KOREA	U
DIANA	CHURCHILL	SOCIAL WORK	NA	S	BARBITURATE	NV	10	20	1963	DEPRESSION DAUGHTER OF WINSTON	ENGLAND	M
JEREMIAH	CLARKE	MUSICIAN	A	S	GUNSHOT	V	12	1	1707			U
ALASDAIR	CLAYRE	MUSICIAN	A	S	TRAIN	V	1	10	1984		ENGLAND	U
CHARMIAN	CLIFT	WRITER	A	S	BARBITURATE	NV	7	8	1969		AUSTRALIA	U
ROBERT	CLIVE	POLITICIAN	NA	S	CUT THROAT	V	11	22	1774		ENGLAND	U
KURT	COBAIN	MUSICIAN	A	S	GUNSHOT	V	4	5	1994	HEROIN VALIUM	SEATTLE	M
BOB	COLLINS	POLITICIAN	NA	S	PRESCRIPTION DRUG	NV	9	21	2007	CHILD SEX OFFENDER ETOH	AUSTRALIA	M
SID	COLLINS	ANNOUNC-ER	NA	S	HANGING	V	5	2	1977	AT MAYO CLINIC ALS		U
RAY	COMBS	COMIC	A	S	HANGING	V	6	2	1996	FAMILY FEUD	CAL	U
TARKA	CORDELL	MUSICIAN	A	S	HANGING	V	4	28	2008		ENGLAND	U
PAMELA	COURSON	ART STU-DENT	A	S	HEROIN	NV	4	25	1974	JIM MORRISON COMPANION	CAL	M
FWS	CRAIG	PSEPHOLO-GIST	NA	S	?	?	3	23	1989			U
HAROLD	CRANE	WRITER	A	S	JUMP	V	4	27	1932		FLA	U
DARBY	CRASH	MUSICIAN	A	S	HEROIN	NV	12	7	1980	THE GERMS		U
RENE	CREVEL	WRITER	A	S	GAS	NV	6	18	1935	FATHER HUNG HIMSELF		U
DENNIS	CROSBY	ACTOR	A	S	GUNSHOT	V	5	7	1991	ETOH BRO SHOT HIMSELF	CAL	M
HARRY	CROSBY	WRITER	A	SM	GUNSHOT	V	12	10	1929	KILLED WIFE THEN SELF	MASS	U
LINDSAY	CROSBY	ACTOR	A	S	GUNSHOT	V	12	11	1989	SON OF BING	NV	U
GEZA	CSATH	MUSICIAN	A	S	POISON	NV	9	11	1919	KILLED WIFE JULY 22		U
ANDREW	CUNANAN	PROSTITUTE	NA	S	GUNSHOT	V	7	23	1997	APRIL 27-JULY 23 KILLING SPREE VERSACE	FLA	U
WILL	CUPPY	WRITER	A	S	SLEEPING PILLS	NV	9	19	1949		NY	U
IAN	CURTIS	MUSICIAN	A	S	HANGING	V	5	18	1980	JOY DIVISION DEPRESSION	ENGLAND	M
ADAM	CZERNIAKOW	ENGINEER	NA	S	POISON	NV	7	23	1942	KILLED SELF INSTEAD OF HANDING OVER CHILDREN		U
STIG	DAGERMAN	WRITER	A	S	?	?	11	4	1954	DEPRESSION		M

DALIDA		MUSICIAN	A	S	BARBITUATE	NV	5	3	1987		PARIS	U
MONIKA	DANNEMANN	PAINTER	A	S	CO POISONING	NV	4	5	1996	JIMI HENDRIX GF	ENGLAND	U
BELLA	DARVI	ACTRESS	A	S	GAS	NV	9	11	1971	GAMBLING	MONACO	M
EDDIE	DAVIDSON	COMPUTER SPAM	NA	SM	GUNSHOT	V	7	24	2008	KILLED WIFE AND DAUGHTER	COLORADO	U
CLIFF	DAVIES	MUSICIAN	A	S	GUNSHOT	V	4	13	2008	TED NUGENT DRUMMER	ATLANTA	U
OSAMU	DAZAI	WRITER	A	S	DROWNING	NV	6	13	1948	PROSTITUTES ETOH PAIN KILLERS	JAPAN	M
GUY	DEBORD	WRITER	A	S	GUNSHOT	V	11	30	1994	ETOH	FRANCE	M
JEANINE	DECKERS	MUSICIAN	A	S	BARBITURATE	NV	3	29	1985	THE SINGING NUN	BEGIUM	U
GILLES	DELEUZE	WRITER	A	S	JUMP	V	4	11	1995	PHILOSOPHER	FRANCE	U
BRAD	DELP	MUSICIAN	A	S	CO POISONING	NV	3	9	2007	BOSTON VOCALIST	NH	U
PENELOPE	DELTA	WRITER	A	S	POISON	NV	4	27	1941		GREECE	U
DENICE	DENTON	ENGINEER	NA	S	JUMP	V	6	24	2006	DEPRESSION	CAL	M
ANGELA	DEVI	PORN MODEL	A	S	ASPHYXIATION	V	3	31	2006	XANAX	AZ	M
PATRICK	DEWAERE	ACTOR	A	S	GUNSHOT	V	7	16	1982		PARIS	U
RUDOLPH	DIESEL	INVENTOR	A	S	JUMP	V	9	29	1913			U
DEBORAH	DIGGES	WRITER	A	S	JUMP	V	4	10	2009			U
DIPENDRA	SHAH	KING NEPAL	NA	SM	GUNSHOT	V	6	4	2001	KILLED FATHER MOTHER BRO SIS	NEPAL	M
THOMAS	DISCH	WRITER	A	S	GUNSHOT	V	7	4	2008		NY	U
HUGO	DISTLER	MUSICIAN	A	S	GAS	NV	11	1	1942			U
DESMOND	DONNELLY	POLITICIAN	NA	S	BARBITURATE	NV	4	3	1974	ETOH		M
TERENCE	DONOVAN	PHOTOGRA-GHER	A	S	HANGING	V	11	22	1996	ADDICTED TO LOVE VIDEO		U
PATRIK	DOONAN	ACTOR	A	S	?	?	3	10	1958			U
MICHAEL	DORRIS	WRITER	A	S	SUFFOCATION	V	4	10	1997	ALLEGATIONS OF SEXUAL ABUSE DAUGHTER	NH	U
OSVALDO	TORRADO	POLITICIAN	NA	S	GUNSHOT	V	6	23	1983		CUBA	U
CHRIS	DOTY	WRITER	A	S	HANGING	V	2	2	2006	BIPOLAR DEPRESSION	LONDON	M
CHARMAINE	DRAGUN	JOURNALIST	A	S	JUMP	V	11	2	2007	DEPRESSION MED CHANGE PARENT MUSICIAN	AUSTRALIA	M
PIERRE	LA ROCHELLE	WRITER	A	S	?	?	3	15	1945			U
JONATHON	WEBB	SURGEON	NA	S	OXYCODONE	NV	12	26	2004	DEPRESSION		M
MICKE	DUBOIS	COMEDIAN	A	S	HANGING	V	12	2	2005			U
QUANG	DUC	MONK	NA	S	IMMOLATION	V	6	11	1963		SAIGON	U
PETE	DUEL	ACTOR	A	S	GUNSHOT	V	12	31	1971	POET	SO CAL	U
K SELLO	DUIKER	WRITER	A	S	HANGING	V	1	19	2005		S AFRICA	U
DAVOR	DUJMOVIC	ACTOR	A	S	HANGING	V	5	31	1999	DEPRESSION SUBSTANCE ABUSE	SLOVENIA	M
BUDD	DWYER	POLITICIAN	NA	S	GUNSHOT	V	1	22	1987	KILLED SELF ON TV	PA	U
GEORGE	EASTMAN	INVENTOR	NA	S	GUNSHOT	V	3	14	1932			U
MERRITT	EDSON	GENERAL	NA	S	CO POISONING	NV	8	14	1955		WASH DC	U
PAUL	EHRENFEST	PHYSICIST	NA	SM	GUNSHOT	V	9	25	1933	KILLED DOWNS SYNDROME CHILD 1ST DEPRESSION		M

JIM	ELLISON	MUSICIAN	A	S	CO POISONING	NV	6	20	1996			U
PEG	ENTWISTLE	ACTRESS	A	S	JUMP	V	9	16	1932	JUMPED OFF HOLLYWOOD SIGN ETOHISM	CAL	M
TOM	EVANS	MUSICIAN	A	S	HANGING	V	11	19	1983	BADFINGER DEPRESSION	ENGLAND	M
LANDIS	EVERSON	WRITER	A	S	GUNSHOT	V	11	17	2007		CAL	U
AUDREY	FAGEN	POLICE OFFICER	NA	S	GUNSHOT	V	4	20	2007		AUSTRALIA	U
ANGUS	FAIRHURST	PHOTOGRA-PHER	A	S	HANGING	V	3	29	2008		SCOTTLAND	U
RICHARD	FARN-SWORTH	ACTOR	A	S	GUNSHOT	V	10	6	2000		NEW MEX-ICO	U
JUSTINUS	FASHANU	SOCCER	NA	S	HANGING	V	5	2	1998		ENGLAND	U
RENE	FAVALORO	DR WRITER	A	S	GUNSHOT	V	7	29	2000		ARGENTINA	U
JEFF	FEHRING	SOCCER	NA	S	?	?	7	25	2008		ENGLAND	U
ANDREA	FELDMAN	ACTRESS	A	S	JUMP	V	8	8	1972	AMPHET-AMINES	NY	M
HANS	FISCHER	CHEMIST	NA	S	?	?	3	31	1945		GERMANY	U
GEORGE	FISKE	PHOTOGRA-PHER	A	S	GUNSHOT	V	10	21	1918			U
ROBERT	FITZROY	ADMIRAL	NA	S	RAZOR	V	4	30	1865	DEPRESSION	ENGLAND	M
EDWARD	FLANDERS	ACTOR	A	S	GUNSHOT	V	2	22	1995	DEPRESSION	CAL	M
FREDERICK	FLEET	SAILOR	NA	S	HANGING	V	1	10	1965	LOOKOUT TITANIC 4/14/1912	ENGLAND	U
JOHN	FLETCHER	WRITER	A	S	DROWNING	NV	5	20	1950	DEPRESSION	ARKANSAS	M
BERNARD	FLOUD	POLITICIAN	NA	S	CO POISONING	NV	10	10	1967	PSYCHIATRIC TREATMENT	ENGLAND	M
DEDE	FORTIN	MUSICIAN	A	S	STABBING	V	5	8	2000			U
VINCE	FOSTER	LAWYER	NA	S	GUNSHOT	V	7	20	1993	DEPRESSION (TRAZODONE) CLINTON ADMINIST	WASH DC	M
WADE	FRANKUM	STUDENT	NA	SM	GUNSHOT	V	8	17	1991	KILLED 7	AUSTRALIA	U
SIGMUND	FREUD	PSYCHIA-TRIST	NA	S	MORPHINE	NV	9	23	1939	PSYCHOSEXU-AL DVLPMNT COCAINE		M
JOHN	FRIEDRICH	BUSINESS-MAN	NA	S	GUNSHOT	V	7	27	1991		VICTORIA	U
MISAO	FUJIMURA	WRITER	A	S	DROWNING	NV	5	22	1903	POETRY OF DEPRESSION	TOKYO	M
ANTON	FURST	PRODUC-TION	A	S	JUMP	V	11	24	1991	DESIGNED 1989 BATMOBILE	CAL	U
PHILLIP	GALE	INVENTOR	A	S	JUMP	V	3	13	1998	MUSICIAN	MASS	U
HUGHIE	GALLACHER	SOCCER	NA	S	TRAIN	V	6	11	1957			U
TED	GARDESTAD	MUSICIAN	A	S	TRAIN	V	6	22	1997	BIPOLAR? (SCHIZOPHREN-IC)	SWEDEN	M
DAVID	GARROWAY	JOURNALIST	A	S	GUNSHOT	V	7	21	1982	DEXEDRINE DEPRESSION	PA	M
ROMAIN	GARY	WRITER	A	S	GUNSHOT	V	12	2	1980	DEPRESSION		M
DANNY	GATTON	MUSICIAN	A	S	GUNSHOT	V	10	4	1994	DEPRESSION	MARYLAND	M
MICHAEL	GAUQUELIN	PSYCHOLO-GIST	NA	S	?	?	5	20	1991			U
MARTHA	GELLHORN	WRITER	A	S	POISON	NV	2	15	1998		ENGLAND	U
KOSTAS	GEORGAKIS	STUDENT	NA	S	IMMOLATION	V	11	19	1970		ITALY	U
PETER	GEORGE	WRITER	A	S	?	?	6	11	1966			U
MARK	GERTLER	PAINTER	A	S	?	?	6	23	1939	DEPRESSED		M
MICHAEL	GILDON	ACTOR	A	S	HANGING	V	12	5	2006			U

KIMVEER	GILL	STUDENT	NA	SM	GUNSHOT	V	9	13	2006	KILLED 1 PER-SON SCHOOL SHOOTING	CANADA	U
CHARLOTTE	GILMAN	WRITER	A	S	CHLOROFORM	NV	8	17	1935	POST PARTUM DEPRESSION		M
ODILO	GLOBOCNIK	NAZI	NA	S	CYANIDE	NV	5	31	1945			U
KURT	GODEL	PHILOSO-PHER	A	S	STARVATION	NV	1	14	1978	PARANOIA	NJ	M
JOSEPH	GOEBBELS	NAZI	NA	SM	GUNSHOT	V	5	1	1945	KILLED 6 KIDS	GERMANY	U
HERMANN	GORING	NAZI	NA	S	CYANIDE	NV	10	15	1946	MORHINE ADDICTION		M
JULEN	GOIKOETXEA	CYCLIST	NA	S	JUMP	V	10	7	2006	DEPRESSION		M
FRITHA	GOODEY	ACTRESS	A	S	STABBING	V	9	7	2004	ANOREXIA	ENGLAND	M
GORDIAN		EMPORER	NA	S	HANGING	V	4	12	238		CARTHAGE	U
ADAM	GORDN	WRITER	A	S	GUNSHOT	V	6	24	1890	MOODY	CONN	M
ARSHILE	GORKY	PAINTER	A	S	HANGING	V	7	21	1948	MOODS OF MELANCHOLY		M
ANDRE	GORZ	PHILOSO-PHER	NA	S	LETHAL INJEC-TION	NV	9	22	2007	SUICIDE WITH WIFE	AUBE	U
ANDERS	GOTHBERG	MUSICIAN	A	S	JUMP	V	3	30	2008		STOCK-HOLM	U
EDDIE	GRAHAM	WRESTLER	NA	S	GUNSHOT	V	1	21	1985	ETOHISM		M
SHAUNA	GRANT	PORN AC-TRESS	A	S	GUNSHOT	V	3	23	1984	COCAINE ADDICTION	PS CAL	M
SPALDING	GRAY	WRITER	A	S	JUMP	V	1	10	2004	BIPOLAR MOM SUICIDE	NY	M
RICHARD	GREEN	REFEREE	NA	S	?	?	7	1	1983		NV	U
PETER	GREGG	RACE DRIVER	NA	S	GUNSHOT	V	12	15	1980			U
ROBERT	GREIM	NAZI PILOT	NA	S	CYANIDE	NV	5	24	1945		AUSTRIA	U
LOUIS	GUILLER-MAIN	MUSICIAN	A	S	STABBING	V	10	1	1770		VERSAILLE	U
ANTONIO	GUZMAN	POLITICIAN	NA	S	GUNSHOT	V	7	4	1982		DOMINICAN	U
CLARA	IMMERWAHR	CHEMIST	NA	S	GUNSHOT	V	5	2	1915		GERMANY	U
JERRY	HADLEY	MUSICIAN	A	S	GUNSHOT	V	7	18	2007		NY	U
RYAN	HALLIGAN	STUDENT	NA	S	HANGING	V	10	7	2003	CYBER-BULLIED	VT	U
KENNETH	HALLIWELL	WRITER	A	SM	NEMBUTOL	NV	8	9	1967	KILLED LOVER FATHER SUICIDE AN-TIDEPRESSANT	ENGLAND	M
MITCH	HALPERN	REFEREE	NA	S	GUNSHOT	V	8	20	2000			U
PETER	HAM	MUSICIAN	A	S	HANGING	V	4	24	1975	BADFINGER	ENGLAND	U
RUSTY	HAMER	ACTOR	A	S	GUNSHOT	V	1	18	1990	MAKE ROOM FOR DADDY	LOUISIANA	U
LOIS	HAMILTON	WRITER MODEL	A	S	ASPHYXIATION	NV	12	23	1999			U
TOM	HAMILTON	?	?	SM	GUNSHOT	V	3	13	1996	DUNBLANE SCHOOL MASSACRE KILLED 17	ENGLAND	U
ANTHONY	HANCOCK	ACTOR	A	S	BARBITURATES	NV	6	24	1968	ETOH	AUSTRALIA	M
ST JOHN	HANKIN	WRITER	A	S	DROWNING W WEIGHTS	NV	6	15	1909			U
EDWARD	HANNIGAN	POLITICIAN	NA	S	MORPHINE	NV	2	25	1859		MS	U
LEWIS	HARCOURT	POLITICIAN	NA	S	?	?	2	24	1922	CHILD MOLESTATION	ENGLAND	U
JAMES	HICKEY	WRITER	A	S	MORPHINE	NV	2	9	1898	WROTE A BOOK ON SUICIDE	TX	U
MARY	HARDY	ACTOR	A	S	?	?	1	7	1985			U
ERIC	HARRIS	STUDENT	NA	SM	GUNSHOT	V	4	20	1999	COLUMBINE DEPRESSION LUVOX IN SYSTEM	CO	M

TONY	HARRIS	BASKET-BALL	NA	S	HANGING	V	11	9	2007	PARANOID	BRAZIL	M
MICHAEL	HARTER	POLITICIAN	NA	S	?	?	2	22	1896		OHIO	U
BRYNN	HARTMAN	WIFE	NA	SM	GUNSHOT	V	5	27	1998	KILLED PHIL HARTMAN ZOLOFT DEPRESSION	LA CAL	M
MARY	HARTMAN	ACTRESS	A	S	JUMP	V	6	10	1987	DEPRESSION	PA	M
ARIHIRO	HASE	VOICE ACTOR	A	S	JUMP	V	7	30	1996			U
DONNY	HATHAWAY	MUSICIAN	A	S	JUMP	V	1	13	1979	DEPRESSION SCHIZOPHREN-IC BIPOLAR? MEDS	NY	M
FELIX	HAUSDORFF	MATHEMA-TICIAN	NA	S	?	?	1	26	1942			U
PHYLLIS	HAVER	ACTRESS	A	S	BARBITURATE	NV	11	19	1960		CONN	U
BRANDI	HAWBAKER	POKER	NA	S	?	?	4	13	2008	MENTAL ILLNESS		M
BENJAMIN	HAYDON	PAINTER	A	S	?	?	6	22	1846			U
JEANNE	HEBUTERNE	WIFE	NA	S	JUMP	V	1	25	1920	WIFE OF AMEDEO MODIGLIANA PAINTER		U
SADEQ	HEDAYAT	WRITER	A	S	GAS	NV	4	4	1951			U
JOHN	HEDDLE	POLITICIAN	NA	S	?	?	12	19	1989			U
MARVIN	HEEMEYER	MECHANIC	NA	S	GUNSHOT	V	6	4	2004	BULLDOZED TOWN	CO	U
ERNEST	HEMINGWAY	WRITER	A	S	GUNSHOT	V	7	2	1961	DAD SIS BRO GD ALL SUICIDE ECT ETOH BIPOLAR	IDAHO	M
MARGAUX	HEMINGWAY	ACTRESS	A	S	BARBITURATE	NV	7	1	1996	DEPRESSION		M
BENJAMIN	HENDRICK-SON	ACTOR	A	S	GUNSHOT	V	7	3	2006	AS THE WORLD TURNS DEPRESSION	NY	M
KONRAD	HENLEIN	POLITICIAN	NA	S	SLIT WRISTS	V	5	10	1945	SLIT WRISTS WITH GLASSES		U
GEORGE	HENNARD	SAILOR	NA	SM	GUNSHOT	V	10	16	1991	LUBYS MASSACRE 23 KILLED	TX	U
JAMES	HERLIHY	WRITER	A	S	SLEEPING PILLS	V	10	21	1993		CAL	U
WILLARD	HERSHBERG-ER	BASEBALL	NA	S	SLIT WRISTS	V	8	3	1940		MASS	U
PAUL	HESTER	MUSICIAN	A	S	HANGING	V	3	26	2005	DEPRESSION MOOD SWINGS	AUSTRALIA	M
GEORGE	HILL	DIRECTOR	A	S	GUNSHOT	V	8	10	1934			U
HEINRICH	HIMMLER	NAZI	NA	S	CYANIDE	NV	5	23	1945			U
JOE	HINRICH	STUDENT	NA	S	EXPLOSION	V	10	1	2005	OKLAHOMA U BOMBING	OK	U
ADOLF	HITLER	NAZI	NA	S	CYANIDE	NV	4	30	1945	UROLAGNIA	GERMANY	U
DON	HOLLEN-BROOK	JOURNALIST	A	S	GAS	V	6	22	1954	GOOD NIGHT AND GOOD LUCK	NY	U
DOUG	HOPKINS	MUSICIAN	A	S	GUNSHOT	V	12	5	1993	DEPRESSION ETOH GIN BLOSSUMS		M
HARRY	HORSE	AUTHOR	A	SM	STABBING	V	1	10	2007	KILLED WIFE AND PETS		U
ELMYR	DE HORY	PAINTER	A	S	SLEEPING PILLS	NV	12	11	1976			U
SOAD	HOSNY	ACTRESS	A	S	JUMP	V	6	21	2001	DEPRESSION	ENGLAND	M
ROBERT	HOWARD	WRITER	A	S	GUNSHOT	V	6	11	1936	DEPRESSION	TEXAS	M
IVAN	HRIBER	POLITICIAN	NA	S	DROWNING	NV	12	28	1941			U

NICHOLAS	HUGHES	BIOLOGIST	NA	S	HANGING	V	3	16	2009	DEPRESSION	ALASKA	M
PHYLLIS	HYMAN	MUSICIAN	A	S	BARBITUATE	NV	6	30	1995		NY	U
ROBIN	HYDE	WRITER	A	S	BENZEDRINE	NV	8	23	1939	PSYCH HOSP	ENGLAND	M
YOUSSEF	IDILBI	ACTOR	A	S	JUMP	V	5	15	2008			U
WILLIAM	INGE	WRITER	A	S	CO POISONING	NV	6	10	1973	DEPRESSION		M
JUZO	ITAMI	ACTOR	A	S	JUMP	V	12	20	1997		JAPAN	U
BRUCE	IVANS	BIOLOGIST	NA	S	CODEINE	NV	7	29	2008	2001 ANTHRAX DEPRESSION PSYCHOSIS	MARYLAND	M
JANG	JA-YEON	ACTRESS	A	S	HANGING	V	3	7	2009	DEPRESSION	KOREA	M
VITTORIO	JANO	ENGINEER	NA	S	?	?	3	13	1965		TURIN ITALY	U
ALICE	DE JANZE	HEIRESS	NA	S	GUNSHOT	V	9	30	1941	DEPRESSION PROMISCUITY MORPHINE	KENYA	M
RICHARD	JENI	COMEDIEN	A	S	GUNSHOT	V	3	10	2007	DEPRESSION PSYCHOSIS	CAL	M
JOHNNY	JACKSON	PRODUCER	A	S	JUMP	V	10	3	2008	ETOH (DWI)		M
ANSON	JONES	BUSINESS- MAN	NA	S	GUNSHOT	V	1	9	1858		TEXAS	U
JIM	JONES	LEADER PT	NA	SM	GUNSHOT/CN	V	11	18	1978	PEOPLES TEMPLE MJ LSD PHENOBARB		M
ALEX	JORDAN	PORN AC- TRESS	A	S	HANGING	V	7	2	1995			U
TIMOTHY	JORDAN	MUSICIAN	A	S	?	?	12	13	2005			U
NAFISA	JOSEPH	MODEL	NA	S	HANGING	V	7	29	2004	MTV VJ	INDIA	U
LUC	JOURET	LEADER	NA	S	?	?	10	5	1994		SWITZER- LAND	U
ATTILA	JOZSEF	WRITER	A	S	TRAIN	V	12	3	1937	SCHIZOPHRE- NIA BPD ?		M
JUNG	DA BIN	ACTRESS	A	S	HANGING	V	2	10	2007	DEPRESSION	KOREA	M
CLAUDE	JUTRA	WRITER	A	S	DROWNING	NV	11	5	1986			U
ALEXEY	KALEDIN	LEADER	NA	S	?	?	1	29	1918			U
JOERG	KALT	DIRECTOR	A	S	?	?	7	1	2007			U
SARAH	KANE	WRITER	A	S	HANGING	NV	2	20	1999	DEPRESSION	ENGLAND	M
KOSTAS	KARYOTAKIS	WRITER	A	S	GUNSHOT	V	7	20	1928	"MELANCHOLY"		M
ROMAS	KALANTA	PROTESTOR	NA	S	IMMOLATION	V	5	14	1972	DEPRESSED STATE	LITHUANIA	M
YASUNARI	KAWABATA	WRITER	A	S	GAS	NV	4	16	1972		JAPAN	U
BIZAN	KAWAKAMI	WRITER	A	S	?	?	6	15	1908			U
BRIAN	KEITH	ACTOR	A	S	GUNSHOT	V	6	24	1997	FAMILY AFFAIR DAUGHTER SUICIDE 4/97	CAL	U
DAVID	KELLY	WEAPONS EXP	NA	S	SLIT WRISTS/ PAIN K	V	7	17	2003		ENGLAND	U
SAMUEL	KENDALL	POLITICIAN	NA	S	GUNSHOT	V	1	8	1933		WASH DC	U
LEVI	KEREAMA	SINGER	A	S	JUMP	V	10	4	2008	AUSTRALIAN IDOL		U
KIMVEER	JIHOO	ACTOR	A	S	HANGING	V	10	6	2008		S KOREA	U
PRESTON	KING	POLITICIAN	NA	S	JUMP	V	11	12	1865			U
JAMES	KJELGAARD	WRITER	A	S	?	?	7	12	1959	DEPRESSION	WISCONSIN	M
HEINRICH	VON KLEIST	WRITER	A	S	GUNSHOT	V	11	21	1811			U
JOCHEN	KLEPPER	JOURNALIST	A	S	GAS	NA	12	11	1942			U
DYLAN	KLEBOLD	STUDENT	NA	SM	GUNSHOT	V	4	20	1999	COLUMINE SHOOTINGS	CO	U
GUNTHER	KLUGE	NAZI	NA	S	CYANIDE	NV	8	19	1944		FRANCE	U
IVAN	KORADE	GENERAL	NA	SM	GUNSHOT	V	4	3	2008	KILLED 4 ETOH	CROATIA	M
FLETCHER	KNEBEL	WRITER	A	S	SLEEPING PILLS	NV	2	26	1993			U
WILLIAM	KNOWLAND	POLITICIAN	NA	S	GUNSHOT	V	2	23	1974		CAL	U
ARTHUR	KOESTLER	WRITER	A	S	OD	NV	3	3	1983	HALLUCINO- GENS	ENGLAND	M

SARAH	KAUFMAN	PHILOSO-PHER	A	S	?	?	10	15	1994			U
HANNELORE	KOHL	WIFE HELMUT	NA	S	SLEEPING PILLS	NV	7	5	2001			U
FUMIMARO	KONOE	POLITICIAN	NA	S	CYANIDE	NV	12	16	1945			U
ALEXAN-DROS	KORIZIS	POLITICIAN	NA	S	GUNSHOT	V	4	18	1941		GREECE	U
RUSLANA	KORSHUN-OVA	MODEL	NA	S	JUMP	V	6	28	2008		NY	U
JERZY	KOSINSKI	WRITER	A	S	BARBITUATES	NV	5	3	1991		NY	U
LOUIS	KRAGES	BUSINESS-MAN	NA	S	GUNSHOT	V	1	11	2001	DEPRESSION	GEORGIA	M
IVAR	KREUGAR	BUSINESS-MAN	NA	S	GUNSHOT	V	3	12	1932			U
FRIEDRICH	KRUGER	NAZI	NA	S	GUNSHOT	V	5	9	1945			U
FRIEDRICH	KRUPP	BUSINESS-MAN	NA	S	?	?	11	22	1902			U
PAUL	LAFARGUE	WRITER	A	S	?	?	11	26	1911			U
ROBERT	LA FOLLETTE	POLITICIAN	NA	S	GUNSHOT	V	2	24	1953	DEPRESSION	WASH DC	M
KAREN	LANCAUME	PORN AC-TRESS	A	S	OD	NV	1	28	2005			U
CAROLE	LANDIS	ACTRESS	A	S	SECONAL	NV	4	5	1948	DEPRESSION	LA CAL	M
JAMES	LANE	POLITICIAN	NA	S	GUNSHOT	V	7	11	1866	DEPRESSION		M
HANS	LANGSDORF	CAPTAIN	NA	S	GUNSHOT	V	12	19	1939		ARGENTINA	U
NAPOLEON	LAPATHIOTIS	WRITER	A	S	GUNSHOT	V	1	7	1944	OPIUM		M
ROD	LAUREN	ACTOR	A	S	JUMP	V	7	11	2007		TRACY CA	U
FLORENCE	LAWRENCE	ACTRESS	A	S	POISON	NV	12	28	1938	"THE FIRST MOVIE STAR"	SO CAL	U
GEORGE	LAWRENCE	POLITICIAN	NA	S	JUMP	V	11	21	1917		NY	U
ADAM	LEDWON	SOCCER	NA	S	HANGING	V	6	11	2008		AUSTRIA	U
LEE	EUN-JU	ACTRESS	A	S	HANGING	V	2	22	2005	DEPRESSION	S KOREA	M
JON	LEE	MUSICIAN	A	S	HANGING	V	1	7	2002	FEEDER	FLA	U
LEE	HAE	ACTIVIST	NA	S	STABBING	V	9	10	2003			U
TRENT	LEHMAN	ACTOR	A	S	HANGING	V	1	18	1982	"NANNY AND THE PROFESSOR"	SO CAL	U
MEGAN	LEIGH	PORN AC-TRESS	A	S	HANGING	V	3	2	1990	VALIUM	CAL	M
NORMAN	VAN LENNAP	CHESS	NA	S	JUMP	V	9	29	1987		HOLLAND	U
MARC	LEPINE	STUDENT	NA	SM	GUNSHOT	V	12	6	1989	MONREAL MASSACRE PSYCHOTIC? VIOLENT	MONTRE-AL,C	M
PRIMO	LEVI	WRITER	A	S	JUMP	V	4	11	1987	GF SUICIDE DEPRESSION	ITALY	M
ROBERT	LEY	POLITICIAN	NA	S	HANGING	V	10	25	1945	ERRATIC BEHAVIOR HEAVY ETOH		M
FRIEDRICH	LEIBACHER	BUSINESS-MAN	NA	SM	GUNSHOT	V	9	27	2001	ZUG MASSA-CRE 14 DEAD ALCOHOLISM	SWITZER-LAND	M
MAX	LINDER	ACTOR	A	S	?	?	10	31	1925	DEPRESSION	FRANCE	M
VACHEL	LINDSAY	WRITER	A	S	LYSOL	NV	12	5	1931	DEPRESSION		M
LOUIS	LINGG	ANARCHIST	NA	S	DYNAMITE	V	11	10	1887		CHICAGO	U
DIANE	LINKLETTER	MUSICIAN	A	S	JUMP	V	10	4	1969	DEPRESSION LSD DAUGHTER OF ART	SO CAL	M
JESSE	LIVERMORE	STOCK BROKER	NA	S	GUNSHOT	V	11	28	1940	DEPRESSION	NY	M
MIKAEL	LJUNGBERG	WRESTLER	NA	S	HANGING	V	11	17	2004	DEPRESSION	SWEDEN	M
PETER	DAVIES	PUBLISHER	NA	S	TRAIN	V	4	5	1960	ETOHISM		M
ROSS	LOCKRIDGE	WRITER	A	S	CO POISONING	NV	3	6	1948	DEPRESSION	INDIANA	M

PHILLIP	LOEB	ACTOR	A	S	BARBITURATE	NV	9	1	1955		NY	U
MARK	LOMBARDI	ARTIST	A	S	HANGING	V	3	22	2000	MANIC DEPRESSIVE	NY	M
TERRY	LONG	FOOTBALL	NA	S	ANTIFREEZE	NV	6	7	2005	DEPRESSION	PA	M
GANG	LU	STUDENT	NA	SM	GUNSHOT	V	11	1	1991	U OF IOWA MASSACRE 5 KILLED	IOWA	U
GHERASIM	LUCA	WRITER	A	S	DROWNING	NV	2	9	1994		FRANCE	U
MARCUS	LUCANUS	WRITER	A	S	CUTTING	V	4	30	65		ITALY	U
RON	LUCIANO	WRITER/ UMPIRE	A	S	CO POISONING	NV	1	18	1995		NY	U
ALEKSANDR	LYAPUNOV	MATHEMA-TICIAN	NA	S	?	?	11	3	1918			U
ROMAN	LYASHENKO	HOCKEY	NA	S	HANGING	V	7	5	2003	DEPRESSION EMOTIONAL DO	TURKEY	M
BILLY	MACKENZIE	MUSICIAN	A	S	OD ELAVIL	NV	1	22	1997	DEPRESSION		M
RICHARD	MANUEL	MUSICIAN	A	S	HANGING	V	3	4	1986	"THE BAND" ETOHISM	FLA	M
SIMONE	MAREUIL	ACTRESS	A	S	IMMOLATION	V	10	24	1954	DEPRESSION	FRANCE	M
ANDREW	MARTINEZ	ACTIVIST	NA	S	SUFFOCATION	NV	5	18	2006	MENTAL ILLNESS CPS?	CAL	M
FLAVIUS	MAGNENTIUS	COMMAND-ER	NA	S	STABBING	V	8	11	353		ITALY	U
ANTON	MAIDEN	MUSICIAN	A	S	?	?	11	1	2003	DEPRESSION	SWEDEN	M
WILLY	MAIRESS	RACE DRIVER	NA	S	?	?	9	9	1969			U
SANDOR	MARAI	WRITER	A	S	GUNSHOT	V	2	22	1989			U
HARRY	MARTINSON	WRITER	A	S	STABBING	V	2	11	1978		SWEDEN	U
TOSHIKAT-SU	MATSUOKA	POLITICIAN	NA	S	HANGING	V	5	28	2007		JAPAN	U
DENIS	MATTHEWS	MUSICIAN	A	S	?	?	12	25	1988			U
VLADIMIR	MAYAKOVSKY	WRITER	A	S	GUNSHOT	V	4	14	1930			U
JACQUES	MAYOL	FREE DIVER	NA	S	HANGING	V	12	22	2001		ITALY	U
SUSANNAH	MCCORKLE	MUSICIAN	A	S	JUMP	V	5	19	2001	DEPRESSION	NY	M
KID	MCCOY	BOXER	NA	S	SLEEPING PILLS	NV	4	18	1940	ETOHISM MURDERED 1 PERSON		M
CHRIS	MCKINSTRY	RESEARCH-ER	NA	S	GAS	NV	1	23	2006	LSD		M
GORDON	MCMASTER	POLITICIAN	NA	S	CO POISONING	NV	7	28	1997	ETOH CHRONIC FATIGUE		M
CHARLES	MCVAY	COMMAND-ER	NA	S	GUNSHOT	V	11	6	1968		CONN	U
MATTHEW	WECHTEL	POLITICIAN	NA	S	GUNSHOT	V	2	21	2008		ND	U
JOE	MEEK	MUSICIAN	A	SM	GUNSHOT	V	2	3	1967	DEPRESSION PARANOIA KILLED LANDLORD	ENGLAND	M
ABDULLAH	MEHSUD	SOLDIER	NA	S	EXPLOSION	V	7	24	2007		PAKISTAN	U
NIKLAUS	MEIENBERG	WRITER	A	S	STRANGLING	V	9	22	1993	DEPRESSION	SWITZER-LAND	M
MEGAN	MEIER	STUDENT	NA	S	HANGING	V	10	17	2006	CYBERBUL-LYING ADD DEPRESSION	MISSOURI	M
KITTY	MELSOSE	ACTOR	A	S	?	?	6	3	1912		ENGLAND	U
ADOLF	MERCKLE	BUSINESS-MAN	NA	S	TRAIN	V	1	5	2009		GERMANY	U
CHARLOTTE	MEW	WRITER	A	S	LYSOL	NV	3	24	1928	DEPRESSION 2 SISTERS PSYCH	ENGLAND	M
NOEL	WOOD	MUSICIAN	A	S	CYANIDE	NV	12	5	1953	DEPRESSION		M

JAMES	MILLER	PARACHUT-IST	NA	S	HANGING	V	9	22	2002	"FAN MAN"	ALASKA	U
WALTER	MILLER	WRITER	A	S	GUNSHOT	V	1	9	1996	DEPRESSED		M
MARY	MILLINGTON	PORN AC-TRESS	A	S	OD	NV	8	19	1979	DEPRESSION SUBSTANCE ABUSE	ENGLAND	M
FREDDIE	MILLS	BOXER	NA	S	GUNSHOT	V	7	25	1965		ENGLAND	U
WILLIAM	MILLS	POLITICIAN	NA	S	GUNSHOT	V	5	24	1973		MD	U
JOHN	MILTON	POLITICIAN	NA	S	GUNSHOT	V	4	1	1865		FLA	U
YUKIO	MISHIMA	WRITER	A	S	SEPPUKU	V	11	25	1970		JAPAN	U
KAZUYOSHI	MIURA	BUSINESS-MAN	NA	S	HANGING	V	10	10	2008	ARSON SHOPLIFT MURDER WIFE	CAL	M
ANA	MLADIC	?	?	S	GUNSHOT	V	3	24	1994	DAUGHTER OF RATKO MLADIC		U
VILHELM	MOBERG	WRITER	A	S	DROWNING	NV	8	3	1973	DEPRESSION	SWEDEN	M
WALTER	MODEL	NAZI	NA	S	GUNSHOT	V	4	21	1945		GERMANY	U
ARTHUR	VAN DEN BRUCK	WRITER	A	S	?	?	5	30	1925	"NERVOUS BREAKDOWN"		M
GEORGE	MOHREN-SCHILDT	GEOLOGIST	NA	S	GUNSHOT	V	3	29	1977	LEE OSWALD FRIEND		U
MOSES	MOLELEKWA	MUSICIAN	A	S	HANGING	V	2	13	2001			U
HENRY	MONTHER-LANT	WRITER	A	S	GUNSHOT	V	9	21	1972		FRANCE	U
DONNIE	MOORE	BASEBALL	NA	S	GUNSHOT	V	7	18	1989	DEPRESSION	SO CAL	M
CHRIS	MORGAN	WRITER	A	S	TRAIN	V	5	30	2008	DEPRESSION	ENGLAND	M
DUANE	MORRISON	?	?	SM	GUNSHOT	V	9	27	2006	PLATTE CANYON HIGH SHOOTING (1) MJ	CO	M
TED	MOULT	RADIO HOST	A	S	GUNSHOT	V	9	3	1986	DEPRESSION		M
DAVID	MUNROW	MUSICIAN	A	S	HANGING	V	5	15	1976			U
JAMES	MURRAY	ACTOR	A	S	JUMP	V	7	11	1936		NY	U
MATTHEW	MURRAY	STUDENT	NA	SM	GUNSHOT	V	12	9	2007	NEWLIFE CHURCH SHOOTINGS (4) VIOLENT LETTERS	CO	M
SAULIUS	MYKOLAITS	WRITER	A	S	HANGING	V	2	18	2006			U
HISAYASU	NAGATA	POLITICIAN	NA	S	JUMP	V	1	3	2009			U
MURAT	NASYROV	MUSICIAN	A	S	JUMP	V	1	19	2007			U
OSCAR	NEDBAL	MUSICIAN	A	S	JUMP	V	12	24	1930			U
NEKOJIRU		ARTIST	A	S	?	?	5	10	1998			U
NERO		EMPORER	NA	S	STABBING	V	6	9	68			U
GERARD	DE NERVAL	WRITER	A	S	HANGING	V	1	26	1855		FRANCE	U
JOACHIM	NIELSON	MUSICIAN	A	S	HEROIN OD	NV	10	17	2000	HEROIN ADDICTION		M
GOCE	NIKOLOVSKI	MUSICIAN	A	S	GUNSHOT	V	12	16	2006			U
FRANK	NITTI	GANGSTER	NA	S	GUNSHOT	V	3	19	1943	SEVERE CLAUS-TROPHOBIC	ILL	M
NOGI	MARESUKE	GENERAL	NA	SM	SEPPUKU	V	9	13	1912	KILLED WIFE	JAPAN	U
JON	NODTVEIDT	MUSICIAN	A	S	GUNSHOT	V	8	13	2006	DISSECTION	SWEDEN	U
ALIGHIERO	NOSCHESE	IMPERSON-ATOR	A	S	GUNSHOT	V	12	3	1979	DEPRESSION	ITALY	M
LAWRENCE	OATES	EXPLORER	NA	S	FREEZING	NV	3	16	1912	SACRIFICED LIFE SO OTHERS COULD HIKE	S POLE	U
JOHN	OBRIEN	WRITER	A	S	GUNSHOT	V	4	10	1994	"LEAVING LAS VEGAS" ETOH		M
C.Y.	O'CONNOR	ENGINEER	NA	S	GUNSHOT	V	3	10	1902		AUSTRALIA	U

HUGHI	OCONNOR	ACTOR	A	S	GUNSHOT	V	3	28	1995	ADOPTED TO CARROLL OPIOD COCAINE MJ	SO CAL	M
LUIS	OCANA	CYCLIST	NA	S	GUNSHOT	V	5	19	1994	DEPRESSED	FRANCE	M
PHIL	OCHS	MUSICIAN	A	S	HANGING	V	4	9	1976	BIPOLAR ETOH	NY	M
PER YNGVE	OHLIN	MUSICIAN	A	S	GUNSHOT	V	4	8	1991	DEPRESSION "MAYHEM"	NORWAY	M
YUKIKO	OKADA	MUSICIAN	A	S	JUMP	V	4	8	1986	MULTIPLE SUICIDE ATTEMPTS	JAPAN	M
OTHO		EMPORER	NA	S	STABBING	V	4	16	1969		ROME	U
WAYNE	PAI	BUSINESS-MAN	NA	S	?	?	7	2	2008			U
JAN	PALACH	STUDENT	NA	S	IMMOLATION	V	1	19	1969		CZECH	U
DEBORAH	PALFRY	ESCORT CO	NA	S	HANGING	V	5	1	2008	DRUG ABUSE	FLA	M
BREECE	DJ PANCAKE	WRITER	A	S	GUNSHOT	V	4	8	1979		VA	U
BILLY	PAPKE	BOXER	NA	SM	GUNSHOT	V	11	26	1936	KILLED WIFE		U
VIOLETA	PARRA	MUSICIAN	A	S	GUNSHOT	V	2	5	1967	DEPRESSION		M
PASCIN		ARTIST	A	S	HANGING	V	6	5	1930	DEPRESSION ETOH	BULGARIA	M
JOHN	PATRICK	WRITER	A	S	SUFFOCATION	NV	11	7	1995			U
PAT	PATTERSON	COACH	NA	SM	GUNSHOT	V	10	11	2007	KILLED ALZHEIMERS WIFE	LA	U
CESARE	PAVESE	WRITER	A	S	BARBITURATES	NV	8	27	1950			U
GEORGE	PERIOLAT	ACTOR	A	S	ARSENIC	NV	2	20	1940		SO CAL	U
WILLIAM	PHILLIPS	ENGINEER	NA	SM	GUNSHOT	V	4	20	2007	JOHNSON SPACE CENTER SHOOTINGS (1)	FLA	U
JUSTIN	PIERCE	ACTOR	A	S	HANGING	V	7	10	2000		NV	U
H BEAM	PIPER	WRITER	A	S	GUNSHOT	V	11	6	1964		PA	U
ALEJANDRA	PIZARNIK	WRITER	A	S	SECONAL	NV	9	25	1972		ARGENTINA	U
SYLVIA	PLATH	WRITER	A	S	GAS	NV	2	11	1963	SON COMMIT-TED SUICIDE 3/16/09	ENGLAND	U
DANA	PLATO	ACTRESS	A	S	VICODIN	NV	5	9	1999	ETOH VALIUM PORN	OK	M
DERRICK	POURDE	MUSICIAN	A	S	GUNSHOT	V	3	30	2005	BIPOLAR		M
STEVIE	PLUNDER	MUSICIAN	A	S	JUMP	V	1	26	1996		AUSTRALIA	U
BEN	POLLACK	MUSICIAN	A	S	HANGING	V	6	7	1971		PS CAL	U
MARC	POTVIN	HOCKEY	NA	S	HANGING	V	1	13	2006		MICHIGAN	U
FELIX	POWELL	MUSICIAN	A	S	GUNSHOT	V	2	10	1942		ENGLAND	U
LUCIEN	PARADOL	WRITER	A	S	GUNSHOT	V	7	20	1870			U
MARK	PRIESTLY	ACTOR	A	S	JUMP	V	8	27	2008	DEPRESSION	AUSTRLIA	M
FREDDIE	PRINZE	COMIC	A	S	GUNSHOT	V	1	29	1977	DEPRESSION QUALUDES	SO CAL	M
CARLOS	SOCARRES	POLITICIAN	NA	S	GUNSHOT	V	4	5	1977		FLA	U
NATHAN	PRITIKAN	NUTRITION-IST	NA	S	?	?	2	21	1985			U
BORIS	PUGO	POLITICIAN	NA	SM	GUNSHOT	V	8	22	1991			U
JACK	PURVIS	MUSICIAN	A	S	?	?	3	30	1962	SEVERAL SUICIDE ATTEMPTS SEVERAL FIRES IN HOTELS	SF CAL	M
ANTERO	DE QUENTAL	WRITER	A	S	?	?	9	11	1891	DEPRESSION		M
RICHARD	QUINE	ACTOR	A	S	GUNSHOT	V	6	10	1989	DEPRESSION		M
ROBERT	QUINE	MUSICIAN	A	S	HEROIN	NV	5	31	2004		NY	U
GLENN	QUINN	ACTOR	A	S	HEROIN	NV	12	3	2002		SO CAL	U

GELI	RAUBAL	HITLERS NIECE	NA	S	GUNSHOT	V	9	12	1931		GERMANY	U
JASON	RAIZE	ACTOR	A	S	HANGING	V	2	3	2004		AUSTRALIA	U
FLORENCIO	RAMOS	ACTOR	A	S	GUNSHOT	V	2	23	1989			U
LYNNE	RANDELL	MUSICIAN	A	S	OD	NV	6	8	2007	METHAMPHET-AMINES	AUSTRALIA	M
KULJEET	RANDHAWA	ACTOR	A	S	HANGING	V	2	8	2006			U
DANNY	RAPP	MUSICIAN	A	S	GUNSHOT	V	4	5	1983	DANNY AND THE JRS		U
DAVID	RAPPAPORT	ACTOR	A	S	GUNSHOT	V	5	2	1990	DEPRESSION	SO CAL	M
ABRAM	RASELEMANE	SOCCER	NA	S	?	?	5	27	2008			U
MARGARET	RAY	UNEM-PLOYED	NA	S	TRAIN	V	10	5	1998	BROTHERS BOTH SUICIDE SCHIZOPHREN-IC?	CO	M
LIAM	RECTOR	WRITER	A	S	GUNSHOT	V	8	15	2007		NY	U
ALFRED	REDI	SOLDIER	NA	S	GUNSHOT	V	5	25	1913			U
GEORGE	REEVES	ACTOR	A	S	GUNSHOT	V	6	16	1959	DEPRESSION	SO CAL	U
DAVID	REIMER	?	?	S	GUNSHOT	V	5	4	2004	SEXUAL REASSIGNMENT POST FAILED CIRCUMCISE		U
THOMAS	REYNOLDS	POLITICIAN	NA	S	JUMP	V	3	30	1887	"LOSING MEN-TAL CAPACITY"	MS	M
THOMAS	REYNOLDS	POLITICIAN	NA	S	GUNSHOT	V	2	9	1844			U
DAVID	RITCHESON	STUDENT	NA	S	JUMP	V	7	1	2007	SEXUALLY ASSAULTED "DRUGS"	MEXICO	M
RENE	RIVKIN	STOCK BROKER	NA	S	?	?	5	1	2005			U
CARLOS	REIINA	POLITICIAN	NA	S	GUNSHOT	V	8	19	2003		HONDURAS	U
MALACHI	RITSCHER	MUSICIAN	A	S	IMMOLATION	V	11	3	2006		ILL	U
ANGEL	MENDEZ	SOLDIER	NA	S	GUNSHOT	V	2	23	1930	SEVERE DEPRESSION	PUERTO R	M
JOHN	ROBARTS	LAWYER	NA	S	GUNSHOT	V	10	18	1982		ONTARIO	U
RACHEL	ROBERTS	ACTOR	A	S	BARBITURATE	NV	11	26	1980	DEPRESSION ETOH	SO CAL	M
BILLY	ROBINZINE	BASKET-BALL	NA	S	CO POISONING	NV	9	16	1982			U
CHARLES	ROCKET	ACTOR	A	S	STABBING	V	10	7	2005	DUMB AND DUMBER	CONN	U
LUKASZ	ROMANAK	RACE DRIVER	NA	S	?	?	6	2	2006		POLAND	U
SAMUEL	ROMILLY	SCHOLAR	NA	S	STABBING	V	11	2	1818		ENGLAND	U
EDGAR	ROSENBERG	PRODUCER	A	S	OD	NV	8	18	1987	DEPRESSION		M
MARK	ROTHKO	PAINTER	A	S	OD	NV	2	25	1970			U
JACQUES	ROUX	ACTIVIST	NA	S	STABBING	V	2	19	1794			U
RUAN	LINGYU	ACTOR	A	S	BARBITURATE	NV	3	8	1935		CHINA	U
THOMAS	RUSK	GENERAL	NA	S	GUNSHOT	V	7	29	1857			U
MICHAEL	RYAN	LABOURER	NA	SM	GUNSHOT	V	8	19	1987	HUNGERFORD MASSACRE (16)	ENGLAND	U
JAKUB	RYBA	MUSICIAN	A	S	STABBING	V	4	8	1815		CZECH	U
MATTI	SARRI	STUDENT	NA	SM	GUNSHOT	V	9	23	2008	KAUHAJOKI MASSACRE (10) MENTAL HEALTH TX	FINLAND	M
MARIO	DE SA CAR-NEIRO	WRITER	A	S	STRYCHNINE	NV	4	26	1916	DEPRESSION	FRANCE	M
EMILIO	SALGARI	WRITER	A	S	STABBING	V	4	25	1911		ITALY	U
ALBERT	SALMI	ACTOR	A	SM	GUNSHOT	V	4	22	1990	DEPRESSION	WASH ST	M
JOHANNA	SAASTROM	ACTOR	A	S	?	?	2	13	2007			U
ALEXANDER	SAMSONOV	SOLDIER	NA	S	GUNSHOT	V	8	29	1914			U

GEORGE	SANDERS	ACTOR	A	S	BARBITURATE	NV	4	25	1972	ANGER	SPAIN	M
ALBERTO	DUMONT	INVENTOR	A	S	HANGING	V	7	23	1932	DEPRESSION	BRAZIL	M
BRUCE	SARVER	RACE DRIVER	NA	S	GUNSHOT	V	11	10	2005			U
DRAKE	SATHER	COMEDIAN	A	S	GUNSHOT	V	3	3	2004		SO CAL	U
SHANNON	WILSEY	PORN ACTRESS	A	S	GUNSHOT	V	7	11	1994	"SAVANNAH" SUBSTANCE ABUSE		M
GIA	SCALA	ACTOR	A	S	OD DRUGS AND ETOH	NV	4	30	1972	SUBSTANCE ABUSE ETOH EMOTIONAL PROBLEMS	SO CAL	M
DAVID	SCARBORO	ACTOR	A	S	JUMP	V	4	27	1988	PSYCH HOSP	ENGLAND	M
PETRUS	SCHAESBERG	ARTIST	A	S	JUMP	V	9	22	2008		NY	U
EUGEN	SCHAUMAN	NATIONALIST	NA	S	GUNSHOT	V	6	16	1904	ASSASSINATED RUSSIAN GOVERNOR	RUSSIA	U
MARGIE	SCHOEDINGER	?	?	S	GUNSHOT	V	9	22	2003	G BUSH RAPED HER AND HUSB DELUSION?	TX	M
ROBERT	SCHOMMER	ASTRONOMER	NA	S	?	?	12	12	2001		CHILE	U
DAVE	SCHULTHISE	MUSICIAN	A	S	?	?	3	10	2004	DEAD MILKMEN		U
CONRAD	SCHUMANN	SOLDIER	NA	S	HANGING	V	6	20	1998	DEPRESSION	GERMANY	M
INGO	SCHWICHTENBERG	MUSICIAN	A	S	TRAIN	V	3	8	1995	SCHIZOPHRENIA ETOH COCAINE HASHISH		M
WILLIAM	SEABROOK	WRITER	A	S	OD	NV	9	20	1945	ETOH	NY	M
JEAN	SEBERG	ACTOR	A	S	BARBITURATES	NV	8	30	1979	DEPRESSION	FRANCE	M
SERGI	SEGU	SOCCER	NA	S	TRAIN	V	11	4	2006	DEPRESSION HOSP		M
ANNE	SEXTON	WRITER	A	S	CO POISONING	NV	10	4	1974	BIPOLAR	MASS	M
FRANCES	SEYMOUR	SOCIALITE	NA	S	STABBING	V	4	14	1950	FONDA'S MOTHER MENTAL ILLNESS	NY	M
DEL	SHANNON	MUSICIAN	A	S	GUNSHOT	V	2	8	1990	ETOHISM	SO CAL	M
DISCO D		COMPOSER	A	S	HANGING	V	1	22	2007	BIPOLAR	WASH DC	M
JAMES	TIPTREE	WRITER	A	SM	GUNSHOT	V	5	19	1987	PAST ATTEMPTS MENTALLY ILL	VA	M
SHIBATA	KATSUIE	COMMANDER	NA	S	SEPPUKU	V	6	14	1583		JAPAN	U
HAROLD	SHIPMAN	PHYSICIAN	NA	S	HANGING	V	1	13	2004	SERIAL KILLER (250) DRUG ABUSE	ENGLAND	M
ARTHUR	SHREWSBURY	CRICKET	NA	S	GUNSHOT	V	5	19	1903		ENGLAND	U
ELI	SIEGEL	WRITER	A	S	?	?	11	8	1978		NY	U
WALTER	SLEZAK	WRITER	A	S	GUNSHOT	V	4	21	1983	DESPONDANT	NY	M
EVERETT	SLOAN	ACTOR	A	S	?	?	8	6	1965	DEPRESSED	SO CAL	M
JAMES	SMITH	PALEOANATOMIST	NA	S	CYANIDE	NV	1	7	1968		S AFRICA	U
PAUL	SNIDER	BUSINESSMAN	NA	SM	GUNSHOT	V	8	14	1980	"STAR 80" KILLED DOROTHY STRATTON	SO CAL	U
MITCH	SNYDER	ACTIVIST	NA	S	HANGING	V	7	6	1990		WASH DC	U
SOGA	EMISHI	STATESMAN	NA	S	?	?	7	11	645		JAPAN	U
MARK	SPEIGHT	TV HOST	A	S	HANGING	V	4	7	2008	COCAINE ADDICTION DEPRESSION ADD?	ENGLAND	M

JOHN	SPENCE	MUSICIAN	A	S	GUNSHOT	V	12	21	1987	DEPRESSION	SO CAL	M
BERNARD	SPILSBURY	PATHOLO-GIST	NA	S	GAS	NV	12	17	1947	DEPRESSION	ENGLAND	M
WILHELM	STEKEL	PSYCHOLO-GIST	NA	S	?	?	6	25	1940		ENGLND	U
INGER	STEVENS	ACTOR	A	S	BARBITURATE	NV	4	30	1970		SO CAL	U
GARY	STEWART	MUSICIAN	A	S	GUNSHOT	V	12	16	2003	ETOH POLYSUB-STANCE	FLA	M
JAY	STEWART	ANNOUNC-ER	A	S	GUNSHOT	V	9	12	1989	ETOH DEPRESSION	SO CAL	M
ROBERT	STEWART	POLITICIAN	A	S	STABBING	V	8	12	1822	PRANOIA MENTAL BREAKDOWN	ENGLAND	M
SHAKIR	STEWART	BUSINESS-MAN	NA	S	GUNSHOT	V	11	1	2008		GEORGIA	U
ADALBERT	STIFTER	WRITER	A	S	STABBING	V	1	28	1868	DEPRESSION		M
ALFONSINA	STORNI	WRITER	A	S	DROWNING	NV	10	25	1938	"EMOTIONAL PROBLEMS"	ARGENTINA	M
DAVID	STRICKLAND	ACTOR	A	S	HANGING	V	3	22	1999	BIPOLAR ETOH COCAINE "SUDDENLY SUSAN"	NV	M
STEVEN	SUEPPLE	BUSINESS-MAN	NA	SM	CAR WRECK	V	3	24	2008	BEAT WIFE AND 4 CHILDREN TO DEATH	IOWA	M
DAVID	SUTCH	MUSICIAN	A	S	HANGING	V	6	16	1999	DEPRESSION (BIPOLAR? PER WIFE)	ENGLAND	M
KAREL	SVOBODA	COMPOSER	A	S	GUNSHOT	V	1	28	2007			U
ISTVAN	SZECHENYL	STATESMAN	NA	S	GUNSHOT	V	4	8	1860		HUNGARY	U
VLADO	TANESKI	JOURNALIST	A	S	BUCKET OF H20	NV	6	23	2008	WROTE ARTICLES ON THE 3 WOMEN HE KILLED	MACEDO-NIA	U
YUTAKA	TANIYAMA	MATHEMA-TICIAN	A	S	?	?	11	17	1958	DEPRESSION		M
ALBERTS	TARULIS	SOCCER	NA	S	HANGING	V	9	24	1927			U
VIKTOR	TAUSK	PSYCHIA-TRIST	NA	S	?	?	7	3	1919	AFTER 3SOME W SIG FREUD AND LOU SALOME		U
SARA	TEASDALE	WRITER	A	S	SLEEPING PILLS	NV	1	29	1933		ST LOUIS	U
PAL	TELEKI	POLITICIAN	NA	S	GUNSHOT	V	4	3	1941		HUNGARY	U
LOU	TELLEGAN	ACTOR	A	S	STABBING	V	10	29	1934		SO CAL	U
LUIGI	TENCO	MUSICIAN	A	S	GUNSHOT	V	1	27	1967			U
TEWODROS		EMPORER	NA	S	?	?	4	13	1868		ETHIOPIA	U
JACK	THAYER	WRITER/ HISTORY	A	S	GUNSHOT	V	9	20	1945	TITANIC SURVIVOR DEPRESSED		M
JASON	THIRSK	MUSICIAN	A	S	GUNSHOT	V	7	29	1996	DEPRESSION ETOH "PENNYWISE"	SO CAL	M
JESSE	THOMAS	POLITICIAN	NA	S	?	?	5	2	1853			U
HUNTER	THOMPSON	WRITER	A	S	GUNSHOT	V	2	20	2005	ETOH PSYCHEDELICS	CO	M
GEORG	TINTER	CONDUC-TOR	A	S	JUMP	V	10	2	1999		HALIFAX	U
MUTSUO	TOI	UNEM-PLOYED	NA	SM	GUNSHOT	V	5	21	1938	TSUYAMA (30) DECAP GM HYPERSEX WITHDRAWN	JAPAN	M

ERNEST	TOLLER	WRITER	A	S	HANGING	V	5	22	1939	DEPRESSION	NY	M
MIKHAIL	TOMSKY	UNIONIST	NA	S	GUNSHOT	V	8	22	1936		RUSSIA	U
WOLFE	TONE	ACTIVIST	NA	S	STABBING	V	11	19	1798		IRELAND	U
TORE	TONNE	POLITICIAN	NA	S	?	?	12	20	2002		NORWAY	U
JOHN	TOOLE	WRITER	A	S	CO POISONING	NV	3	26	1969	ETOH MIGRAINES	MISSISSIPPI	M
GEORG	TRAKL	WRITER	A	S	COCAINE	NV	11	3	1914	DEPRESSION		M
KOKICHI	TSUBURAYA	RUNNER	NA	S	STABBING	V	1	9	1968			U
MARINA	TSVETAEVA	WRITER	A	S	HANGING	V	8	31	1941		RUSSIA	U
KURT	TUCHOLSKY	WRITER	A	S	SLEEPING PILLS	NV	12	21	1935		GERMANY	U
JOHN	TURNBULL	SOLDIER	NA	SM	GUNSHOT	V	9	27	1999	KILLED WIFE AND WIFES LOVER	IRELAND	U
RANDY	TURPIN	BOXER	NA	S	GUNSHOT	V	5	17	1966		ENGLAND	U
JIM	TYRER	FOOTBALL	NA	SM	GUNSHOT	V	9	15	1980	KILLED WIFE	MISSOURI	U
U;NEE		ACTOR	A	S	HANGING	V	1	21	2007	DEPRESSION	S KOREA	M
ERNST	UDET	PILOT	NA	S	GUNSHOT	V	11	27	1941		GERMANY	U
URMUZ		WRITER	A	S	?	?	11	23	1923			U
MITSURU	USHIJIMA	GENERAL	NA	S	SEPPUKU	V	6	22	1945		JAPAN	U
VAISHNAVI		ACTRESS	A	S	HANGING	V	4	17	2006		INDIA	U
WOOD-BRIDGE	VAN DYKE	ACTOR	A	S	?	?	2	5	1943		SO CAL	U
VINCENT	VAN GOGH	PAINTER	A	S	GUNSHOT	V	7	29	1890	MENTALLY ILL CUT OFF EAR 12/24		M
VICKI	VAN METER	PILOT	NA	S	GUNSHOT	V	3	15	2008	DEPRESSION	PA	M
IKE	VAN ZANDT	BASEBALL	NA	S	GUNSHOT	V	9	14	1908		NH	U
GEORGE	VANDERBILT	EXPLORER	NA	S	JUMP	V	6	24	1961	ETOH	SF CAL	M
JOHANNES	VARES	PHYSICIAN	NA	S	?	?	11	29	1946		FINLAND	U
MINNIE	VAUTRIN	MISSION-ARY	NA	S	GAS	NV	5	14	1941		INDIANA	U
LUPE	VELEZ	ACTOR	A	S	SLEEPING PILLS	NV	12	13	1944		SO CAL	U
HERVE	VILLECHAIZE	ACTOR	A	S	GUNSHOT	V	9	4	1993	FANTASY ISLAND ETOH DEPRESSION	SO CAL	M
CHRIS	VON ERICH	ACTOR WRESTLE	A	S	GUNSHOT	V	9	12	1991	2 BROS COMMITTED SUICIDE DRUGS DEPRESSED	TX	M
KERRY	VON ERICH	ACTOR WRESTLE	A	S	GUNSHOT	V	2	18	1993	2 BROS COMMITTED SUICIDE DRUGS	TX	M
MIKE	VON ERICH	ACTOR WRESTLE	A	S	PLACYDYL	NV	4	12	1987	ETOH DEPRESSION DRUG CHARGES	TX	M
DAVID	WALLACE	WRITER	A	S	HANGING	V	9	12	2008	DEPRESSION ECT NARDIL	SO CAL	M
PETRI	WALLI	MUSICIAN	A	S	JUMP	V	6	28	1995		FINLAND	U
LARRY	WALTERS	PILOT	NA	S	GUNSHOT	V	10	6	1993	LAWN CHAIR PILOT	SO CAL	U
WANG	GUOWEI	WRITER	A	S	DROWNING	NV	6	2	1927		CHINA	U
ANDRE	WATERS	FOOTBALL	NA	S	GUNSHOT	V	11	20	2006	MULTIPLE CONCUSSIONS	FLA	U
DOODLES	WEAVER	ACTOR	A	S	GUNSHOT	V	1	17	1983		SO CAL	U
GARY	WEBB	WRITER	A	S	GUNSHOT	V	12	10	2004	DEPRESSION	CAL	M
DEBBIE	WEEMS	ACTOR	A	S	JUMP	V	2	22	1978	MENTAL ILLNESS POLYSUB-STANCE ABUSE	NY	M
OTTO	WEININGER	WRITER	A	S	GUNSHOT	V	10	4	1903		AUSTRIA	U

JEFF	WEISE	STUDENT	NA	SM	GUNSHOT	V	3	21	2005	RED LAKE SHOOTING (9) DEPRESSION MOM ETOH	MINN	M
HORACE	WELLS	DENTIST	NA	S	SLIT OPEN LEG ART	V	1	24	1848	CHLORO- FORM ADDICT INVENTED ANAESTHESIA	CONN	M
VINCE	WELNICK	MUSICIAN	A	S	?	?	6	2	2006	DEPRESSION	CAL	M
FRED	WEST	ARTIST	A	S	HANGING	V	1	1	1995	INCEST/ BEASTIALITY AS KID KILLED/RAPED 9 W WIFE	ENGLAND	U
JAMES	WHALE	DIRECTOR	A	S	DROWNING	NV	5	29	1957	STROKES MOOD SWINGS DEPRESSION	SO CAL	M
SAMUEL	WHITBREAD	POLITICIAN	NA	S	STABBING	V	6	6	1815	DEPRESSION	ENGLAND	M
DAN	WHITE	POLITICIAN	NA	S	CO POISONING	NV	10	21	1985	DEPRESSION KILLED SF MAYOR AND MILK 11/27/78	SF CAL	M
MIKE	WHITMARSH	VOLLEY- BALL	NA	S	CO POISONING	NV	2	17	2009		SO CAL	U
KEVIN	WHITRICK	ENGINEER	NA	S	HANGING	V	3	21	2007	SUICIDE ONLINE WEBCASTED	ENGLAND	U
WARREN	WIEBE	MUSICIAN	A	S	?	?	10	25	1998	MENTAL HEALTH ISSUES		M
ROLAND	WEISSEL- BERG	ACTIVIST	NA	S	IMMOLATION	V	10	31	2006		GERMANY	U
PAUL	WILLIAMS	MUSICIAN	A	S	GUNSHOT	V	8	17	1973	DEPRESSION ETOH THE TEMPTATIONS	MICHIGAN	M
PERCY	WILLIAMS	ATHLETE	NA	S	?	?	11	29	1982			U
ROZZ	WILLIAMS	MUSICIAN	A	S	HANGING	V	4	1	1998	HEROIN	SO CAL	M
WENDY	O'WILLIAMS	MUSICIAN	A	S	GUNSHOT	V	4	6	1998	DESPONDENCE	CONN	M
DEANGELO	WILSON	ACTOR	A	S	HANGING	V	11	26	2008	DEPRESSED	SO CAL	M
GREG	WILTON	POLITICIAN	NA	S	?	?	6	14	2000	DEPRESSIVE CONDITION		M
JOHN	WINANT	POLTICIAN	NA	S	?	?	11	3	1947			U
JOHN	WINTER	JOURNALIST	A	S	GUNSHOT	V	4	5	2007	SEVERE DEPRESSION	FLA	M
SHEREE	WINTON	ACTOR	A	S	OD	NV	5	29	1976	CLINICAL DEPRESSION	ENGLAND	M
EDUARD	WIRTHS	PHYSICIAN	NA	S	HANGING	V	9	20	1945	DEPRESSED CONDUCTED RESEARCH ON PRISONERS		M
STANISLAW	WITKIEWICZ	WRITER	A	S	STABBING	V	9	18	1939	NARCOTICS PEYOTE	POLAND	M
FRANK	WOLFF	ACTOR	A	S	?	?	12	12	1971		ITALY	U
WOO	BUM-KON	POLICE OFFICER	NA	SM	GUNSHOT	V	4	27	1982	ETOH UIRYEONG MASSACRE (57)	S KOREA	M
WOO	SEUNG-YEON	ACTRESS	A	S	HANGING	V	4	27	2009	DEPRESSION	S KOREA	M
WALLY	WOOD	CARTOON- IST	A	S	GUNSHOT	V	11	2	1981	ETOHISM MIGRAINE HA	SO CAL	M
VIRGINIA	WOOLF	WRITER	A	S	DROWNING	NV	3	28	1941	BIPOLAR MOOD SWINGS	ENGLAND	M

SHAWN	WOOLLEY	PC GAME PLAYER	NA	S	GUNSHOT	V	11	20	2001	DEPRESSIVE OCD EVERQUEST PLAYING MEDS	WISC	M
KELLY	YEOMANS	STUDENT	NA	S	PAIN KILLERS	NV	9	28	1997	DEPRESSION BULLIED AT SCHOOL	ENGLAND	M
SERGIE	YESENIN	WRITER	A	S	STABBING	V	12	27	1925	MENTAL BREAKDOWN ETOH	RUSSIA	M
HAILU	YIMENU	PRIME MIN-ISTER	NA	S	?	?	5	26	1991		ETHIOPIA	U
FARON	YOUNG	MUSICIAN	A	S	GUNSHOT	V	12	10	1996	DESPONDENCE	TN	M
GIG	YOUNG	SM	A	SM	GUNSHOT	V	10	19	1978	ETOH KILLED WIFE	NY	M
BARBARA	YUNG	ACTRESS	A	S	CO POISONING	NV	5	14	1985	DEPRESSED	HNG KNG	M
BERND	ZIMMER-MANN	COMPOSER	A	S	?	?	8	10	1970	DEPRESSIVE		M
MAHMOUD	ZUABI	PRIME MIN-ISTER	NA	S	GUNSHOT	V	5	21	2000		SYRIA	U
STEFAN	ZWEIG	WRITER	A	S	BARBITURATE	NV	2	22	1942	CO-SUICIDE WITH WIFE	BRAZIL	U
SZMUL	ZYGIELBOJM	POLITICIAN	NA	S	CO POISONING	NV	5	12	1943		ENGLAND	U
MAY	AYIM	ACTIVIST	NA	S	JUMP	V	8	9	1996	PSYCH HOSP HALLUCINA-TIONS DEP		M
JOSE	BALMACEDA	POLITICIAN	NA	S	GUNSHOT	V	9	19	1891		CHILE	U
PAUL	FEDERN	PSYCHOLO-GIST	NA	S	?	?	5	4	1950			U
CHARLES	WHITMAN	STUDENT	NA	M	GUNSHOT	V	8	1	1966	U OF T AUSTIN (13) HOSTILE PSYCHOTIC METH VALIUM		M
DAVID	GRAY	MANUFAC-TERING	NA	M	GUNSHOT	V	11	13	1990	DECLINE IN MENTAL HEALTH ARAMOANA (13)	N ZEALAND	M
TIAN	MINGJIAN	SOLDIER	NA	M	GUNSHOT	V	9	20	1994	TIAN MINGJIAN INCIDENT (23)	CHINA	U
MARTIN	BRYANT	UNEM-PLOYED	NA	M	GUNSHOT	V	4	28	1996	PORT ARTHER (35) MENT DISABLED DAD SUICIDE	AUSTRALIA	M
TOMOHIRO	KATO	UNEM-PLOYED	NA	M	STABBING	V	6	8	2008	PAST SUICIDE ATTEMPT AKIHABRA (7) VILENT	JAPAN	M

Chart 10

Suicide Data Omissions

1) Albert Ayler (no suicide date)
2) Robert Billings (no suicide date)
3) Scotty Beckett (suicide questionable)
4) Brutus (no suicide date)
5) Gaius Longinus (no suicide date)
6) Cato The Younger (no suicide date)
7) Charles Clegg (no suicide date)
8) Cleopatra (no suicide date)
9) Leighton Crandle (suicide questionable)
10) Decebalus (no suicide date)
11) Delphine Delamare (no suicide date)
12) James Forrestal (suicide questionable)
13) Henri Gifford (no suicide date)
14) Paula Goodspeed (suicide questionable)
15) Hannibal (no suicide date)
16) Willis Huggins (no suicide date)
17) Takako Konishi (no suicide date)
18) Phillip Taylor Kramer (no suicide date)
19) Hans Loritz (no suicide date)
20) Maximian (no suicide date)
21) Minamoto no Yorimasa (no suicide date)
22) Al Mulock (no suicide date)
23) Scott Nearing (no single date of death....starvation)
24) Ni Min-jan (no suicide date)
25) Phasael (no suicide date)
26) Petronius (no suicide date)
27) Richard Piggott (no suicide date)
28) Jan Potoki (no suicide date)
29) Nicos Poulantzas (no suicide date)
30) Kiki Preston (no suicide date)
31) Qu Yuan (no suicide date)
32) Sue Rodriguez (assisted suicide)
33) Varnado Simpson (no suicide date)
34) Somesvara (no suicide date)
35) Li Tobler (unclear reference)
36) Silvanus Trevail (no suicide date)
37) Getulio Vargus (unclear reference)
38) Publius Varus (no suicide date)
39) Charles Whittlesey (no suicide date or details)
40) Marion Zioncheck (suicide questionable)

Chart 11

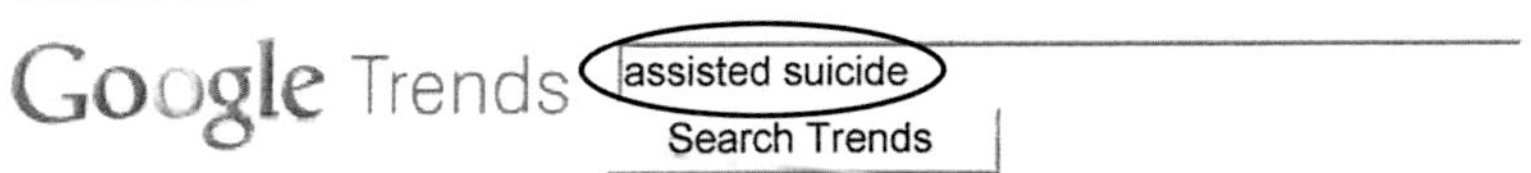

Tip: Use commas to compare multiple search terms.

Searches Websites | All regions

An improvement to our geographical assignment was applied retroactively from 1/1/2011. Learn more

● **assisted suicide**

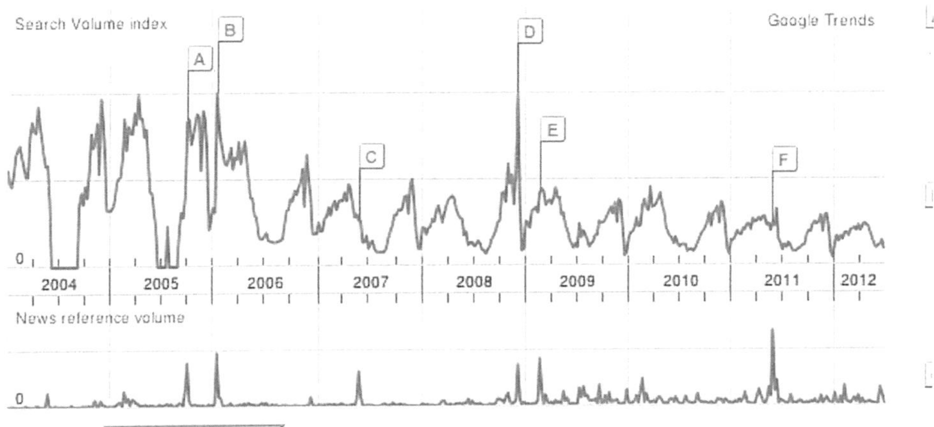

Rank by assisted suicide

Regions

1. United States
2. Canada

Cities

1. Portland, OR, USA

Seattle, WA,

Languages

1. English
2. French

Chart 12

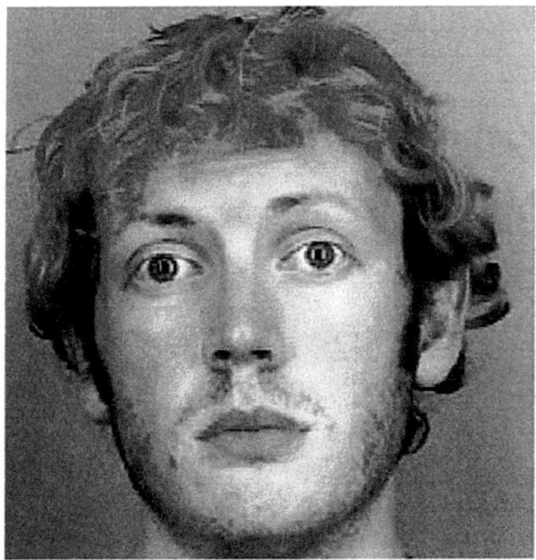

Mugshot of James Holmes by Arapahoe County Detention Center, Colorado, USA, after arrest as suspect in 2012 movie theater shooting,

Source (WP:NFCC#4)

Chart 13

Dow Jones Industrial Average (^DJI) **Aug 28: 9,544.20** ↓ 36.43 (0.38%)

More On ^DJI

Quotes
Summary
Components
Options
Historical Prices

Charts
Interactive
Basic Chart
Basic Tech. Analysis

News & Info
Headlines

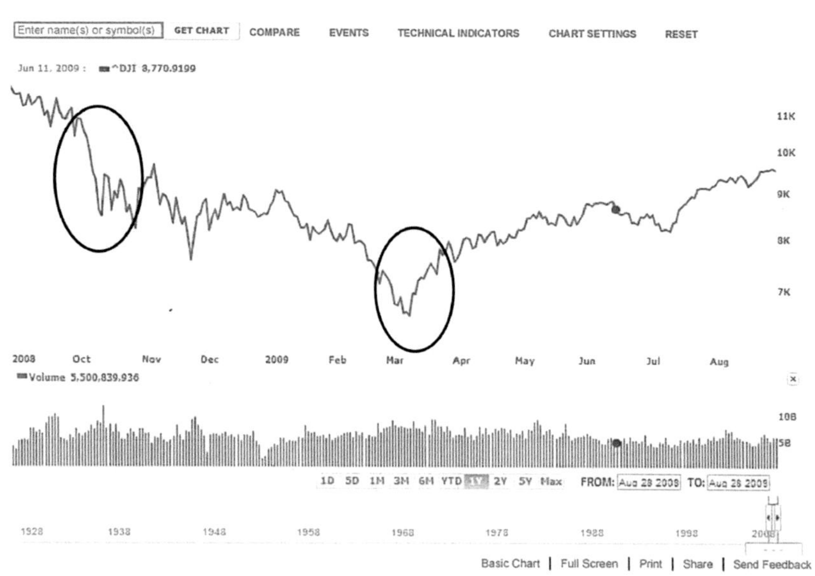

Dow Jones Industrial Average (DJI: ^DJI)

Index Value:	**9,544.20**
Trade Time:	**Aug 28**
Change:	↓ 36.43 (0.38%)
Prev Close:	**9,580.63**
Open:	**9,582.74**
Day's Range:	**9,495.98 - 9,630.20**
52wk Range:	**6,440.08 - 11,831.30**

Quotes delayed, except where indicated otherwise. For consolidated real-time quotes (incl. pre/post market data), sign up for a free trial of Real-time Quotes.

Chart 14

CBOE VOLATILITY INDEX (^VIX)

Aug 28: **24.76** ↑0.08 (0.32%)

More On ^VIX

Quotes
Summary
Components
Options
Historical Prices

Charts
Interactive
Basic Chart
Basic Tech. Analysis

News & Info
Headlines

Enter name(s) or symbol(s) | GET CHART | COMPARE | EVENTS | TECHNICAL INDICATORS | CHART SETTINGS | RESET

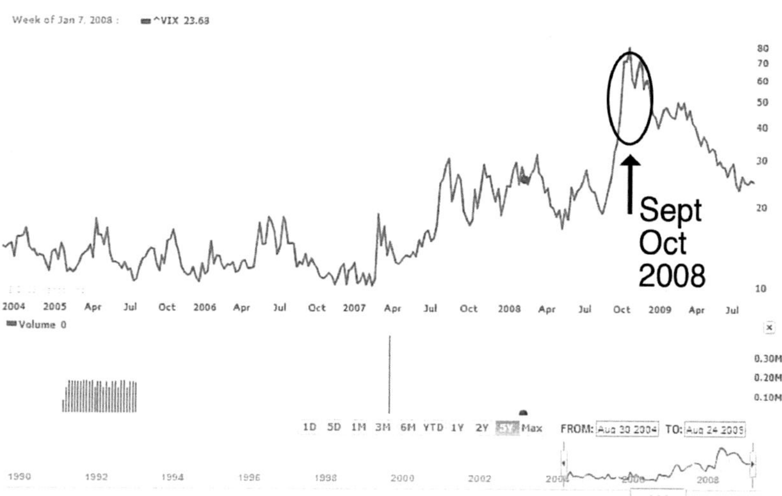

CBOE VOLATILITY INDEX (Chicago Options: ^VIX)

Index Value:	**24.76**
Trade Time:	**Aug 28**
Change:	↑0.08 (0.32%)
Prev Close:	**24.68**
Open:	**24.44**
Day's Range:	**24.28 - 25.50**
52wk Range:	**19.43 - 89.53**

Quotes delayed, except where indicated otherwise. For consolidated real-time quotes (incl. pre/post market data), sign up for a free trial of Real-time Quotes.

Chart 15a

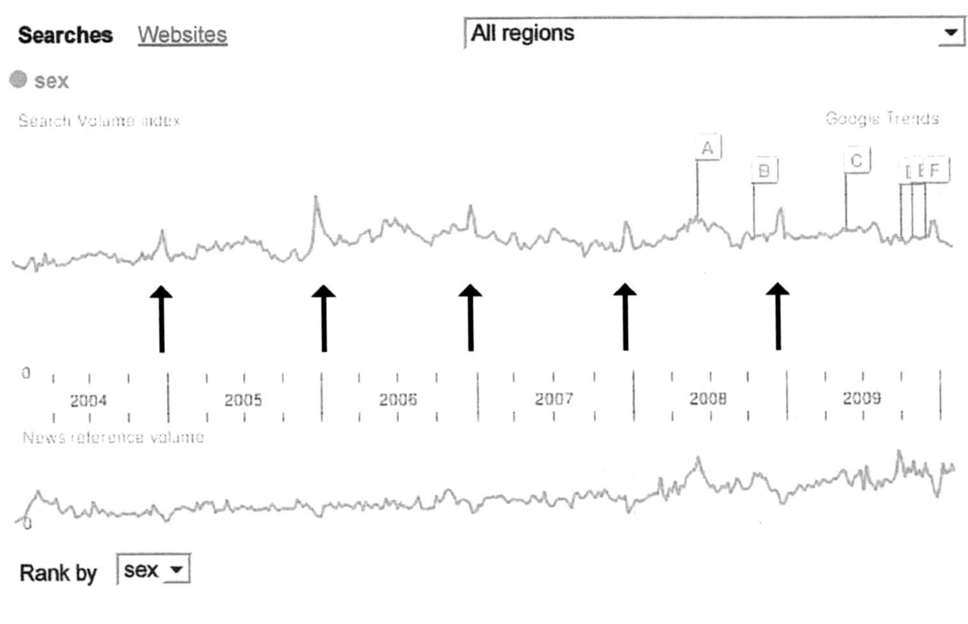

Chart 15b

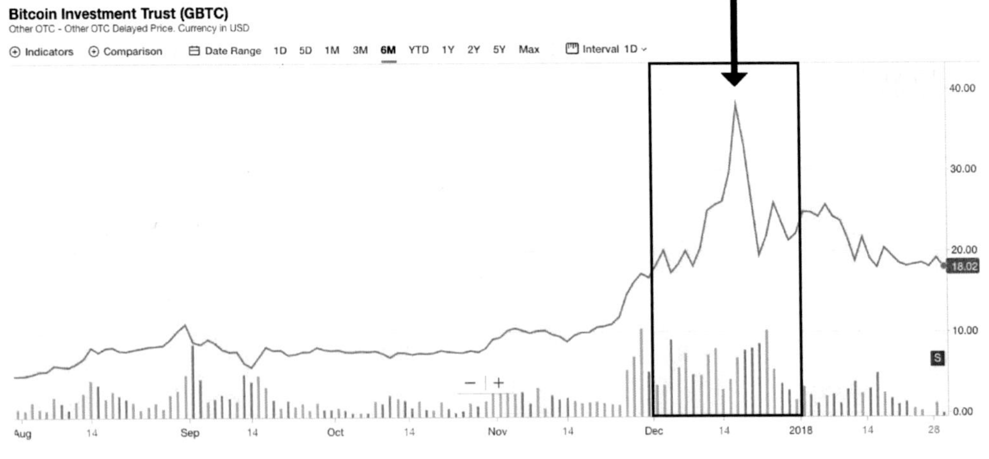

Chart 16

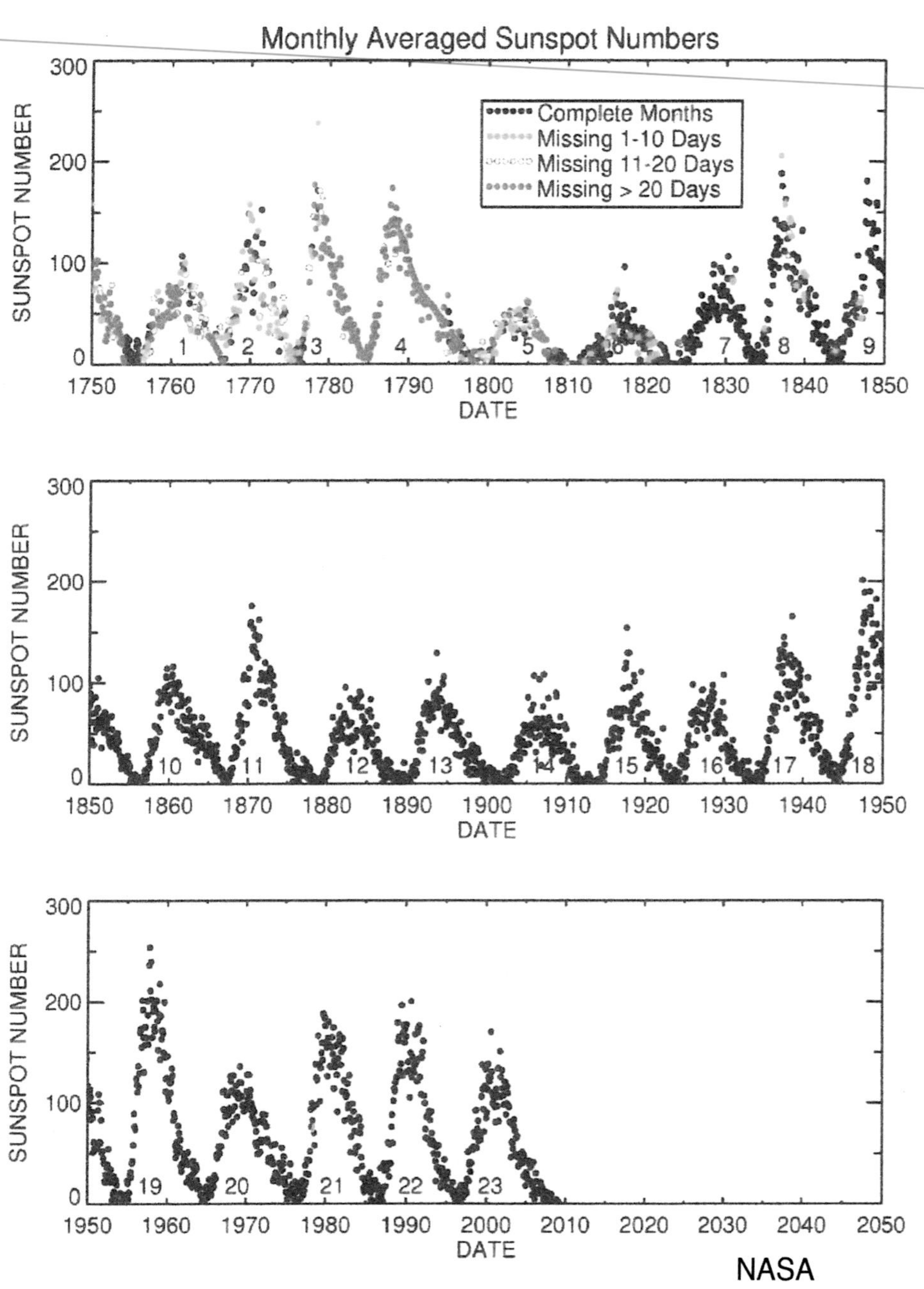

Monthly Averaged Sunspot Numbers
Complete Months
Missing 1-10 Days
Missing 11-20 Days
Missing > 20 Days
SUNSPOT NUMBER
DATE
NASA
NASA/MSFC/NSSTC/HATHAWAY 2009/04

Chart 17

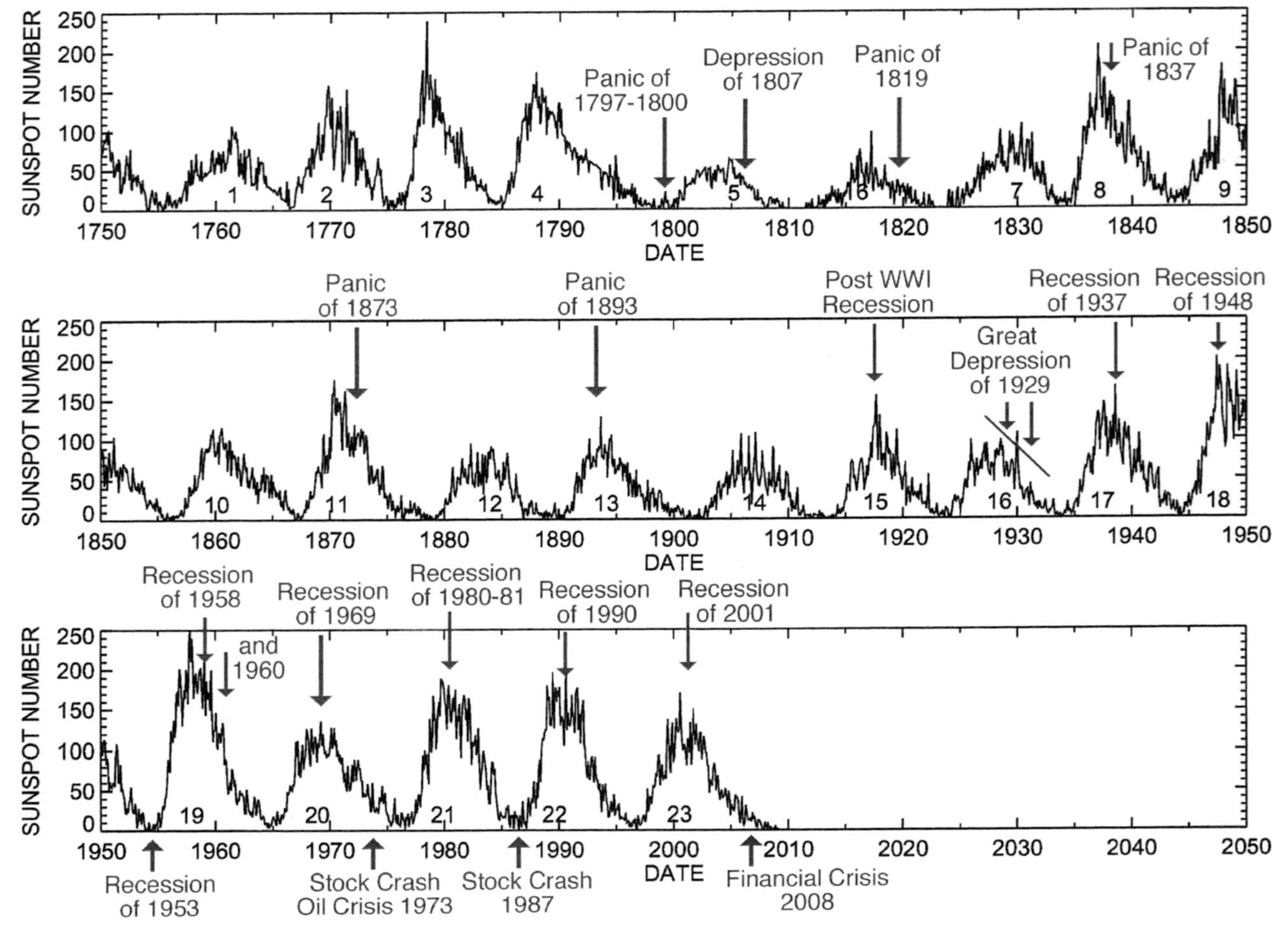

SUNSPOT NUMBER
DATE
Panic of 1797-1800
Depression of 1807
Panic of 1819
Panic of 1837
Panic of 1873
Panic of 1893
Post WWI Recession
Great Depression of 1929
Recession of 1937
Recession of 1948
Recession of 1958
and 1960
Recession of 1969
Recession of 1980-81
Recession of 1990
Recession of 2001
Recession of 1953
Stock Crash Oil Crisis 1973
Stock Crash 1987
Financial Crisis 2008

Chart 18

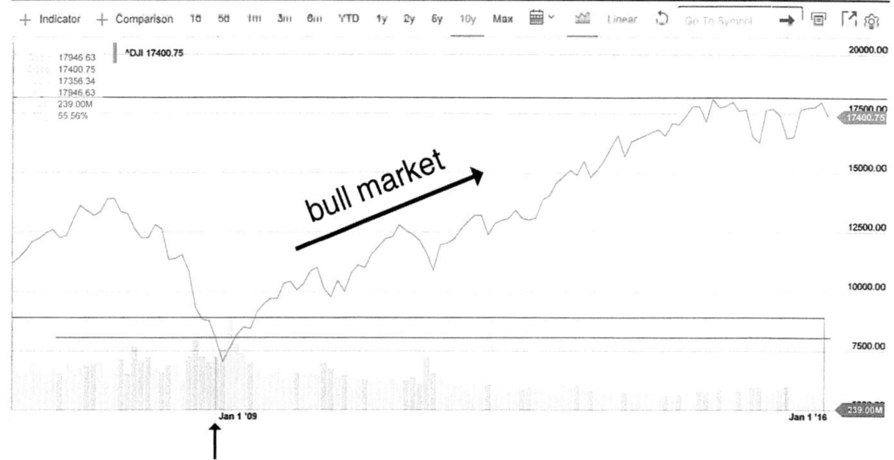

Current Solar Cycle 24
Started here December 2008

Chart 19

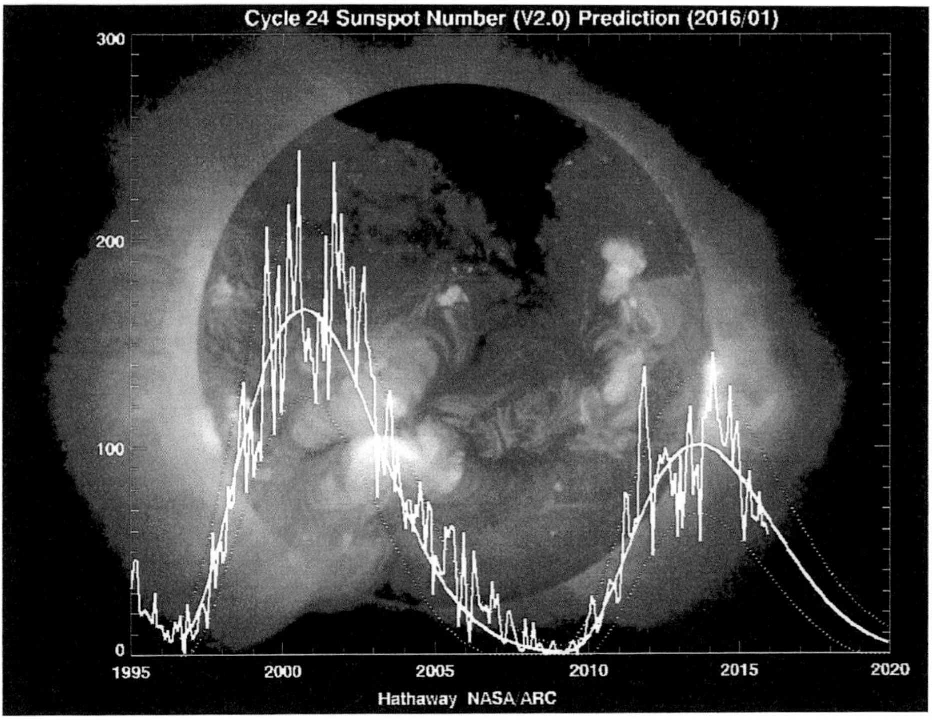

Cycle 24 Sunspot Number (V2.0) Prediction (2016/01)

300
200
100
0
1995 2000 2005 2010 2015 2020
Hathaway NASA/ARC

Solar Cycle 23

Current Solar Cycle 24

Chart 20

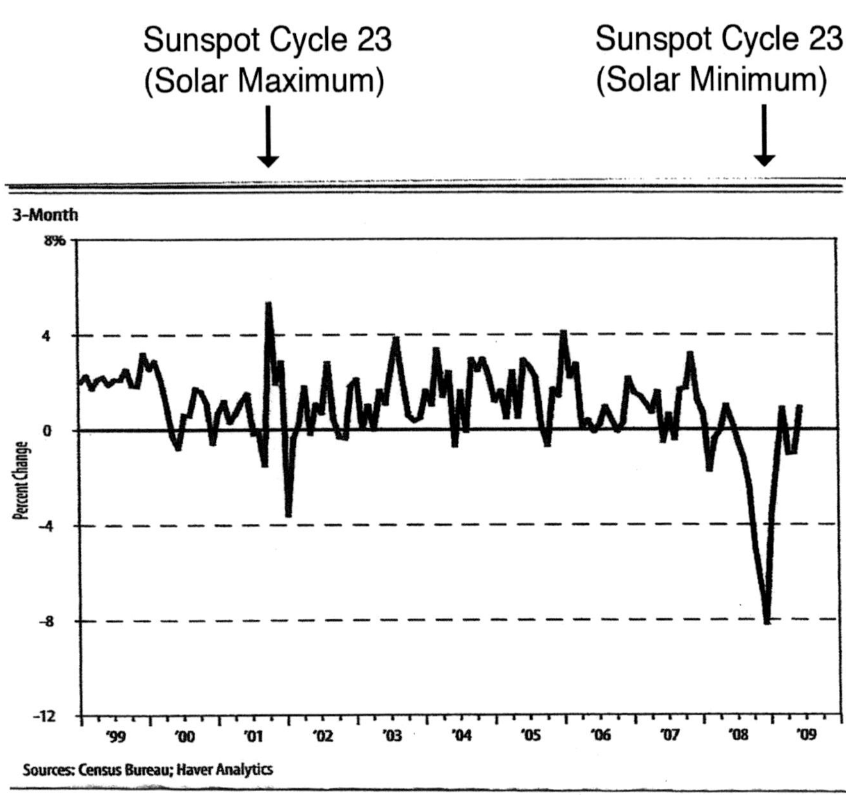

Retail Sales
Sunspot Cycle 23
(Solar Maximum)
Sunspot Cycle 23
(Solar Minimum)
3-Month
8%
4
0
-4
-8
-12
Percent Change
'99
'00
'01
'02
'03
'04
'05
'06
'07
'08
'09
Sources: Census Bureau; Haver Analytics

Chart 21

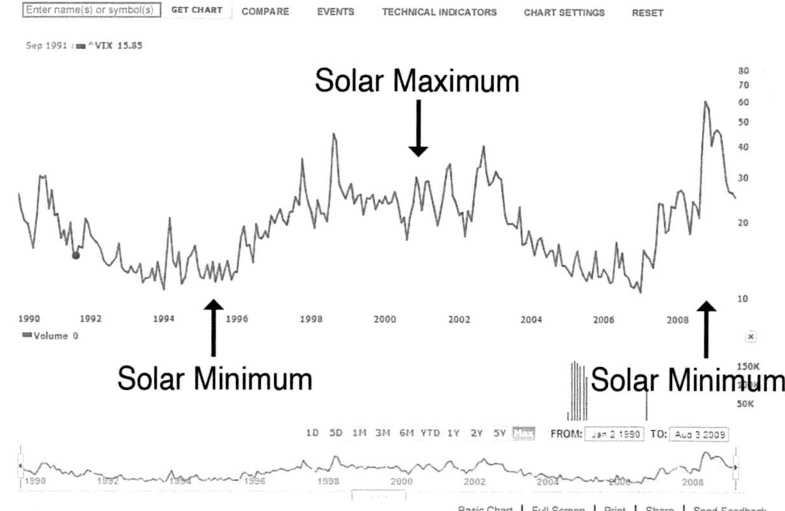

CBOE VOLATILITY INDEX (Chicago Options: ^VIX)

Index Value:	**24.76**
Trade Time:	**Aug 28**
Change:	↑ 0.08 (0.32%)
Prev Close:	**24.68**
Open:	**24.44**
Day's Range:	**24.28 - 25.50**
52wk Range:	**19.43 - 89.53**

Quotes delayed, except where indicated otherwise. For consolidated real-time quotes (incl. pre/post market data), sign up for a free trial of Real-time Quotes.

Chart 22

Dow Jones Industrial Average (^DJI)

May 6: **10,520.32** ↓ 347.80 (3.20%)

More On ^DJI

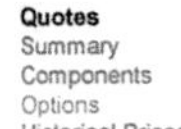

Charts
Interactive
Basic Chart
Basic Tech. Analysis

News & Info
Headlines

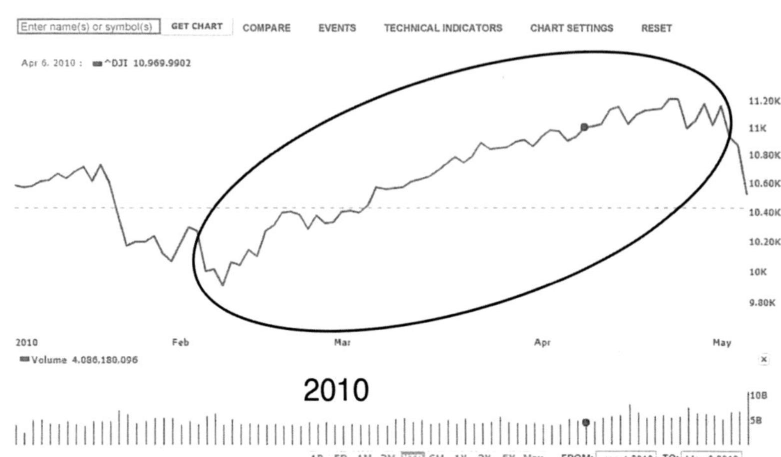

Dow Jones Industrial Average (DJI: ^DJI)

Index Value:	**10,520.32**
Trade Time:	**May 6**
Change:	↓ 347.80 (3.20%)
Prev Close:	**10,868.12**
Open:	**10,862.22**
Day's Range:	**9,869.62 - 10,879.76**
52wk Range:	**8,057.57 - 11,309.00**

Quotes delayed, except where indicated otherwise. Currency in USD.

Chart 23

Dow Jones Industrial Average (^DJI) - DJI

Add to Portfolio

12,777.09 ↑203.82(1.62%) Jul 13

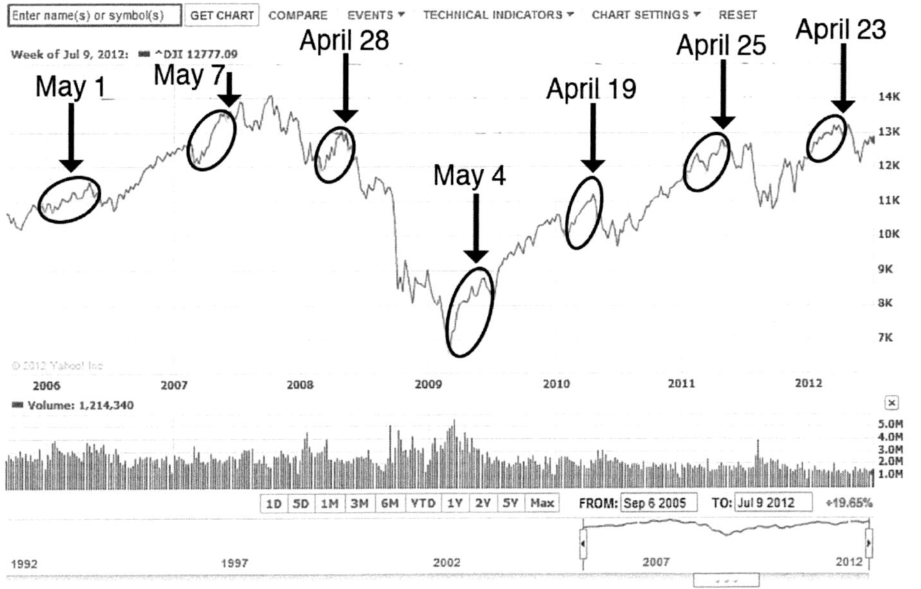

Basic Chart | Full Screen | Print | Share | **Send Feedback**

Dow Jones Industrial Average (^DJI) - DJI

Prev Close:	**12,573.27**	Day's Range:	**12,573.04 - 12,784.73**
Open:	**12,573.73**	52wk Range:	**10,404.50 - 13,338.70**

Quotes delayed, except where indicated otherwise. Currency in USD.

Chart 24

Data from the NOAA-Space Environment Center

Daily Sun Spot Number
Mon, 10 May 2010

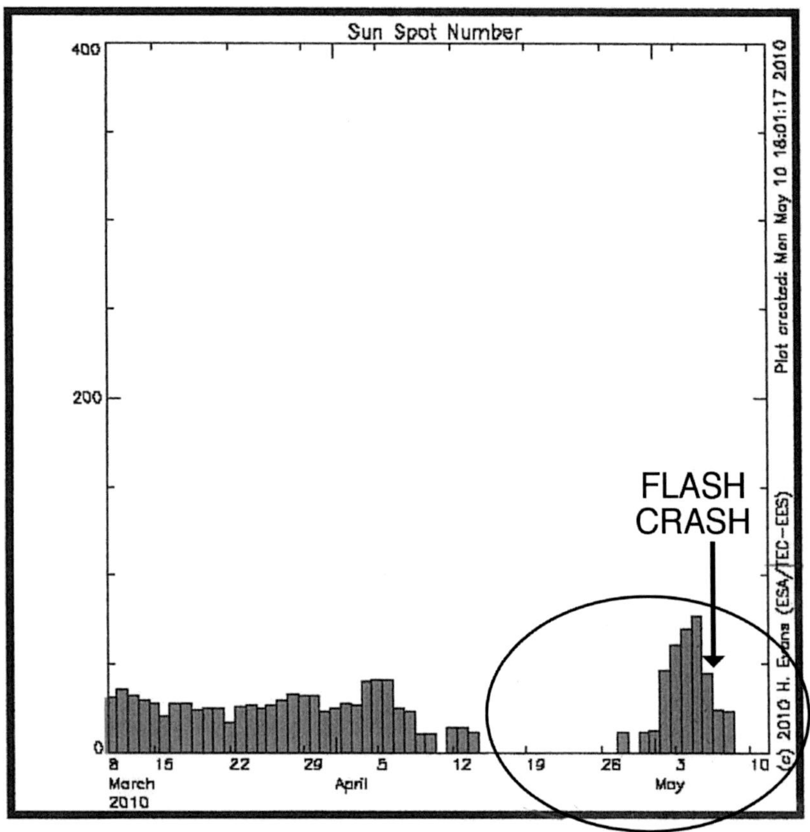

The official SESC sunspot number is computed according to the Wolf Sunspot Number formula R = k(10g + s), where g is the number of sunspot groups (regions), s is the total number of individual spots in all the groups and k is a scaling factor that corrects for seeing conditions.

A sunspot number of zero indicates there were no visible sunspots on that date; a blank indicates that no observations were possible that day.

The sunspot region information used to compute the daily sunspot number incorporates reports from as many as six observatories. These reports are used to form a composite picture of each individual region, taking into account such factors as the time of observation and the quality of seeing.

09-Aug-2002

Chart 25

VOLATILITY S&P 500 (^VIX) 4:14PM EDT: **28.84** ↓ 12.11 (29.57%)

More On ^VIX

Quotes
Summary
Components
Options
Historical Prices

Charts
Interactive
Basic Chart
Basic Tech. Analysis

News & Info
Headlines

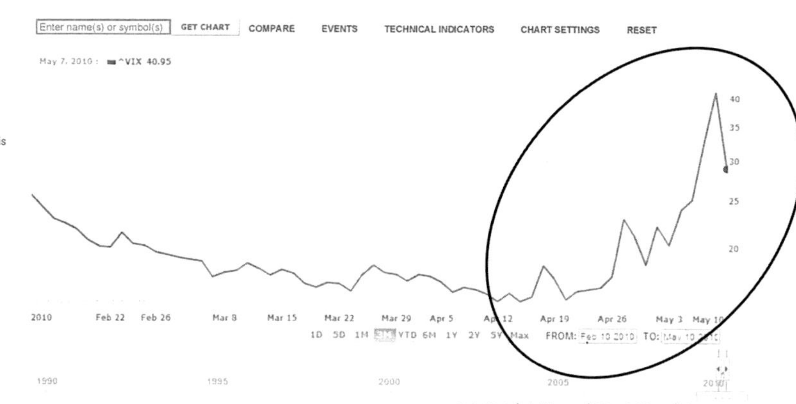

VOLATILITY S&P 500 (Chicago Options: ^VIX)

Index Value:	**28.84**
Trade Time:	**4:14PM EDT**
Change:	↓ 12.11 (29.57%)
Prev Close:	**40.95**
Open:	**28.65**
Day's Range:	**25.68 - 30.89**
52wk Range:	**15.23 - 42.15**

Quotes delayed, except where indicated otherwise. Currency in .

Chart 26

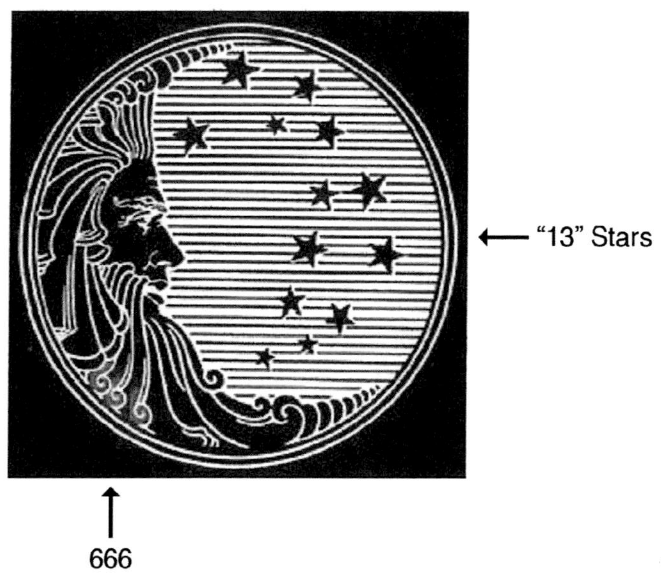

Chart 27

:Product: Daily Solar Data DSD.txt
:Issued: 0225 UT 04 Aug 2014
#
Prepared by the U.S. Dept. of Commerce, NOAA, Space Weather Prediction Center
Please send comments and suggestions to SWPC.Webmaster@noaa.gov
#
Last 30 Days Daily Solar Data
#

Date	Radio Flux 10.7cm	SESC Sunspot Number	Sunspot Area 10E-6 Hemis.	New Regions	Stanford Solar Mean Field	GOES15 X-Ray Bkgd Flux	Flares X-Ray C	M	X	S	Optical 1	2	3
2014 07 05	193	213	2090	1	-999	B9.6	3	0	0	11	0	0	0
2014 07 06	201	256	2230	1	-999	C1.2	5	0	0	14	0	0	0
2014 07 07	198	197	1980	0	-999	B9.8	5	0	0	17	0	0	0
2014 07 08	201	209	2280	2	-999	C1.0	4	1	0	15	1	1	0
2014 07 09	198	183	2230	0	-999	C1.0	5	1	0	29	2	0	0
2014 07 10	177	159	1790	1	-999	B9.2	3	1	0	12	1	0	0
2014 07 11	166	166	1490	1	-999	B9.5	3	0	0	16	0	0	0
2014 07 12	145	145	1420	0	-999	B8.0	4	0	0	22	0	0	0
2014 07 13	127	102	660	0	-999	B5.9	5	0	0	3	1	0	0
2014 07 14	109	70	370	0	-999	B4.0	1	0	0	1	0	0	0
2014 07 15	101	25	20	0	-999	B2.7	1	0	0	0	0	0	0
2014 07 16	92	11	10	0	-999	B1.7	0	0	0	0	0	0	0
2014 07 17	89	0	0	0	-999	B1.3	0	0	0	0	0	0	0
2014 07 18	89	26	30	2	-999	B1.2	0	0	0	0	0	0	0
2014 07 19	86	27	30	0	-999	B1.1	0	0	0	0	0	0	0
2014 07 20	87	17	40	1	-999	B1.5	0	0	0	0	0	0	0
2014 07 21	90	16	70	0	-999	B2.1	0	0	0	0	0	0	0
2014 07 22	93	40	180	2	-999	B1.8	0	0	0	0	0	0	0
2014 07 23	99	55	180	1	-999	B2.0	0	0	0	7	0	0	0
2014 07 24	104	55	280	0	-999	B2.5	1	0	0	3	1	0	0
2014 07 25	107	65	220	0	-999	B2.8	1	0	0	2	1	0	0
2014 07 26	117	76	240	3	-999	B4.2	4	0	0	6	0	0	0
2014 07 27	121	110	380	2	-999	B4.3	2	0	0	6	0	0	0
2014 07 28	132	143	540	1	-999	B5.0	2	0	0	5	1	0	0
2014 07 29	142	160	890	2	-999	B5.1	8	0	0	7	0	0	0
2014 07 30	152	145	900	0	-999	B7.1	5	0	0	2	1	0	0
2014 07 31	156	139	860	1	-999	B6.7	6	1	0	5	0	0	0
2014 08 01	168	165	890	0	-999	B8.2	2	2	0	15	2	0	0
2014 08 02	156	178	850	2	-999	B7.8	4	0	0	14	0	0	0
2014 08 03	152	152	680	0	-999	B6.3	7	0	0	13	1	0	0

Chart 28

Data from the NOAA-Space Environment Center

Daily Ap Geomagnetic Index
Thu, 04 Feb 2010

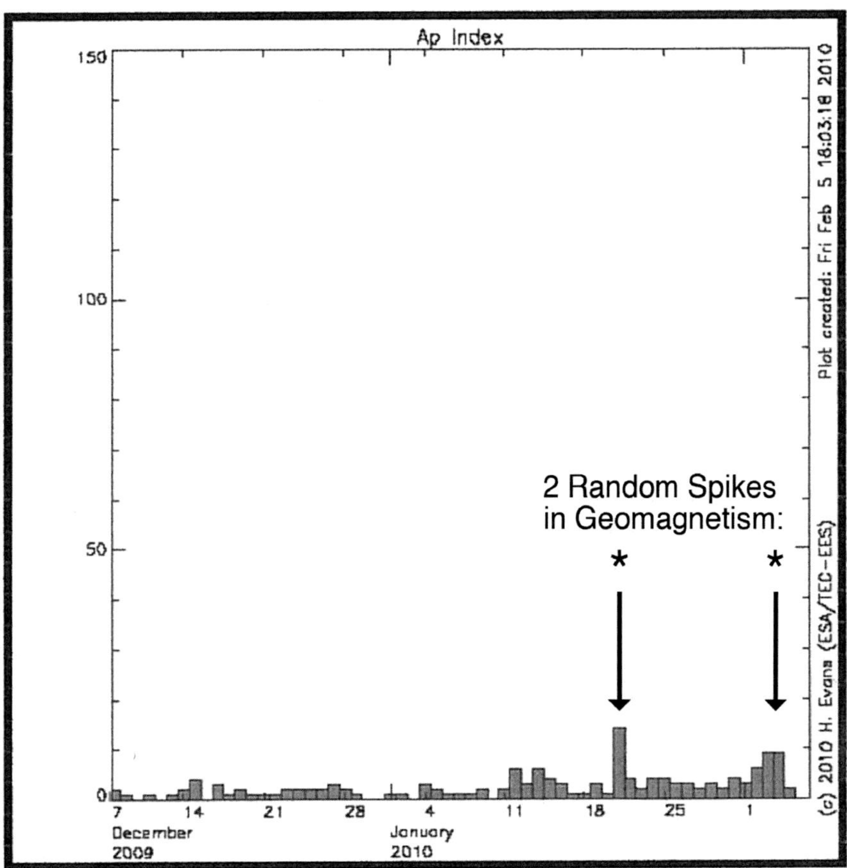

The daily average Ap index from the Fredericksburg (mid-latitude) and Anchorage (high-latitude) stations, which monitor the Earth's magnetic field.

The Ap index ranges from 0 (very quiet) to 400 (extremely disturbed). An Ap index of 30 or greater indicates local geomagnetic storm conditions.

The a index, from which the Ap index is derived, is an "equivalent amplitude" index of local geomagnetic activity; "a" is related to the 3-hourly K index.

08-Aug-2002

Chart 29

VOLATILITY S&P 500 (^VIX) 1:06PM ET: **26.81** ↑ 0.73 (2.80%)

More On ^VIX

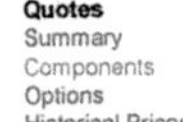

Charts
Interactive
Basic Chart
Basic Tech. Analysis

News & Info
Headlines

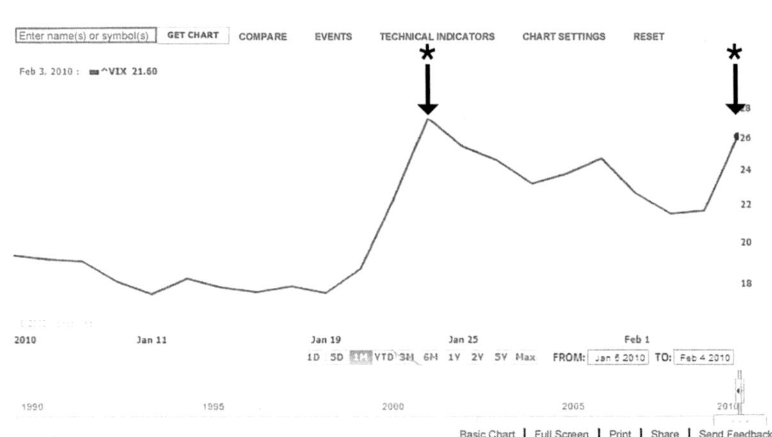

Basic Chart | Full Screen | Print | Share | Send Feedback

VOLATILITY S&P 500 (Chicago Options: ^VIX)

Index Value:	**26.81**
Trade Time:	**1:06PM ET**
Change:	↑ 0.73 (2.80%)
Prev Close:	**26.08**
Open:	**25.69**
Day's Range:	**25.37 - 26.81**
52wk Range:	**16.86 - 53.25**

Quotes delayed, except where indicated otherwise. For consolidated real-time quotes (incl. pre/post market data), sign up for a free trial of Real-time Quotes.

Chart 30

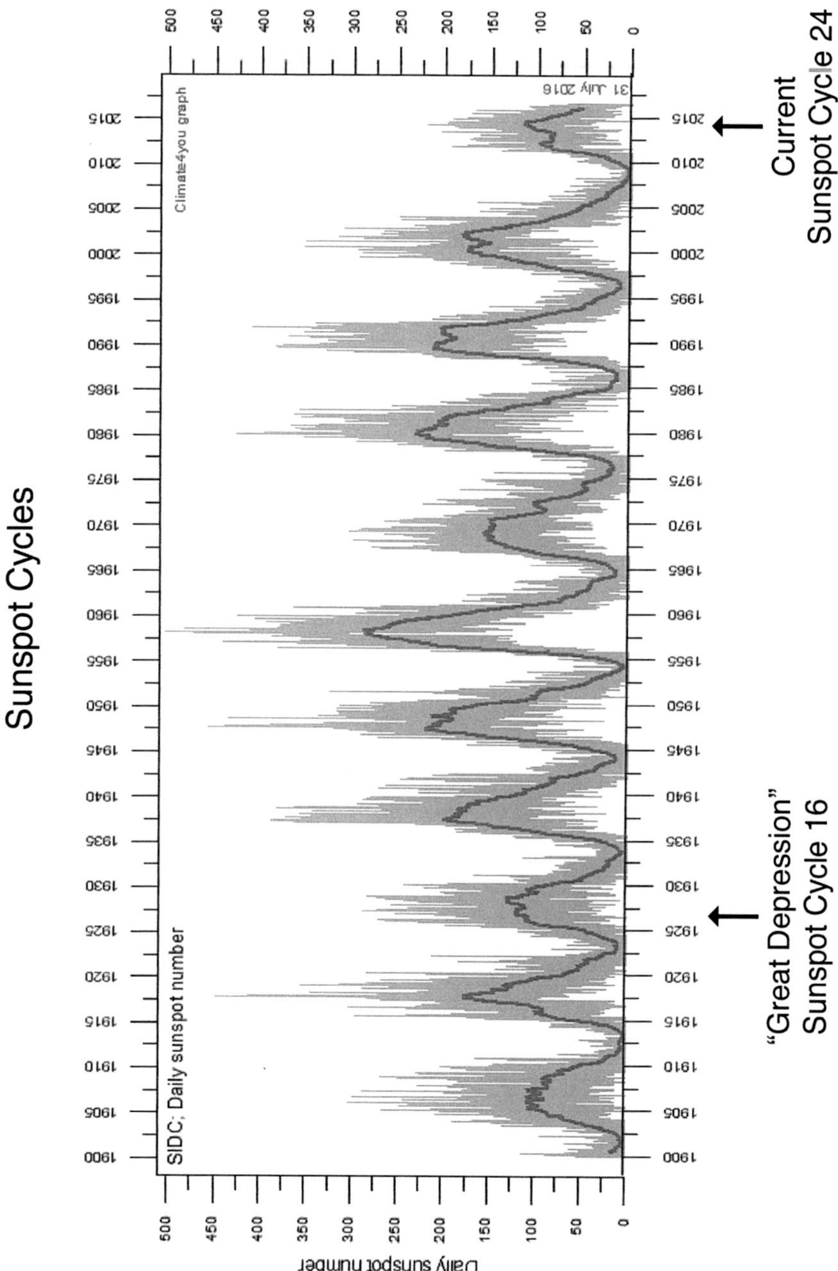

www.climate4you.com Ole Humlum

Chart 31

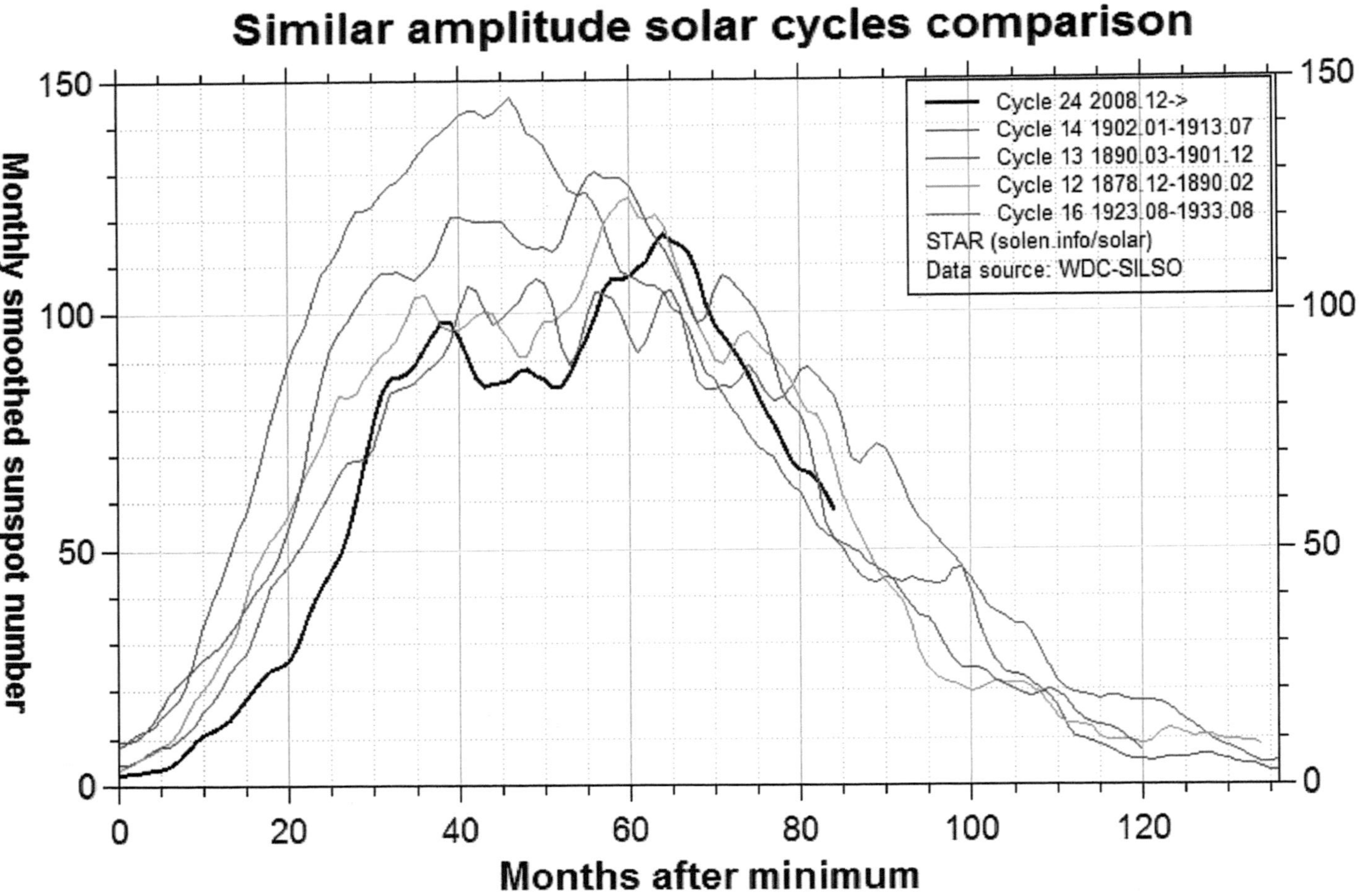
Similar amplitude solar cycles comparison
Cycle 24 2008.12->
Cycle 14 1902.01-1913.07
Cycle 13 1890.03-1901.12
Cycle 12 1878.12-1890.02
Cycle 16 1923.08-1933.08
STAR (solen.info/solar)
Data source: WDC-SILSO
150
100
50
0
0
20
40
60
80
100
120
Months after minimum
Monthly smoothed sunspot number

Chart 32a

Google Trends - Web Search interest: happy - Worldwide, 2004 - present
"Happiness" leveling off and decreasing
Search term: "Happy"
you are here
2005
2007
2009
2011
2013
2015
Solar Cycle 24 begins
Solar Cycle 24 peaks

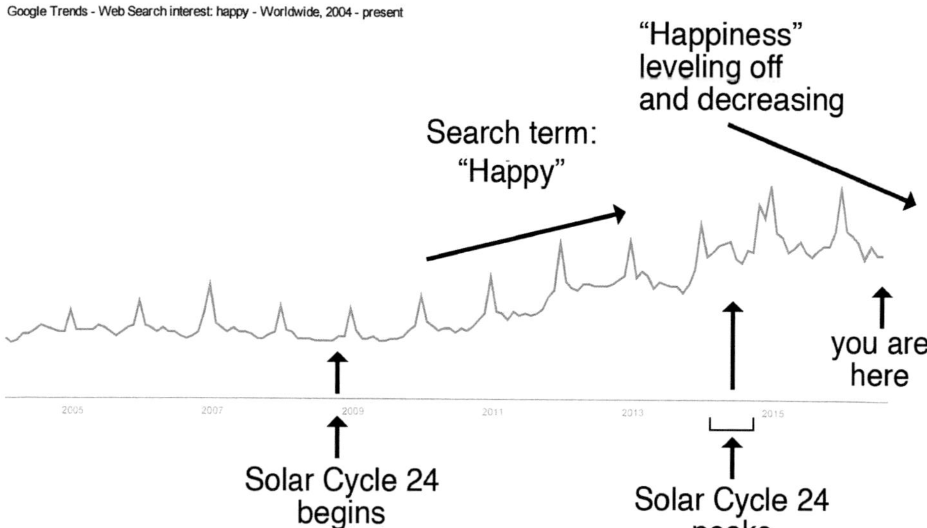

Chart 32b

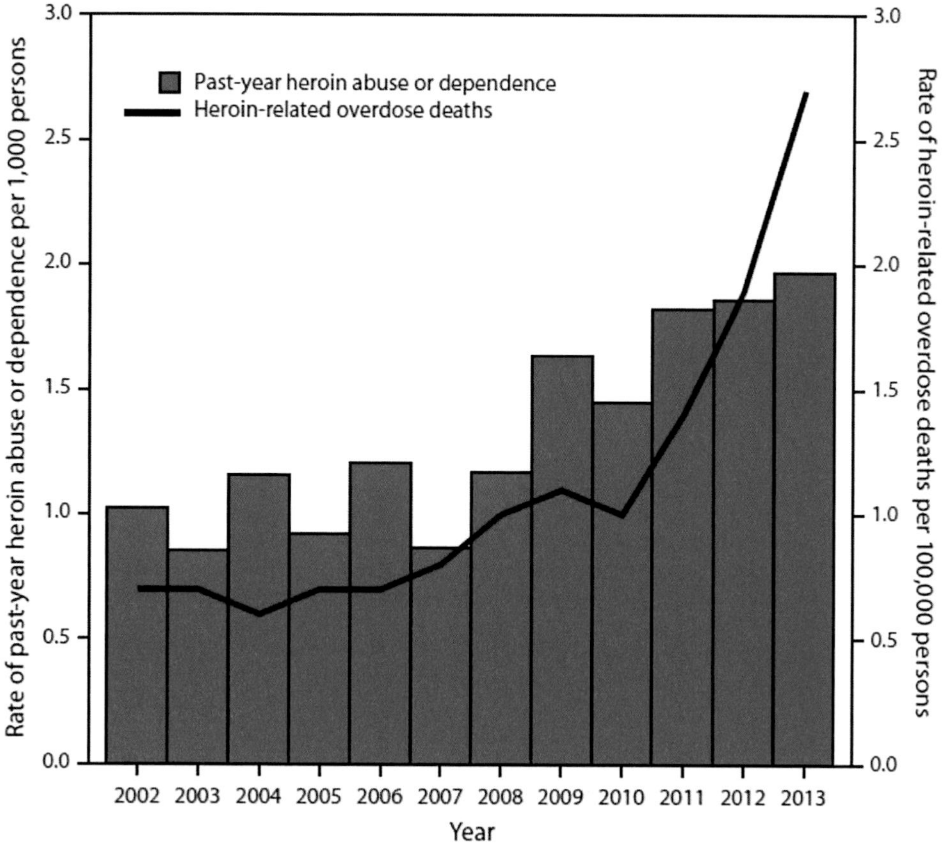

Past-year heroin abuse or dependence
Heroin-related overdose deaths
Rate of past-year heroin abuse or dependence per 1,000 persons
Rate of heroin-related overdose deaths per 100,000 persons
0.0
0.5
1.0
1.5
2.0
2.5
3.0
2002
2003
2004
2005
2006
2007
2008
2009
2010
2011
2012
2013
Year

Chart 33

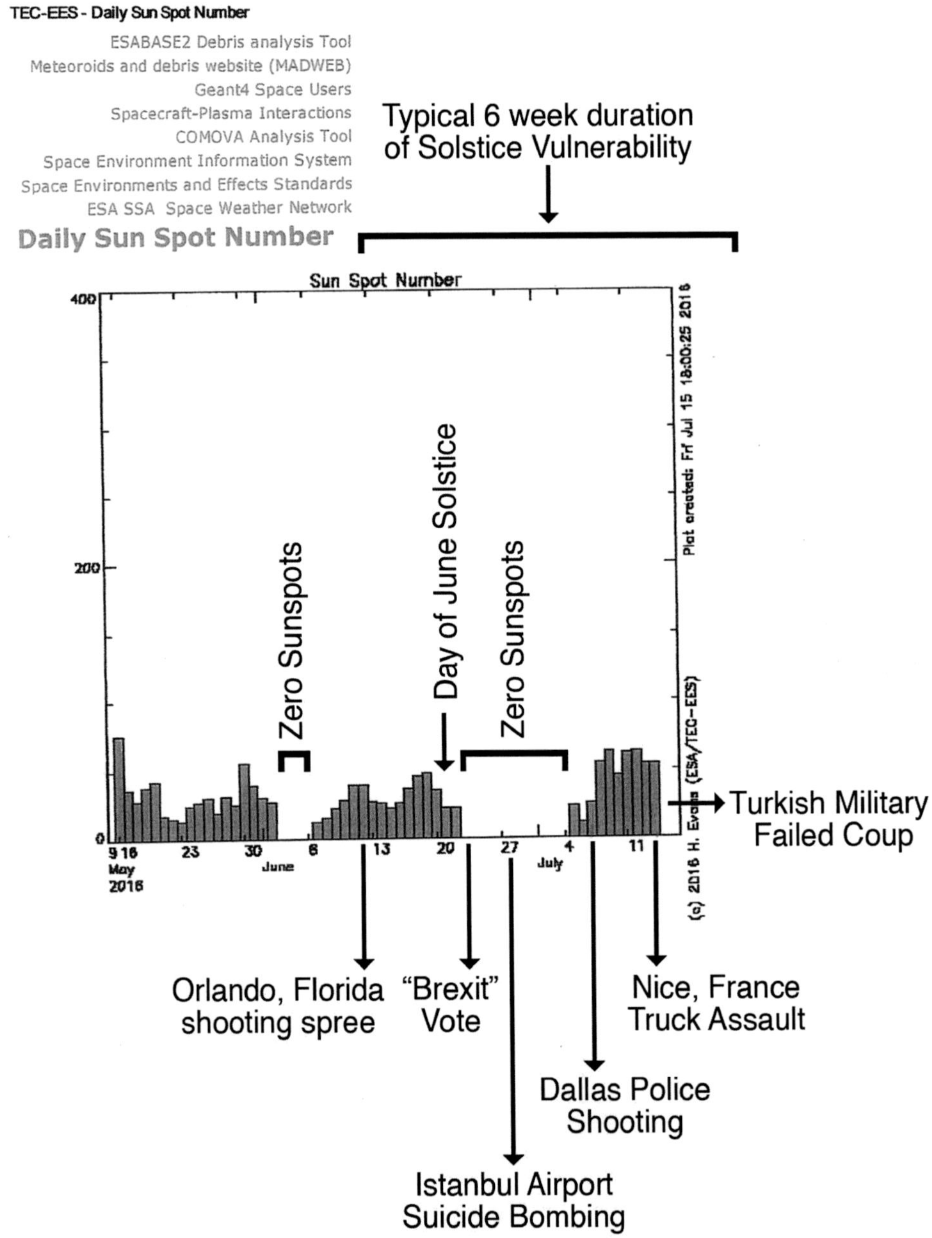

TEC-EES - Daily Sun Spot Number
ESABASE2 Debris analysis Tool
Meteoroids and debris website (MADWEB)
Geant4 Space Users
Spacecraft-Plasma Interactions
COMOVA Analysis Tool
Space Environment Information System
Space Environments and Effects Standards
ESA SSA Space Weather Network
Daily Sun Spot Number
Typical 6 week duration of Solstice Vulnerability
Sun Spot Number
400
200
0
9 16
May
2016
23
30
June
6
13
20
27
July
4
11
Plot created: Fri Jul 15 18:00:25 2016
(c) 2016 H. Evans (ESA/TEC-EES)
Zero Sunspots
Day of June Solstice
Zero Sunspots
Turkish Military Failed Coup
Orlando, Florida shooting spree
"Brexit" Vote
Istanbul Airport Suicide Bombing
Dallas Police Shooting
Nice, France Truck Assault

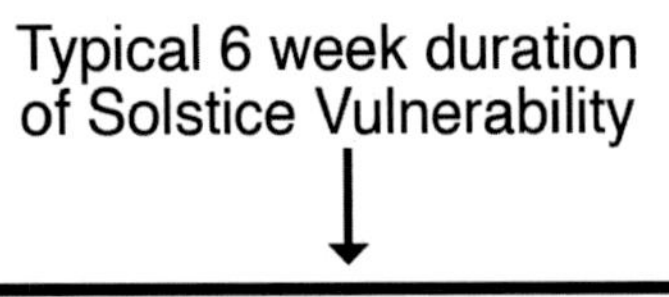

Chart 34

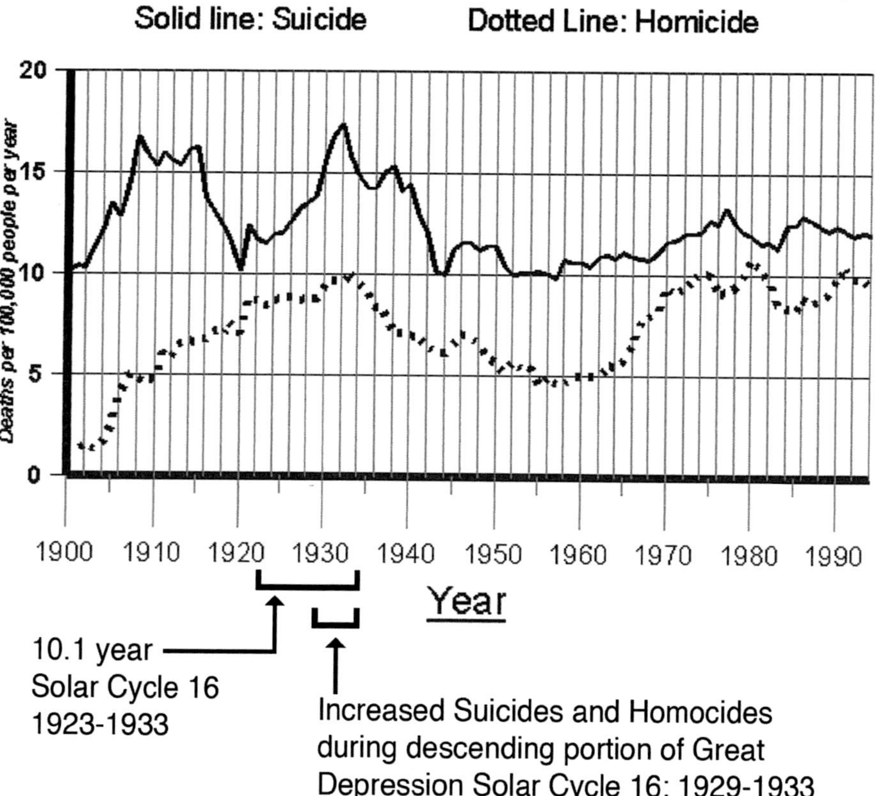

U.S. Suicide and Homicide Rates, 1900-1994
Solid line: Suicide
Dotted Line: Homicide
Deaths per 100,000 people per year
20
15
10
5
0
1900
1910
1920
1930
1940
1950
1960
1970
1980
1990
Year
10.1 year
Solar Cycle 16
1923-1933
Increased Suicides and Homocides during descending portion of Great Depression Solar Cycle 16: 1929-1933

Chart 35

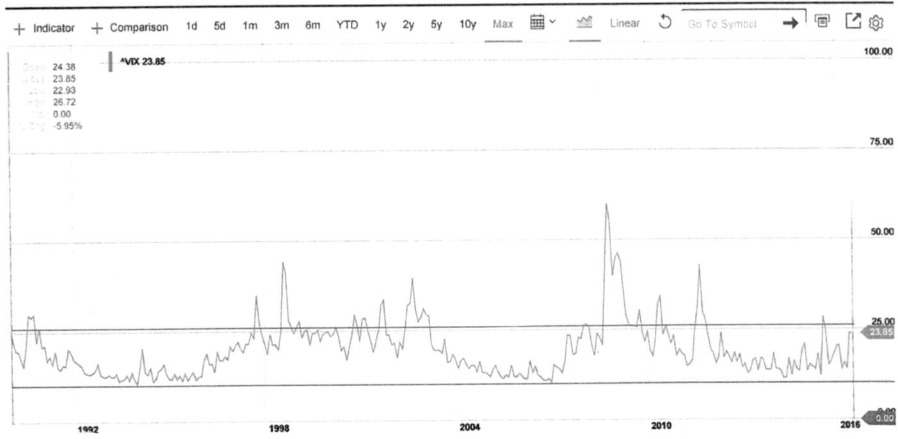

Sunspot Cycle 23
"Normal" VIX Sinusoidal Curve

Sunspot Cycle 24 Partial
"Abnormal"/Non-Sinusoidal
Curve

Chapter 6

THOU SHALL NOT CAST STONES AT THAT HORMONE

"Bad behavior" (aka evil behavior) as I have mentioned can pretty much be parceled into 4 broad categories: mental illness, substance abuse, flawed logic and hormones. The purpose of this brief chapter is to demonstrate how hormones play a fundamental part of human physiology but also can promote bad behavior. A hormone is a chemical that is produced in one cell, but exerts its influence on another type of cell. Hormones can be amine, peptide or lipid/cholesterol based (Chart 1). Endocrine hormones are released into the bloodstream (such as testosterone or cortisol) whereas exocrine hormones exert their action through a duct (pancreatic juices). In this chapter we will be dealing with hormones that are endocrine in nature and cholesterol (steroid) based (Chart 2).

Testosterone is "the male hormone" and is in the family of "androgens". It is produced primarily in the testes via LH (Chart 3). In the fetus, testosterone is responsible for development of the male sex organs. Testosterone also initiates puberty which confers growth, muscle development, facial hair, deepening of the voice and an increase in libido. As an adult, testosterone contributes to libido and physical energy (Chart 4). Interestingly, men are more likely than women to commit suicide presumably secondary to this testosterone effect (Chart 5).

So…how could testosterone possibly get any male into trouble? Hm-mmm…. sounds rhetorical doesn't it? The Bible says that even "looking" at a woman with "lust" is a sin. It's comparable to breaking the 7th commandment of committing adultery. Billy Graham went on and describes thinking of sex that is outside of a marriage as "evil daydreaming". So therefore what we have is a God given drive that gets us in trouble with God. Our body's testosterone increases our libido which increases our thinking of sex which in turn is considered a sin. Where does the Devil fit in to this? I don't get it? Does The Devil tamper with our gonads too? A better and simpler explanation however is that God gave us a libido, and made sure it was enjoyable as it would be solely responsible for the perpetuation of our species. When He developed the system, He really didn't seem to care if we were married (or responsible) as this sex drive starts at about 13 years of age. If you have a libido and are a God-fearing person and still wish to act on your urge for sex.... you'll need to get married first. Unfortunately, in order to Biblically justify yourself, marriage would have to occur in your early teens. The only problem is, being "right with God" and marrying at 13, will probably run you into a host of other problems including finding employment as a minor, being arrested for sex with a minor, and probably picking an incompatible spouse. You can't win. This whole idea of "Satan" tempting us with sex is so silly.... if anyone is to blame its God for giving us testosterone to begin with and NOT TO MENTION its induction at such a young age. The pornography Industry that ensued was simply a way to deal with our testosterone based God given libido, but even that has been demonized. The only other option is to simply live a life of repression which is what pedophiliac clergy traditionally have tried to do.... but that never works either.

As far as legitimately BAD sexual behavior is concerned, I would definitively include sex with a minor (pedophilia) and a non-consented party (rape) to that list. Clearly, testosterone plays a part in these crimes as there is an over representation of males as pedophiles (Footnote 1) and rapists (Footnote 2). This male hormone clearly can cause a great deal of reprehensible acts.

In addition to testosterone and its influence on sex drive, the hyper-sexuality of manic depression also plays a part in inappropriate sexual behavior and this has already been discussed. They both probably function through adrenaline release but this is beyond the scope of the conversation. What I will add though is that bipolar families from my observation have a higher rate of incest (another mostly illegal sexual act) compared to non-bipolar. The reasoning being is that not only is the perpetrating adult bipolar hyper-sexualized.... but so is the unwittingly participating genetically bipolar child. An example of this MIGHT be Mackenzie Phillips' alleged incestuous relationship with her father John Phillips. Both were artists with opiate abuse histories. This explanation gives the strange scenario a skosh more understandability. This unusual relationship however should not be confused with the recent rash of older women (in positions of authority) seducing and having sex with under aged school aged boys. This phenomenon is more likely generated by a hyper sexual bipolar woman and a testosterone saturated male teen. Either way, by testosterone or bipolarity, we are wired for sex.

Testosterone contributes to male energy, but some experts believe it does not actually cause aggression. Counter intuitively, studies show that LOW levels of testosterone actually cause the "aggression", but men who take anabolic steroids clearly are more aggressive than non-steroid users so I don't quite know what to make of these conflicting observations. Having said that, as a former medical advisor to The Palm Springs SWAT team, whenever I was on patrol and an arrest was made, most of the time it was a male (Chart 6). I think we can all agree that testosterone plays a substantial part in daily societal bad behavior and this is substantiated in laboratory tests with mice as well (Chart 7). Apocalyptic riots are usually caused, frequented and perpetuated by young men (just watch news footage of a riot and you will see). This again supports the idea that testosterone plays a part in the wicked nature of man. My dog quieted down quite nicely after he was neutered although I'm not suggesting this as a treatment (actually I am..... in the right cases).

Women have their own crosses to bear too. Estrogen is "the female hormone" and it's produced by the ovaries. Estrogens initiate puberty for a woman and are responsible for sex organ, breast and pubic hair development (Chart 8). The primary hormonal "bad behavior" seen in women is from fluctuating levels of estrogen and progesterone seen in various physiologic states. A women's menstrual cycle (Chart 9) is characterized by numerous changes in hormones but none as great as in the event the female egg isn't fertilized during the last two weeks of this cycle. At this time, levels of progesterone plummet and this in conjunction with already low levels of estrogen can set up "The premenstrual syndrome". A hormone depleted state which is typified by bloating, breast tenderness and me getting yelled at. In all seriousness, women can become quite emotionally irritable and depressed and may demonstrate "bad behavior" such as intolerance or over-reactivity. Of interest is that the removal of a uterus is called a hysterectomy and it was thought to properly deal with a female's "hysteria". We also see changes in hormone levels and hence potentially bad behavior during the female perimenopausal years (45-55yrs) (Chart 10). If bad behavior does occur it's simply a reflection of feeling poorly from the decline in hormones and may require hormone replacement therapy. I once overheard a patient call his mother an "evil b*tch" but she really wasn't evil.... just hormone depleted.

The same fluctuations in hormones occur after giving birth as well (Chart 11). Estrogen levels that were 50x normal fall to normal after 3 days, progesterone that was 10x normal falls to normal within a week, cortisol levels that were 2-3x normal fall to normal after several weeks and prolactin that was 7x normal falls to normal after 3 months. These changes can result in depressive symptoms known as "The baby blues" in 80% of new mothers. Symptoms include about 2 weeks' worth of sadness, crying spells and difficulty sleeping. It's usually quite brief and uneventful. Other patients however, go onto have more serious signs of depression including irritability, depression, withdrawal or apathy towards self or baby. This is usually in about 15% of new mothers and in my opinion is associated with a pre-existing Psychiatric diagnosis of a mood disorder. Postpartum psychosis is rare but is a profoundly abnormal state manifested by thought disturbance, delusions and hallucinations. These patients are usually bipolar and can't handle the drastic hormonal changes seen in child-birth. In both cases, medications (and not an exorcism) can be quite helpful to assist these newly suffering mothers.

The Andrea Yates case recapitulates many points that we have addressed in this book. Andrea Yates was married in 1993 and was allegedly under significant influence from a pastor friend of her new husband. That implies to me that this new relationship was merely an extension of her existing hyper-religiosity. She later made the statement that due to this religious belief.... she would have "as many babies as nature would allow" (she went on to have 5). This pangs to me hyper-sexuality. In 1999, she had 2 suicide attempts (implying a depression of some type) and 2 Psychiatric hospitalizations for postpartum psychosis. Did you make the diagnosis yet? Depression + hyper-spirituality+ hyper-sexuality in no uncertain terms equates to bipolar disorder. Now, move forward to 2001. Andrea has another child earlier that year and true to form has another postpartum psychosis in March 2001 (near a solstice). On June 20th (the summer solstice, the brightest day of the year) in 2001 (close to the Solar Sunspot peak of that decade) ......Andrea went on to drown all 5 children. It was a perfect storm of bad behavior of epic proportions: the murders occurred at a solstice, sunspot peak, she had an established history of mental illness, and she was 6 months post-partum. Although she stated that she was "marked by Satan" and the only way to "keep my kids out of Hell was to kill them" ......her hyper religious delusion was just a delusion, and any reasonable person can now understand the true nature of this tragedy. If you still think Satan was somehow involved, you haven't been paying attention (see ADHD medication list).

I'd finally like to readdress homosexuality when discussing hormones. Most strict followers of doctrine see homosexuality as a sin. They say its "unnatural", but they fail to tell you what's so natural about an Immaculate Conception. They also say it is a weakness of temptation but as a male I see nothing tempting about it. Keeping in line with the chapter, there has been speculation that a GOD GIVEN fetal exposure to abnormal concentrations of hormone may ultimately influence sexual preference. Maybe God intended it this way just as He's intended any other challenge we as humans face. Those who are gay or lesbian clearly live challenging lives. Without being crass, I've found it amusing that God would see to it that a sexually sensitive organ (the prostate gland) is located rectally in a male... what business would He have putting it there unless it served another purpose? This is now sort of getting awkward so let's move on shall we. In conclusion, homosexuality is not a depraved sin but rather an inborn human sexual variant and it is not a matter of choice. Come on people, if homosexuality were a choice...nobody would be gay.

Chart 1

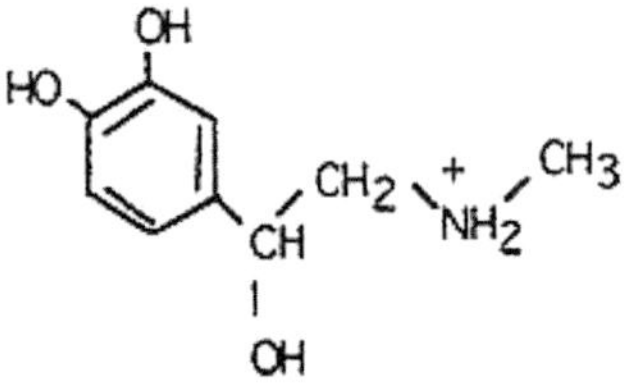

OH
HO
CH2
+
CH3
CH
NH2
OH

EPINEPHRINE
(amine)

NH₂-His-Ser-Gln-Gly-Thr-Phe-Thr-
Ser-Asp-Tyr-Ser-Lys-Tyr-Leu-
Asp-Ser-Arg-Arg-Ala-Gln-Asp
Phe-Val-Gln-Trp-Leu-Met-Asn-Thr-COOH

GLUCAGON
(peptide)

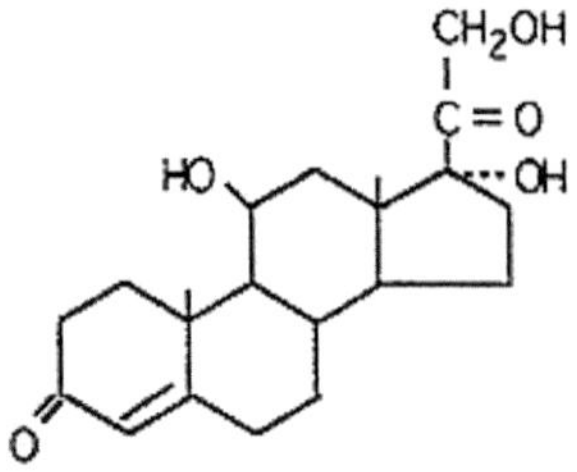

CH2OH
C=O
HO
OH
O

CORTISOL (steroid)

Chart 2

Pathway for Sex Steroid Hormone Production

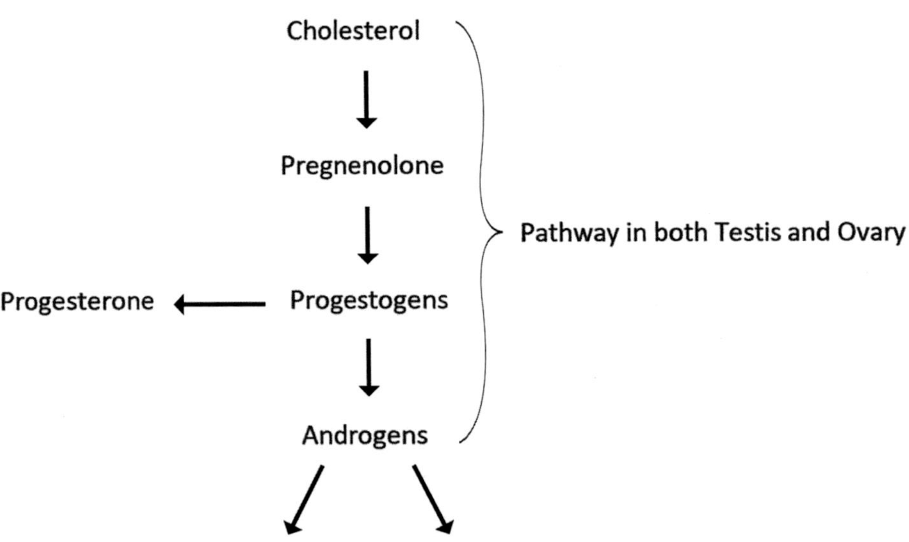

Cholesterol
Pregnenolone
Pathway in both Testis and Ovary
Progesterone
Progestogens
Androgens
ESTROGEN made in female Ovary
TESTOSTERONE made in male Testis nale Testis

Chart 3

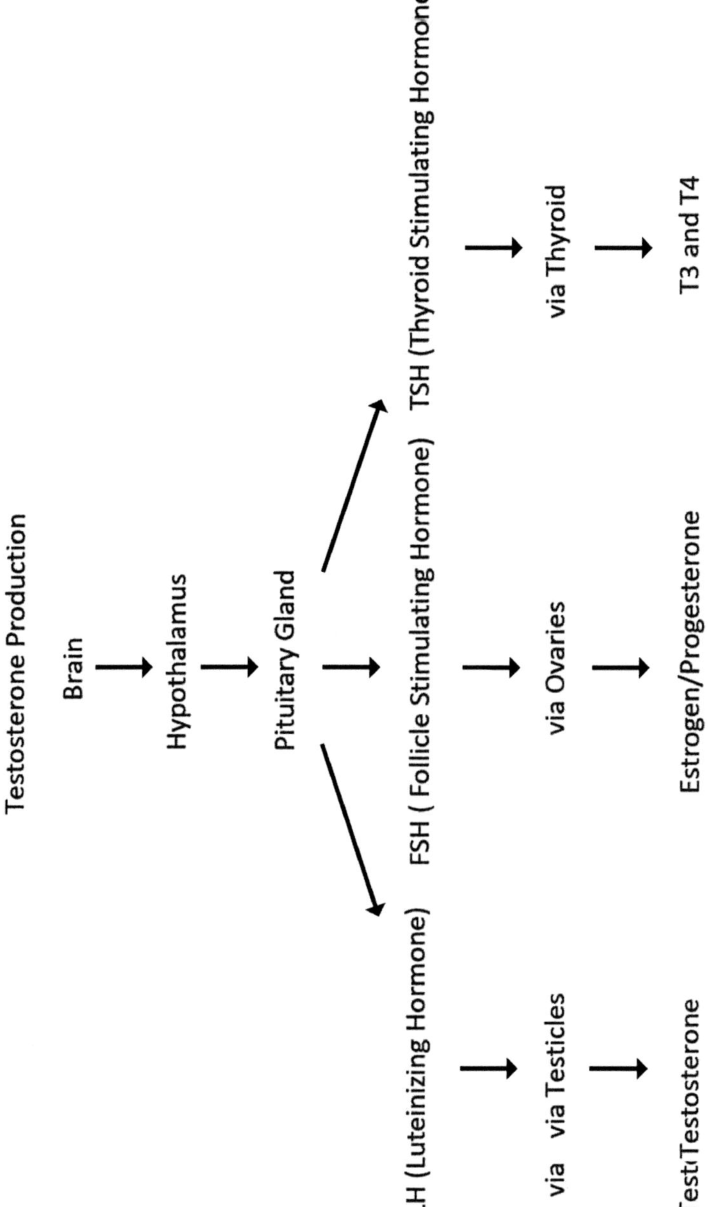

Testosterone Production
Brain
Hypothalamus
Pituitary Gland
LH (Luteinizing Hormone)
FSH (Follicle Stimulating Hormone)
TSH (Thyroid Stimulating Hormone)
via via Testicles
via Ovaries
via Thyroid
Testosterone
Estrogen/Progesterone
T3 and T4

Chart 4

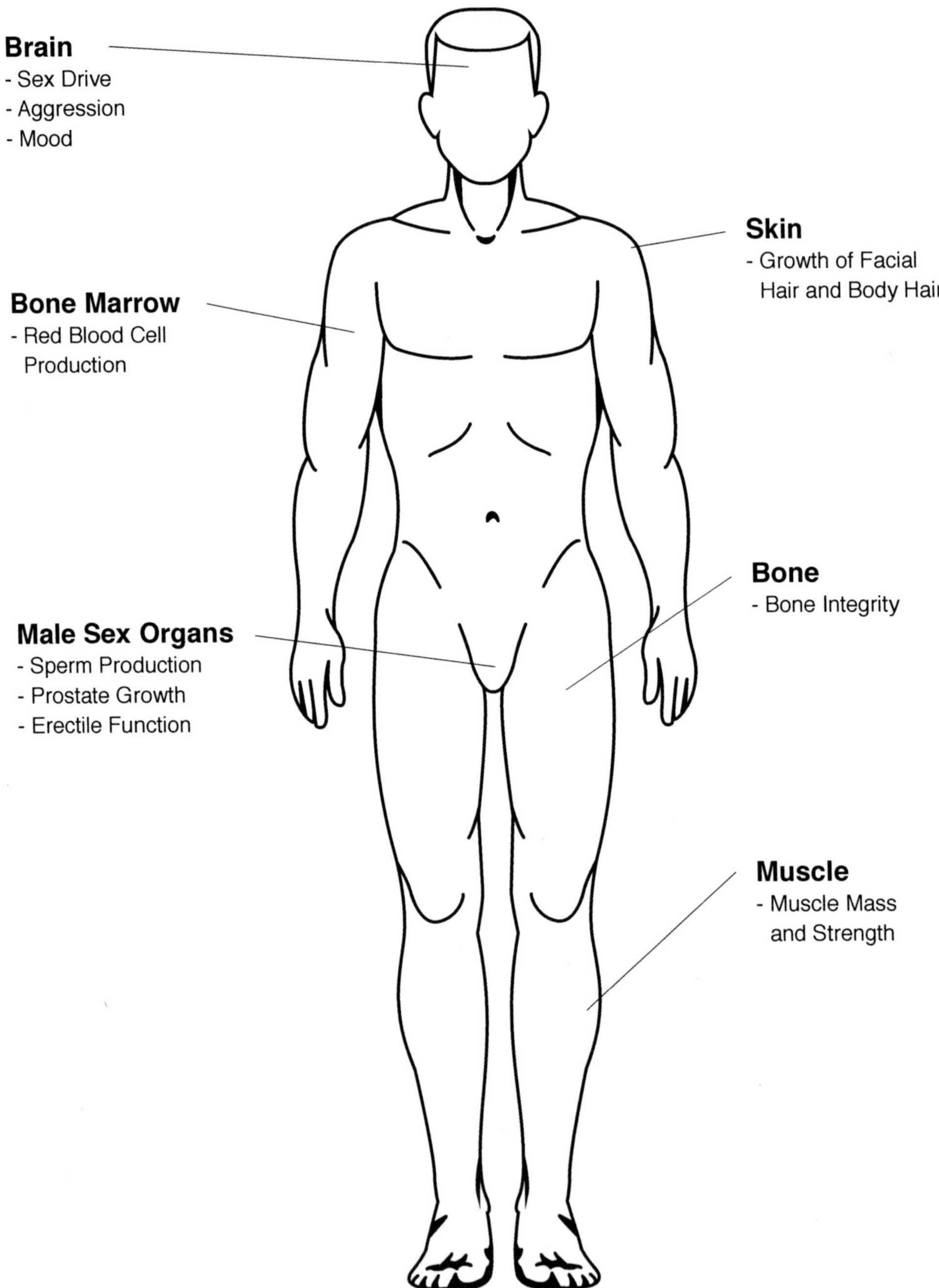
Effects of Testosterone
Brain
- Sex Drive
- Aggression
- Mood
Skin
- Growth of Facial Hair and Body Hair
Bone Marrow
- Red Blood Cell Production
Bone
- Bone Integrity
Male Sex Organs
- Sperm Production
- Prostate Growth
- Erectile Function
Muscle
- Muscle Mass and Strength

Chart 5

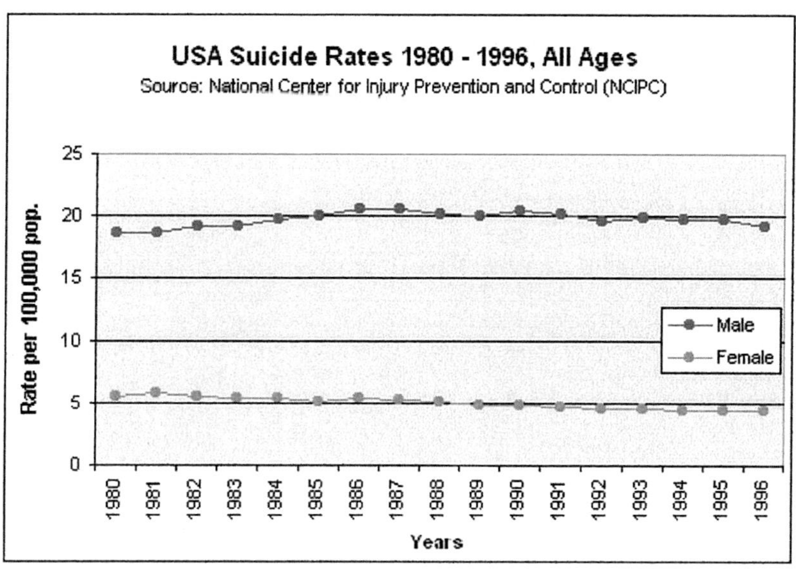

Chart 6

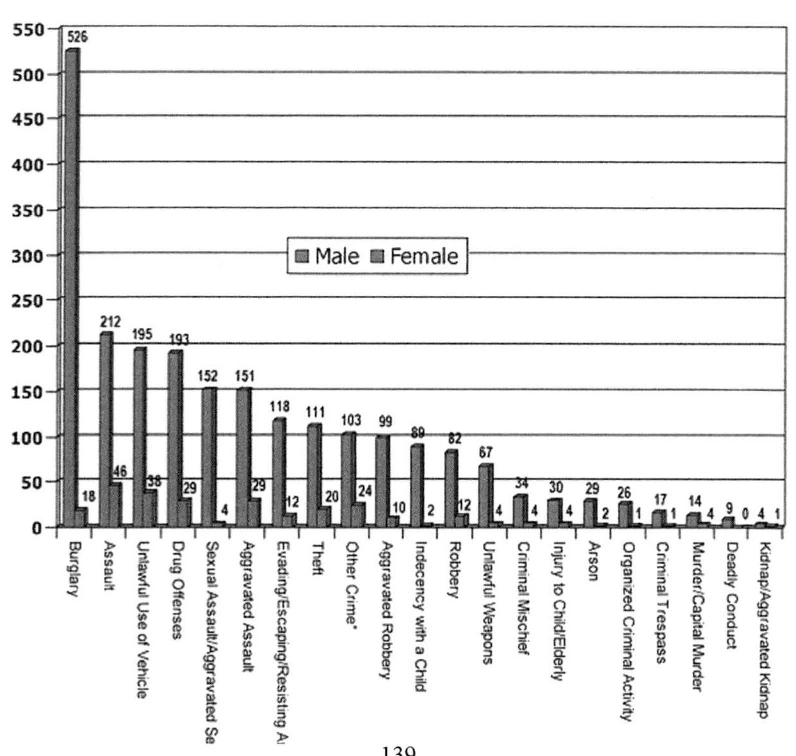

Chart 7

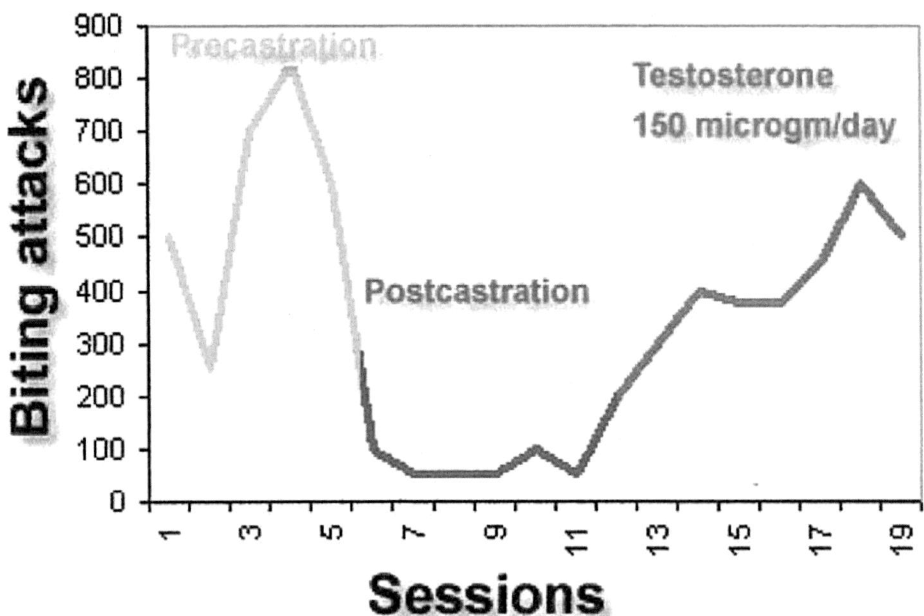

Testosterone Effects on Aggression in Male Mice
Precastration
Testosterone
150 microgm/day
Postcastration
Biting attacks
0
100
200
300
400
500
600
700
800
900
1
3
5
7
9
11
13
15
17
19
Sessions

Chart 8

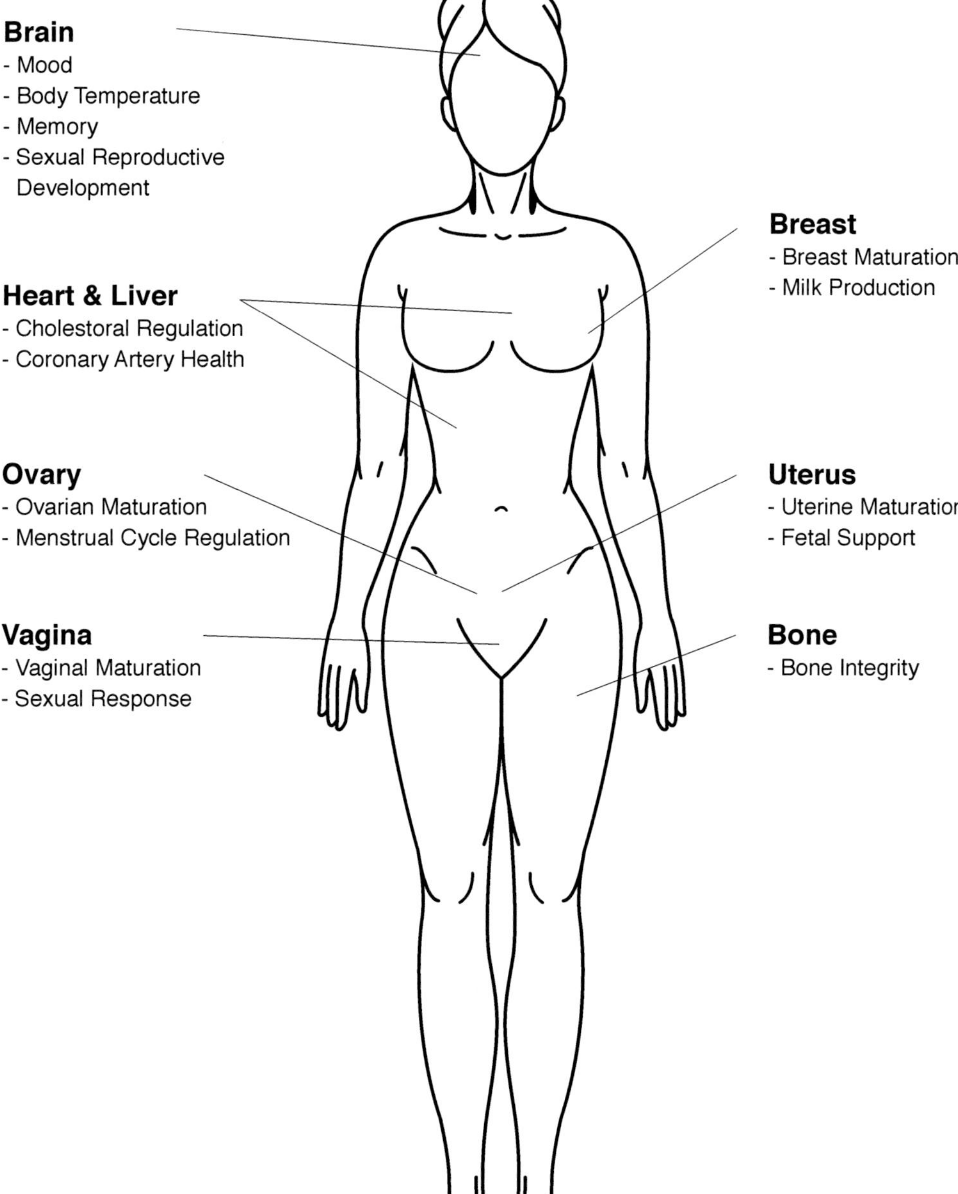

Effects of Estrogen
Brain
- Mood
- Body Temperature
- Memory
- Sexual Reproductive Development
Heart & Liver
- Cholestoral Regulation
- Coronary Artery Health
Ovary
- Ovarian Maturation
- Menstrual Cycle Regulation
Vagina
- Vaginal Maturation
- Sexual Response
Breast
- Breast Maturation
- Milk Production
Uterus
- Uterine Maturation
- Fetal Support
Bone
- Bone Integrity

Chart 9

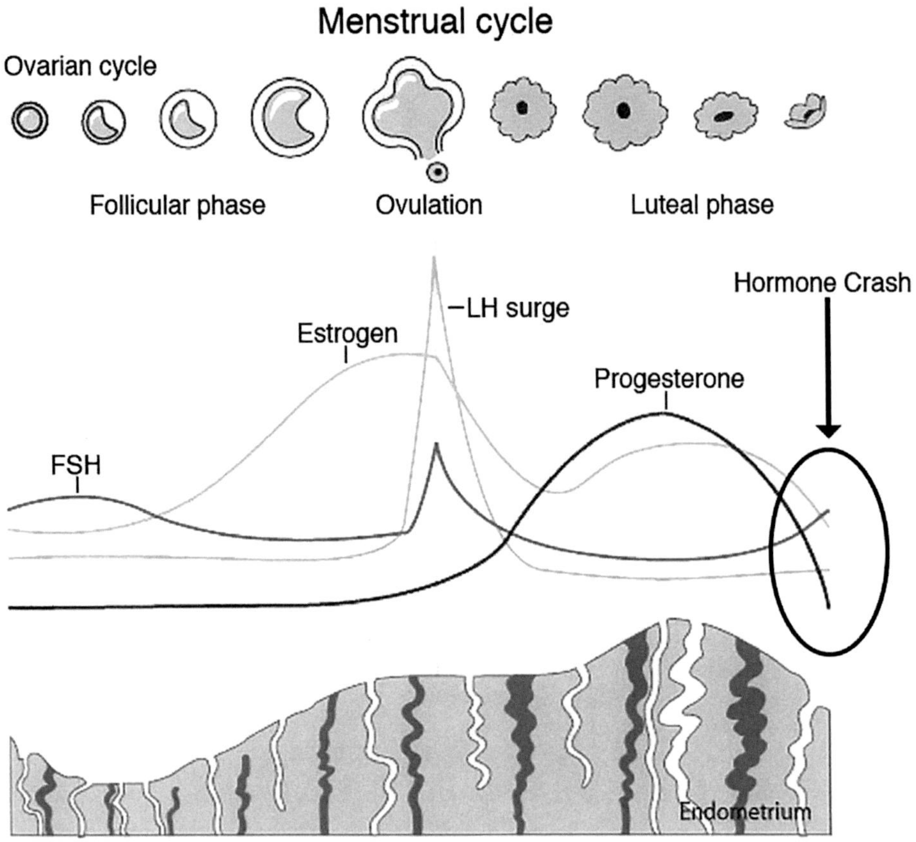

Menstrual cycle
Ovarian cycle
Follicular phase
Ovulation
Luteal phase
Hormone Crash
–LH surge
Estrogen
Progesterone
FSH
Endometrium

Chart 10

Estrogen
Progesterone
35% reduction from age 35-50
HORMONE
At menopause, there is
a relative high estrogen
compare to progesterone
75% reduction
from age 35-50
Hormone
Depletion
25
35
50
60
75
AGE

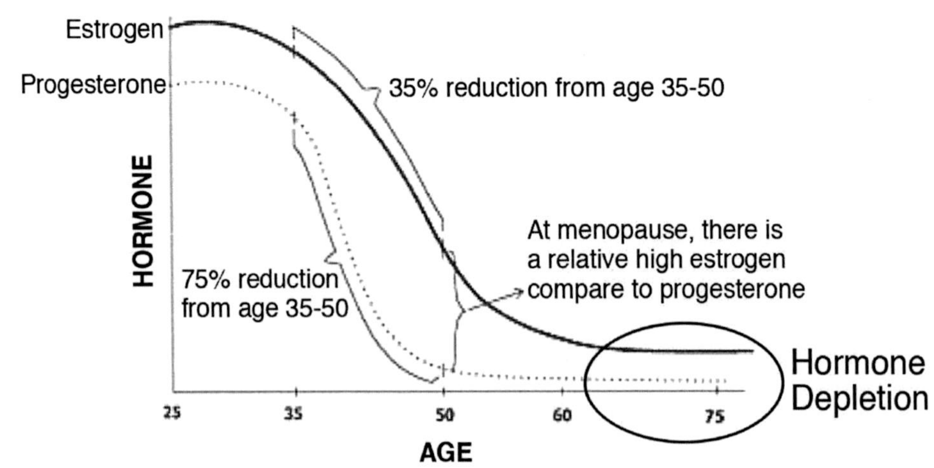

Chart 11

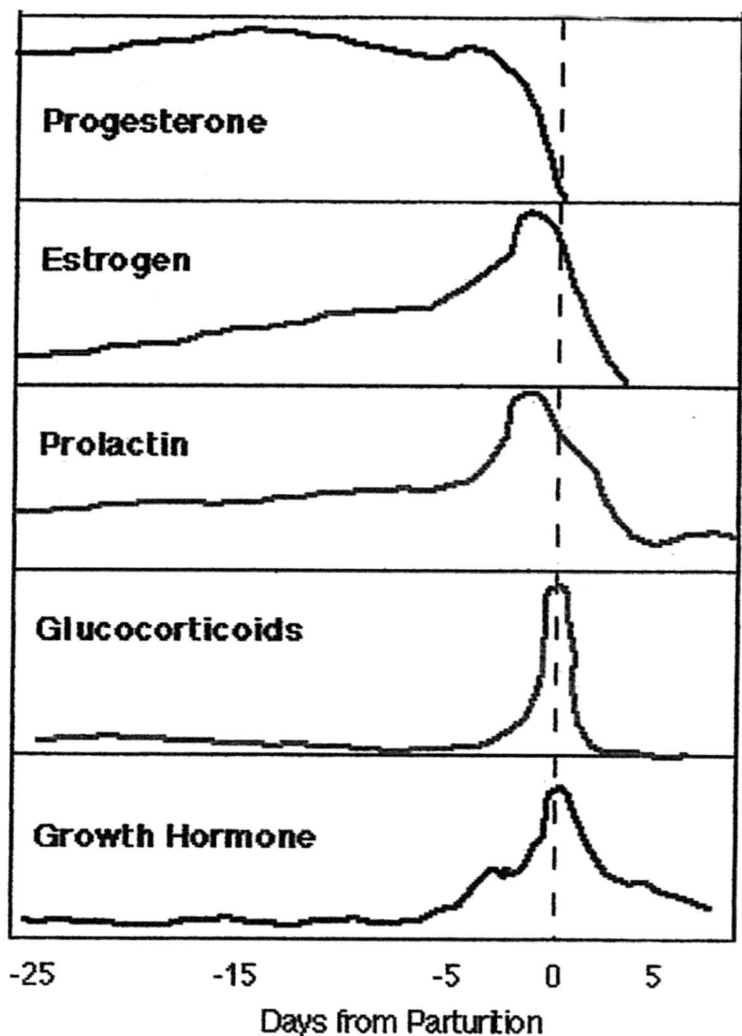

Progesterone
Estrogen
Prolactin
Glucocorticoids
Growth Hormone
-25
-15
-5
0
5
Days from Parturition

Chapter 7

THOU SHALL NOT ACT LIKE A CHILD (UNLESS YOU ARE ONE)

Excuse the Apocalyptic pun.... but what the hell is a personality disorder anyway? For that matter, what is personality? I wondered that for years in residency as we distinguish Axis I disorders (depression, schizophrenia etc.) from Axis II Disorders (personality disorders). If one looks it up on Wikipedia...personality would be defined as "a dynamic and organized set of characteristics possessed by a person that uniquely influences his or her cognitions, motivations and behaviors in various situations". That to me sounds too obtuse and generic to be useful. After mulling it through.... personality in my opinion is "the unique perspective we all have in viewing ourselves and The Universe". This unfortunately might be seen as equally vague, but clarifications and qualifications are to follow.

Modern day Psychiatry identifies 11 personality disorders in all. They are grouped into clusters A, B, and C. Conventional understanding is that they are all considered to be (generally speaking) refractory to medication treatment and more appropriately treated with psychotherapy. We cluster these disorders because all the constituents of each cluster are somewhat similar in their presentations. I'll briefly address Clusters A and C then spend much more time on Cluster B. Cluster A are "the weirds". They constitute the paranoid personality (Chart 1) (irrational suspicions of others), the schizotypal personality (Chart 2) ("odd" thinking or behavior) and schizoid personality (Chart 3) (lack of interest in social relationships). In Psychiatry we desperately try to codify all presentations of patients, and sometimes in doing so we make diagnostic conclusions more complicated than they need to be. Clinically speaking, these disorders are for the most part irrelevant conditions. Patients who allegedly present with these conditions (especially the paranoid personality disorder) are much more likely to suffer a sub-syndromal GENETIC/BIOLOGICAL condition such as a mild variant of schizophrenia or a thought disorder. They also may constitute a variant of normal "personality" in our population. For the most part, paranoid personality patients can generally function fine with their suspiciousness, but if they don't, think schizophrenia or a variant thereof. A schizotypal personality is characterized by odd thinking, but who is to say what is odd? I have plenty of friends who have odd thoughts, and they probably think I do too (Exhibit A: Psychiatric Apocalypse). The bottom line is that EVERYONE is odd …. because everyone is different. Part of the challenge with life is that everybody is weird, but it's just a question of whose weirdness you can put up with. As far as the schizoid personality is concerned, these patients again could be mildly schizophrenic, or have no interest in relationships because they have had either numerous social disappointments or simply and benignly prefer their own company. The asocial nature of schizoids may therefore represent Axis I conditions such as a mild form of schizophrenia or a burnt out social-phobe and not a "personality disorder". These two alternative diagnoses can be treated with medications. In summary, I believe these previously designated Cluster A Personality Disorders do not exist.

Cluster C personality disorders are considered "the wimps". They are traditionally considered the most anxious of the groupings. These personality disorders include avoidant (Chart 4), passive-aggressive (Chart 5), obsessive compulsive (Chart 6) and dependent (Chart 7). In order to disprove each condition like I did with Custer A's, I'll take one at a time. Avoidant personality disordered patients (unlike schizoids) actually wouldn't mind having relationships, but unfortunately they have difficulty making them. These patients probably suffer from early social phobia where they haven't reached that burnt out state of not caring if they are social or not (like a schizoid). Serotonin reuptake inhibitors are a wonderful choice for these patients. Passive aggressive personality patients aren't clinically significant at all. Sometimes we see patients who use passive aggressive defense mechanisms in their life and also in therapy. Subsequently we tag them with a personality disorder "label" out of pure frustration with their inability to speak their mind directly. These patients usually function reasonably well, so they shouldn't have a diagnosis in my opinion. Obsessive compulsive personality's probably just have a variant of OCD (obsessive compulsive disorder), bipolar or ADD. Once again, SRI's (serotonin reuptake inhibitors), other types of antidepressants or new generational antipsychotics should treat this condition quite well if the patient chooses to do so. Lastly, are the dependents (dependent personality disorder). This is defined by "a pervasive dependence on other people". In my opinion, this is a legitimate "personality disorder" (but more of a Cluster B issue) which we will discuss now and in the following chapter.

Cluster B is the most clinically relevant of all groupings (the "wilds"). Mental health workers generally see them when they become stressed and subsequently seek evaluation for another unrelated psychiatric condition that might have worsened with said stress. Again, don't forget, stress worsens all pre-existing Axis I conditions. The personality disorder itself usually doesn't generate the visit unless they are forced to come in by a loved one or legal agency. They typically don't come in for treatment for their personality disorder as they are quite incapable of self-observation and for the most part don't see how their personality negatively impacts themselves or the ones around them. Having said that, Cluster B patients are "stress machines" caused by chronic disappointment from life's reality not quite measuring up to their life's expectations. These Cluster B patients include the histrionics (Chart 8) (superficial emotions and pervasive attention seeking behavior), the antisocials (Chart 9) (pervasive disregard for laws and the rights of others), the borderlines (Chart 10) (black and white thinking, self-image and identity disorder, and mood instability), and the narcissists (Chart 11) (pervasive need for admiration and lack of empathy). Histrionic patients in my opinion are simply dramatic narcissists, so they will no longer be discussed in this text as an individual category.

All Cluster B patients have in common behavior that is child-like in nature. These patients routinely get themselves into trouble primarily in relationships and the law (ultimately out of entitlement issues). Like children, they have very little tolerance for emotional discomfort. If they seek psychiatric evaluation, it's usually for psychotherapy to investigate life's "unfairness". It may also be as a result of attempting to treat an unrelated Axis I Disorder that has worsened in the face of stress fueled by their distorted outlook on life. You actually know who these people are.... they are 5% of your life but take up 70% of your time. Like children, they are inflexible, unrealistic, reactive, demanding, self-centered, manipulative, controlling, unappreciative, immature (phew I'm tired...but I must go on), overly competitive, dramatic, complainers, critical, overly opinionated, unfair, superficial, jealous, disempathetic, needy, and consider themselves perpetual victims. Many experts will say it's due to emotional trauma sustained in childhood which stopped the person in their tracks from developing, but I don't buy it for a second. Plenty of people have traumatic upbringings and mature just fine. Also, I've interviewed plenty of Cluster B's who never quite relate any unusually malignant insults from childhood to speak of anyway. From my perspective, these patient's upbringings are no more toxic than anyone else's. From their perspective however, they have always been wronged and victimized. As a result, they are the pioneers of the frivolous law suit.

So how do Cluster B patients promote Apocalyptic bad behavior? Very easy.... they are the tyrants, dictators, fundamental religious extremists, and serial killers. But guess what.... they don't know any better.... here's why.

Chart 1

DSM-IV & DSM-IV-TR: Paranoid Personality Disorder

Individuals with this Cluster A Personality Disorder distrust others and are suspicious of their motives.

Diagnostic criteria for 301.0 Paranoid Personality Disorder
(cautionary statement)

A. A pervasive distrust and suspiciousness of others such that their motives are interpreted as malevolent, beginning by early adulthood and present in a variety of contexts, as indicated by four (or more) of the following:

(1) suspects, without sufficient basis, that others are exploiting, harming, or deceiving him or her
(2) is preoccupied with unjustified doubts about the loyalty or trustworthiness of friends or associates
(3) is reluctant to confide in others because of unwarranted fear that the information will be used maliciously against him or her
(4) reads hidden demeaning or threatening meanings into benign remarks or events
(5) persistently bears grudges, i.e., is unforgiving of insults, injuries, or slights
(6) perceives attacks on his or her character or reputation that are not apparent to others and is quick to react angrily or to counterattack
(7) has recurrent suspicions, without justification, regarding fidelity of spouse or sexual partner

B. Does not occur exclusively during the course of Schizophrenia, a Mood Disorder With Psychotic Features, or another Psychotic Disorder and is not due to the direct physiological effects of a general medical condition.
Note: If criteria are met prior to the onset of Schizophrenia, add "Premorbid," e.g., "Paranoid Personality Disorder (Premorbid)."

Chart 2

DSM-IV & DSM-IV-TR: Schizotypal Personality Disorder

Individuals with this Cluster A Personality Disorder, like individuals with schizoid personalities have little capacity for close relationships but they are also eccentric in their behaviors, perceptions, and thinking.

Diagnostic criteria for 301.22 Schizotypal Personality Disorder
(cautionary statement)

A. A pervasive pattern of social and interpersonal deficits marked by acute discomfort with, and reduced capacity for, close relationships as well as by cognitive or perceptual distortions and eccentricities of behavior, beginning by early adulthood and present in a variety of contexts, as indicated by five (or more) of the following:

(1) ideas of reference (excluding delusions of reference)
(2) odd beliefs or magical thinking that influences behavior and is inconsistent with subcultural norms (e.g., superstitiousness, belief in clairvoyance, telepathy, or "sixth sense"; in children and adolescents, bizarre fantasies or preoccupations)
(3) unusual perceptual experiences, including bodily illusions
(4) odd thinking and speech (e.g., vague, circumstantial, metaphorical, overelaborate, or stereotyped)
(5) suspiciousness or paranoid ideation
(6) inappropriate or constricted affect
(7) behavior or appearance that is odd, eccentric, or peculiar
(8) lack of close friends or confidants other than first-degree relatives
(9) excessive social anxiety that does not diminish with familiarity and tends to be associated with paranoid fears rather than negative judgments about self

B. Does not occur exclusively during the course of Schizophrenia, a Mood Disorder With Psychotic Features, another Psychotic Disorder, or a Pervasive Developmental Disorder.
Note: If criteria are met prior to the onset of Schizophrenia, add "Premorbid," e.g., "Schizotypal Personality Disorder (Premorbid)."

Chart 3

DSM-IV & DSM-IV-TR:

Schizoid Personality Disorder

Individuals with this Cluster A Personality Disorder express only a limited range of emotion in social interactions and form few if any close relationships with others.

Diagnostic criteria for 301.20 Schizoid Personality Disorder
(cautionary statement)

A. A pervasive pattern of detachment from social relationships and a restricted range of expression of emotions in interpersonal settings, beginning by early adulthood and present in a variety of contexts, as indicated by four (or more) of the following:

(1) neither desires nor enjoys close relationships, including being part of a family
(2) almost always chooses solitary activities
(3) has little, if any, interest in having sexual experiences with another person
(4) takes pleasure in few, if any, activities
(5) lacks close friends or confidants other than first-degree relatives
(6) appears indifferent to the praise or criticism of others
(7) shows emotional coldness, detachment, or flattened affectivity

B. Does not occur exclusively during the course of Schizophrenia, a Mood Disorder With Psychotic Features, another Psychotic Disorder, or a Pervasive Developmental Disorder and is not due to the direct physiological effects of a general medical condition.
Note: If criteria are met prior to the onset of Schizophrenia, add "Premorbid," e.g., "Schizoid Personality Disorder (Premorbid)."

Chart 4

DSM-IV & DSM-IV-TR: Avoidant Personality Disorder

Individuals with this Cluster C Personality Disorder are socially inhibited, usually feel inadequate and are overly sensitive to criticism.

Diagnostic criteria for 301.82 Avoidant Personality Disorder
(cautionary statement)

A pervasive pattern of social inhibition, feelings of inadequacy, and hypersensitivity to negative evaluation, beginning by early adulthood and present in a variety of contexts, as indicated by four (or more) of the following:

(1) avoids occupational activities that involve significant interpersonal contact, because of fears of criticism, disapproval, or rejection

(2) is unwilling to get involved with people unless certain of being liked

(3) shows restraint within intimate relationships because of the fear of being shamed or ridiculed

(4) is preoccupied with being criticized or rejected in social situations

(5) is inhibited in new interpersonal situations because of feelings of inadequacy

(6) views self as socially inept, personally unappealing, or inferior to others

(7) is unusually reluctant to take personal risks or to engage in any new activities because they may prove embarrassing

Chart 5

PTypes - Personality Types

PTypes	A Correspondence of Psychiatric, Keirsey, and Enneagram Typologies	Passive-Aggressive

Diagnostic Criteria for Passive-Aggressive Personality Disorder

A pervasive pattern of passive resistance to demands for adequate social and occupational performance, beginning by early adulthood and present in a variety of contexts, as indicated by at least *five* of the following:

1. procrastinates, i.e., puts off things that need to be done so that deadlines are not met
2. becomes sulky, irritable, or argumentative when asked to do something he or she does not want to do
3. seems to work deliberately slowly or to do a bad job on tasks that he or she really does not want to do
4. protests, without justification, that others make unreasonable demands on him or her
5. avoids obligations by claiming to have "forgotten"
6. believes that he or she is doing a much better job than others think he or she is doing
7. resents useful suggestions from others concerning how he or she could be more productive
8. obstructs the efforts of others by failing to do his or her share of the work
9. unreasonbly criticizes or scorns people in positions of authority

Source: American Psychiatric Association. *Diagnostic and Statistical Manual of Mental Disorders, Third Edition, Revised*. Washington, DC, American Psychiatric Association, 1987. pp. 357-358.

Chart 6

DSM-IV & DSM-IV-TR: Obsessive-Compulsive Personality Disorder (OCPD)

Individuals with this Cluster C Personality Disorder sacrifice openness, spontaneity, and flexibility to pursue orderliness, control, and perfectionism.

Diagnostic criteria for 301.4 Obsessive-Compulsive Personality Disorder (cautionary statement)

A pervasive pattern of preoccupation with orderliness, perfectionism, and mental and interpersonal control, at the expense of flexibility, openness, and efficiency, beginning by early adulthood and present in a variety of contexts, as indicated by four (or more) of the following:

(1) is preoccupied with details, rules, lists, order, organization, or schedules to the extent that the major point of the activity is lost

(2) shows perfectionism that interferes with task completion (e.g., is unable to complete a project because his or her own overly strict standards are not met)

(3) is excessively devoted to work and productivity to the exclusion of leisure activities and friendships (not accounted for by obvious economic necessity)

(4) is overconscientious, scrupulous, and inflexible about matters of morality, ethics, or values (not accounted for by cultural or religious identification)

(5) is unable to discard worn-out or worthless objects even when they have no sentimental value

(6) is reluctant to delegate tasks or to work with others unless they submit to exactly his or her way of doing things

(7) adopts a miserly spending style toward both self and others; money is viewed as something to be hoarded for future catastrophes

(8) shows rigidity and stubbornness

Chart 7

DSM-IV: Dependent Personality Disorder

Individuals with this Cluster C Personality Disorder use their submissive and clinging behavior toward others to elicit care, depending on them for initiative, reassurance, decision making, and advice.

Diagnostic criteria for 301.6 Dependent Personality Disorder
(cautionary statement)

A pervasive and excessive need to be taken care of that leads to submissive and clinging behavior and fears of separation, beginning by early adulthood and present in a variety of contexts, as indicated by five (or more) of the following:

(1) has difficulty making everyday decisions without an excessive amount of advice and reassurance from others

(2) needs others to assume responsibility for most major areas of his or her life

(3) has difficulty expressing disagreement with others because of fear of loss of support or approval.
Note: Do not include realistic fears of retribution.

(4) has difficulty initiating projects or doing things on his or her own (because of a lack of self-confidence in judgment or abilities rather than a lack of motivation or energy)

(5) goes to excessive lengths to obtain nurturance and support from others, to the point of volunteering to do things that are unpleasant

(6) feels uncomfortable or helpless when alone because of exaggerated fears of being unable to care for himself or herself

(7) urgently seeks another relationship as a source of care and support when a close relationship ends

(8) is unrealistically preoccupied with fears of being left to take care of himself or herself

Chart 8

DSM-IV & DSM-IV-TR: Histrionic Personality Disorder

Individuals with this Cluster B Personality Disorder exaggerate their emotions and go to excessive lengths to seek attention.

Diagnostic criteria for 301.50 Histrionic Personality Disorder (cautionary statement)

A pervasive pattern of excessive emotionality and attention seeking, beginning by early adulthood and present in a variety of contexts, as indicated by five (or more) of the following:

(1) is uncomfortable in situations in which he or she is not the center of attention

(2) interaction with others is often characterized by inappropriate sexually seductive or provocative behavior

(3) displays rapidly shifting and shallow expression of emotions

(4) consistently uses physical appearance to draw attention to self

(5) has a style of speech that is excessively impressionistic and lacking in detail

(6) shows self-dramatization, theatricality, and exaggerated expression of emotion

(7) is suggestible, i.e., easily influenced by others or circumstances

(8) considers relationships to be more intimate than they actually are

Reprinted with permission from the Diagnostic and Statistical Manual of Mental Disorders, fourth Edition. Copyright 1994 American Psychiatric Association

Chart 9

DSM-IV & DSM-IV-TR: Antisocial Personality Disorder

Individuals with this Cluster B Personality Disorder in their actions regularly disregard and violate the rights of others. These behaviors may be aggressive or destructive and may involve breaking laws or rules, deceit or theft.

Diagnostic criteria for 301.7 Antisocial Personality Disorder
(cautionary statement)

A. There is a pervasive pattern of disregard for and violation of the rights of others occurring since age 15 years, as indicated by three (or more) of the following:

(1) failure to conform to social norms with respect to lawful behaviors as indicated by repeatedly performing acts that are grounds for arrest
(2) deceitfulness, as indicated by repeated lying, use of aliases, or conning others for personal profit or pleasure
(3) impulsivity or failure to plan ahead
(4) irritability and aggressiveness, as indicated by repeated physical fights or assaults
(5) reckless disregard for safety of self or others
(6) consistent irresponsibility, as indicated by repeated failure to sustain consistent work behavior or honor financial obligations
(7) lack of remorse, as indicated by being indifferent to or rationalizing having hurt, mistreated, or stolen from another

B. The individual is at least age 18 years.

C. There is evidence of Conduct Disorder with onset before age 15 years.

D. The occurrence of antisocial behavior is not exclusively during the course of Schizophrenia or a Manic Episode.

Also: anti-social, "Not me!", sociopath, sociopathy, sociopathic, psychopath, psychopathy, psychopathic, dyssocial

Chart 10

DSM-IV & DSM-IV-TR: Borderline Personality Disorder

Individuals with this Cluster B Personality Disorder behave impulsively and their relationships, self-image, and emotions are unstable.

Diagnostic criteria for 301.83 Borderline Personality Disorder
(cautionary statement)

A pervasive pattern of instability of interpersonal relationships, self-image, and affects, and marked impulsivity beginning by early adulthood and present in a variety of contexts, as indicated by five (or more) of the following:

(1) frantic efforts to avoid real or imagined abandonment.
Note: Do not include suicidal or self-mutilating behavior covered in Criterion 5.

(2) a pattern of unstable and intense interpersonal relationships characterized by alternating between extremes of idealization and devaluation

(3) identity disturbance: markedly and persistently unstable self-image or sense of self

(4) impulsivity in at least two areas that are potentially self-damaging (e.g., spending, sex, Substance Abuse, reckless driving, binge eating).
Note: Do not include suicidal or self-mutilating behavior covered in Criterion 5.

(5) recurrent suicidal behavior, gestures, or threats, or self-mutilating behavior

(6) affective instability due to a marked reactivity of mood (e.g., intense episodic dysphoria, irritability, or anxiety usually lasting a few hours and only rarely more than a few days)

(7) chronic feelings of emptiness

(8) inappropriate, intense anger or difficulty controlling anger (e.g., frequent displays of temper, constant anger, recurrent physical fights)

(9) transient, stress-related paranoid ideation or severe dissociative symptoms

Reprinted with permission from the Diagnostic and Statistical Manual of Mental Disorders, fourth

Chart 11

DSM-IV & DSM-IV-TR: Narcissistic Personality Disorder

Individuals with this Cluster B Personality Disorder have an excessive sense of how important they are. They demand and expect to be admired and praised by others and are limited in their capacity to appreciate others' perspectives.

Diagnostic criteria for 301.81 Narcissistic Personality Disorder (cautionary statement)

A pervasive pattern of grandiosity (in fantasy or behavior), need for admiration, and lack of empathy, beginning by early adulthood and present in a variety of contexts, as indicated by five (or more) of the following:

(1) has a grandiose sense of self-importance (e.g., exaggerates achievements and talents, expects to be recognized as superior without commensurate achievements)

(2) is preoccupied with fantasies of unlimited success, power, brilliance, beauty, or ideal love

(3) believes that he or she is "special" and unique and can only be understood by, or should associate with, other special or high-status people (or institutions)

(4) requires excessive admiration

(5) has a sense of entitlement, i.e., unreasonable expectations of especially favorable treatment or automatic compliance with his or her expectations

(6) is interpersonally exploitative, i.e., takes advantage of others to achieve his or her own ends

(7) lacks empathy: is unwilling to recognize or identify with the feelings and needs of others

(8) is often envious of others or believes that others are envious of him or her

(9) shows arrogant, haughty behaviors or attitudes

Chapter 8

JOHN'S NEW REVELATION: BORN AS A BEAST

For years, mental health professionals have tried to elucidate the cause of personality disorders. In my opinion, the two clues that crack this case are as follows. Firstly, medications don't help Cluster B personality disorders (the most clinically important [and legitimate] of all personality disorders as discussed in the last chapter). This therefore implies that it might not have a chemical/biological basis. Secondly, as we defined, all personality disorders (Cluster B's) behave like children. Perhaps if the timeless concept of a soul exists, maybe YOUNG souls act like children too. Maybe we as humans experience multiple lives (prominent in Hinduism / Buddhism) and the earliest of them represent modern day psychiatric personality disorders. And just as humans sludge their way through a series of embarrassingly awkward emotional/social developmental stages in one life... maybe young souls do so as well. I guess we could therefore classify personality disorders as a "spiritual deficiency".

If this theory is correct, the rationale behind the concept of multiple lives starts with God. Certainly if something so nutty as "multiple lives" actually does exist, then the whole mess isn't random after all. If there truly is a God....He must be Brilliant and be the Supreme discerner of fact (right) verses fiction (wrong). Our existence on Earth therefore may simply be His attempt for us to become more like Him (smart) through the trials of life and the logic it teaches us. Think of the most emotionally painful event you have been through.... isn't it also the most important lesson you have ever learned? THIS IS WHY BAD THINGS HAPPEN TO GOOD (AND BAD) PEOPLE! It would follow that if one lifetime is fruitful for such learning, then many lifetimes must be even better! Now you know why I discounted the existence of Cluster A and Cluster C personality disorders...they don't make any sense given this paradigm. They DON'T act like children and they probably DO respond to medications if properly diagnosed as Axis 1 disorders. With this new approach to possibly understanding patients, we have solved a common and perpetually vexing psychiatric diagnostic dilemma with a supernatural solution. However, the sad reality is, whether describing a young soul or young human, we are all born monsters. It is only with successful navigation of painful earthly lessons that we with time are sculpted to become more responsible, more mature, and to have a better understanding of right vs. wrong. This may explain how people can be so different.... we are all in a different stage of "figuring things out". It also explains how "common sense" can vary so greatly from person to person. In short.... a soul is a template for awareness, conscience and knowledge.

In order to somehow prove this unlikely concept, I'll first need to give an overview of human emotional development from newborn to adult. My goal is to pinpoint the various emotional milestones in a HUMAN'S life, and then align them with the correspondingly RELEVANT personality disorder that we observe in Psychiatry. This should give us an idea of how "evolved" each personality disorder is relative to one another. My contention is that a soul evolves on a macro basis analogously to the human development of a single life's micro basis. The concept is a kin to the unproven concept of "ontogeny following phylogeny". That is, the evolutionary steps of a fetal organism (a fetus) recapitulates the evolutionary steps of the species as a whole. The example being that we as humans assume the shape of a tadpole just after conception, and the analogous initial stages of our species AS A WHOLE resembled a tadpole many millions of years ago as well. This concept has never been proven (and certainly flies in the face of Creationism), but it's the concept of "macro mirroring micro" that matters. This theory is another example of "a cycle within a cycle" as we saw with seasonality and sunspots (and also is seen in The Mayan Calendar which I will touch on later). We have numerous human life cycles that make up one souls LARGE life cycle. As a result, a person with a young soul (a personality disorder) can't evolve any faster than the experiences they have mastered over those previous lifetimes REGARDLESS of whatever human age they have accrued in their current HUMAN life. For example, an 80-year-old person in his/her 1st lifetime is therefore less spiritually evolved than a 7-year-old in his/her 4th lifetime.

The rudimentary stages of child and adolescent development are as follows. Please note this is a general outline and a more precise guideline would include 6 month intervals in children younger than 6 years. Child to child variability is also noted.

1 year old: Immediate gratification. Egocentric (disregard for others). Abandonment issues.

2 years old: No impulse control. Magical thinking (no discernment between reality and fantasy). Attention seeking. Temper tantrums. Will hit for a toy. Awkward social relationships. "Black and white" thinking. Doesn't play fair. Changing of friends. Immediate gratification. Egocentric. Contradictory beliefs (they don't realize that they can't play indoors and outdoors SIMULTANEOUSLY for example).

3 years old: Less temper tantrums but they still exist. Starting to understand others feelings but they still don't totally play fairly. Fantasied and magical thinking. STARTING to understand "mine vs theirs". Attention seeking. A bit less "black and white" thinking. Begins to play with others and frequent changing of friends. Egocentric.

4 years old: Shows more sympathy. Exaggerates and boasts. Recognizes others property. More competitive.... doesn't like losing. Attention seeking. Fantasied and magical thinking. Changing of friends. Beginning to share. Egocentric.

5 years old: Improving fair play. Magical thinking lessening in favor of reality. A bit less egocentric. Attention seeking. Should start to understand right vs. wrong. Changing friends.

6 years old: More reality based. Less egocentric. Starting to have consistent friends. Becoming more rule based. Gives up immediate reward for delayed reward.

7-8 years old: Highly rule based. Self-esteem based on ability commences. Logical thinking begins. Dramatically less fantasy and egocentricity.

9-11 years old: Rules negotiated but still followed strictly. Team Sports. Aware of peer group leader.

12-14 years old: Social status related to group membership. Self-esteem related to social acceptance. Social acceptance depends on conformity. Alternates between child and adult behavior.

15-18 years old: Personal identity forming. More logical. Generation of personal opinions and desires.

18 years and beyond: Social status a bit little less important. Less need for external objects to prop-up sense of self. Acceptance of self. Self-observation. Improved stress management. More realistic and tolerant.

As you can see, humans are more civil and hence less "evil" as they get older. The earliest stage of development clearly represents the most self-indulgent, unfair, self-centered, and unrealistic. In other words, the younger the person, the less regard for others feelings. This is analogous to the sociopath (antisocial personality disorder) and I call it "The Age of Lawlessness". We all start our first human lifetimes as sociopaths, therefore we begin our spiritual journey with very little awareness, conscience and knowledge (like a baby). No wonder Adam and Eve were sinners…they were sociopaths! In my opinion, sociopathy is the most destructive Psychiatric condition on the planet. Unlike a dangerous schizophrenic, these people behave in a blending and non-obtrusive way SUPERFICIALLY. As a result, they are not discredited by acquaintances upon first glance…. but this changes with time. Sociopathy represents ages 1-2 years of age on the above human development scale. Just like an infant/toddler, they are all about personal gratification and it is usually predatory which means it is at the expense of others. I dare you to give ten toddlers each a mallet and lock them in a room for an hour……guaranteed only one will be standing upright by hours end. And even then, the last toddler standing will have little regard for the aftermath. Similarly, sociopaths have no sense of fair play and have no ability to understand how their self-centered indulgence affects the people around them. Their self-indulgence could revolve around money laundering, stealing sex through rape or simply enjoying the exaltation of domination. Egocentrism is the term used to describe a baby's total involvement with itself. This concept of egocentrism is also what makes a sociopath so dangerous…. a total disregard for other's feelings. If you see a friend or colleague with a personal picture of them SMILING with hunted game…run for the hills. There should be no joy in the killing of our fellow mammals…. even if it is for food. Trophy hunters hunt for the sake of domination. Sociopaths enjoy dominating, bullying, intimidating and humiliating.

In my paradigm, sociopathy (1-2 years) precedes narcissism (3-6 years). As a result, sociopaths will share almost all of the narcissist's "blind spots", and narcissists may only have a few of the sociopath's developmental vulnerabilities. It makes sense that sociopaths would have narcissistic characteristics, they evolutionarily speaking haven't dealt with those (or even their own) milestones yet. The only personality disorder that can actually START to be seen in childhood and beyond is sociopathy (it is referred to as conduct disorder). The reason is, we should normally outgrow its lawlessness VERY QUICKLY (by AT MOST the 7th year of life). In my opinion, if a child or adolescent after that age repeatedly abuses animals (because they need the feeling of dominating other living beings) …. that's your best clue that said person is a future sociopath. Sociopaths revel in other's pain and misadventures due to their own sense of spiritual emptiness. That is, they haven't accrued enough past lives to experience the sense of feeling "full" (the intangible sense of having a conscience). As a result…. it is only the agony of others that allows them to feel powerful and relevant since they can't quite attain that "feeling" on their own.

I once watched a video on "America's Favorite Home videos" of an infant in a high chair eating dinner. Apparently the mother had asked the toddler not to eat the desert (chocolate cake) while she tended to something else. However, when she got back, the baby's face was covered with frosting. Now, on tape, she asks the child "Did you eat that cake"?.....and the child with a blank remorseless chocolate covered face states…."no mommy, I didn't eat the cake". That's what sociopaths do…. they lie to your face and cheat their way to self-gratification. The serial killer Ted Bundy was a perfect example. He found that raping and killing women made complete sense as it served to satiate his own gratification. Killing them also served to prop up his meager sense of self as now that made him their God.

In addition to serial killers, we also may observe how some World's leaders might have sociopathy as well (AND NARCISSISM). Young souls routinely seek political office as it satiates their need to feel important and only requires the ability to persuade others. Once in power, they feast on controlling and dominating others. Their own people are subjugated as they have very little sense of empathy as long as their own needs of power and wealth are taken care of. You can pretty much bank that a ruler has a personality disorder (a young soul) if their picture, likeness or name is everywhere you look. I'm quite certain that if Apocalyptic geopolitical events occur, a sociopathic/narcissistic leader will tangentially be involved…. if anything just to prove to the world how relevant that person is (hmmmm). Unfortunately, to these personality disordered world leaders, fantasy rules, and the truth is irrelevant.

Sociopathy, or the need for personal gratification at the expense of others, can also be seen in the many recent events on Wall Street. Bernie Madoff and his false profits represented swindling of egregious proportions. I can't say for certain he was a sociopath (since I never examined him), however, the extent to which he conned others for self-gratification is stunning. Young "sociopathic" souls might GIVE a little upfront initially to gain one's confidences.... but after that it's just take, take, take. Sociopaths do what they have to do to get what they want. Madoff showed me a very unique clue that he may be a "newbie" while I watched him on television. As he was being walked to the court house for his arraignment......I noticed that he was actually smiling and joking. How inappropriate I thought. If he was innocent, appropriate behavior would have been to demonstrate a mood which was congruent to the seriousness of the charges. And, if he was guilty, he clearly shouldn't be jovial as that would show no remorse for his transgressions. The bottom line is, young souls are like young children, they don't really know how to act in emotionally charged and unfamiliar situations. I saw the same inappropriate affect (emotion) with court dates for John Gotti, OJ Simpson, Drew Petterson and Michael Jackson (dancing on a car). Personally, I think young souls are very uncomfortable as human adults. It's not something they have ever experienced and it's way "too new". Conversely, human childhood to an old soul is probably hackneyed and dissatisfying.

Narcissism is another personality disorder, but in my opinion it represents ages roughly 3-6 years on the above human developmental scale. As previously stated, sociopaths share many of the same symptoms as narcissists and I think that just represents the very close transitioning from one developmental milestone to another on a macro basis (and sociopaths have yet to fulfill those spiritual evolutionary stages). I'm mentioning it twice because it's such an important explanation as to why there are few "pure-play" sociopaths or narcissists.... they blend quite often. Narcissists and sociopaths both demand attention and see life in very "black and white" terms. That is, they have problems identifying people as having good AND bad qualities simultaneously.... just one or the other. Young children demonstrate the same tendency. As a result, these young souls are also very opinionated (critical) of others, as it serves to buoy their own poor self-esteem. This also predictably results in numerous short lived social relationships (as seen in children as well). In addition, they both demonstrate magical thinking as they preoccupy themselves with fantasies of power and success. Both of these personality disorders also "don't play fair" and do exploit.... but narcissists VERY IMPORTANTLY have less of these socially acidic qualities since they are SLIGHTLY more evolved. They are less likely to undertake nefarious deeds such as murder and larceny. But, the bottom line is, anything between 1-6 years of age represents self-centered behavior (fantasied self-preoccupied thinking) and as a result sociopaths and narcissists act like little self-serving drunken demons. I find it ironic that age "6" is when children begin to phase out of developmentally reprehensible behavior...."6", the number of the Beast. It's not until age 7 that children in earnest start to become more realistic, more fair and easier.

As sociopathy represents "personal gratification", narcissism represents "personal glorification". I call this phase "The Age of Self-Centeredness". They love their possessions and are very poor losers (just like children). Possessions serve as a crutch for their weak sense of self....as a result they are trophy collectors as they think this will impress the viewer. Possessions also must be "brand name" as this improves their perceived status. Narcissists are self-promoters and tend to exaggerate personal accomplishments. However, they seem to have a bit more need for attention than sociopaths. I'm guessing this is because they developmentally understand the concept of other people more than sociopaths, and they are less socially awkward. John Wayne Gacy, the notorious serial killer, wore a clown costume for local charity functions and birthdays which is essentially a proxy for stating "pay attention to me.... not the kid who is having a birthday". Their self-esteem is primarily based on being paid attention to and HOW others see them. They love to give advice to people even when not asked. It's a primitive attempt to appear bright and a not so subtle attempt to prove how stupid you are. Watching two narcissists converse with one another is actually pretty hilarious.... they try to "out do" each other without fully realizing how silly the whole exchange looks to others.

Narcissists are also very easily offended and as a result have an exquisite sensitivity to rejection and criticism ("thin skinned"). Since narcissists are more evolved than sociopaths, the good news is they may be unfair but at least are not lawless. Some might argue that narcissism should represent the self-centered "adolescent" years in human development, but the bottom line is, they still demonstrate profoundly unfair behavior towards others and have an active fantasy life (magical thinking) which both precede my chart's teen years developmentally. They have fleeting relationships because no one can put up with their demands for admiration, their jealousy, or their inappropriate anger when their ego is threatened. Narcissists are exhausting to be with because they are also so competitive. To them, WINNING IS EVERYTHING! Kids older than 13 can EASILY observe an ADULT narcissist's (and sociopath's) behavior and understand how immature it is.... the reason is.... they have ALREADY mastered those developmental steps in their current human life (assuming that they are an old soul and don't have these personality disorders). Narcissists tend to have tremendous feelings of entitlement, and as a result routinely feel they should have things they don't deserve. They commonly buy or lease things they can't afford because they feel they need to look the appropriate status. It's actually quite expensive to be one. There is no doubt in my mind that the US mortgage crunch of 2008 and beyond is IN PART due to this sense of personal entitlement. Many felt they deserved to have a nice home they couldn't afford.

Narcissists are also notoriously controlling. If someone is trying to "witness" to you or if Hare Krishna are soliciting you at the airport, in many instances this is simply a primitive way of trying to control and manipulate you. To save us all a lot of time, they should just come out and say "I'm special, you're not, and you need to be like me". This is the "Narcissist's Psalm" and a childlike attempt to bolster a fragile sense of self through personal anointing. These religious manipulators will tell you that they just want to glorify God.... but unbeknownst to them, it's a self-deceived attempt to glorify themselves. They typically start off by stating they love you (without even knowing you) and that they are looking out for your future well-being. Next time this happens to you (and after you write a "note to self" for a restraining order), ask them for $1500 to help with your mortgage bill. Usually, the only thing left after that retort is a facial flush and a dust cloud. You'll quickly learn how interested they REALLY are in you. Trying to control others is not only an attempt to rob the other person of their freedom to choose AND the opportunity to think for themselves, but it also shows profound arrogance in that it attempts to impose a behavior or belief that is pleasing to the controller (and not necessarily to the Universe). I'm not saying you can't believe what you want, but try to resist the narcissistic temptation to impose those beliefs on others. I find it comical that people revere their own controlling religion as Godly, but describe someone else's controlling religion as a cult.

And then there is the diagnosis of borderline personality disorder. If you ever saw the movie Fatal Attraction, you will know that Glenn Close played a borderline. Borderlines have a mish-mash of primitive defenses representing anywhere between 6 mos to 4 years (Otto Kernberg identifies them as having characteristics of 6 mos to 36 months). Like a 1 to 2-year-old, they have epic feelings of abandonment and inappropriate anger when this is tested. They are impulsive, especially in relationships, and almost always have dramatic endings to their relationships secondary to their unreasonable expectations of the other person. Like a narcissist though, their sense of self and identity is very fragile, and instead of propping it up with possessions, they prop it up with relationships (other people). That's why being alone or perceiving abandonment is so difficult for them. As a coping mechanism, suicidality, either threatened or actualized, is often employed. Clearly, borderlines behave equally as "young" and unevolved as a sociopath.... but just with different symptoms.

In my experience, most sociopaths tend to be male and most borderlines tend to be female. So then the logical question is: why is it that the youngest souls that are male appear to have sociopathic features, and female cases demonstrate more borderline characteristics? As long as we are going out on a limb with regards to the concept of soul progression.... for as much of a stretch as it sounds, maybe we have male and female souls. The Bible states Arch Angels are spiritual beings but are male in gender (Michael, Raphael, Gabriel) ....so MAYBE we are on to something. Just as the "instructions" for PHYSICAL development of a man requires an XY chromosome, and for a female requires an XX chromosome, maybe the SENSE of feeling like a man or woman is determined by the gender of one's soul. Perhaps being a female is a combination of having a female soul and female body/hormones and the same applies to being male. Maybe our first lifetimes represent the primitive needs of our soul's gender which in the case of females are relationships, and for a male maybe it's domination/respect. Another way of thinking about it is that "male" souls have different lessons to learn than "female" souls, hence the rudimentary but different types of struggles seen in each gender existence. If one looks at a prison, the type of place a young wayward soul (sociopath or borderline) might end up, these basic characteristics are all too obvious. A male prison's gestalt consists of domination and the subsequent respect required, whereas female inmates tend to be defined by their relationships. Perhaps life is simply a lesson in dealing with, managing and learning from the innate drives we have imprinted on our souls (in addition to our DNA).

If this were true, this may open the door to many other revelations. Having worked with the transgendered community, this may explain why those who claim to be transgendered feel like they are a man trapped in a women's body or a female in a man's body. Maybe these people's souls are the victim of being assigned to an incompatible body type. Caitlyn Jenner hinted at this in her now infamous interview with Diane Sawyer in 2015.

Maybe the soul determines the SENSE of feeling like a male or female, but the chromosomal assignment and subsequently produced biochemical hormones determine the body type. We can even take this one step further and explain the alleged "heretical" concept of being gay as well. If one's soul determines the sense of gender type, then maybe an internal balance of hormones (in a particular part of the brain) determines sexual preference as I mentioned in the chapter pertaining to hormones. This would explain how a physically appearing male, who feels like a male, would prefer to have sex with a male.... it's three totally separate issues. They have the correct soul and body (XY) assignments, but somewhere in their brains development a certain unknown hormonal imbalance caused an attraction to the same sex. Once again I digress like an ADD kid tracking a shiny object .... back to borderlines.

The only problem with the concept of male and female souls is that after the first initial lifetime of either being a sociopath (male)or a borderline (female).... there would appear to be no gender differences in any of the subsequent personality disorders. Narcissistic personalities and beyond show no difference in gender bias.... they are equally male and female. I can't explain this other than saying "it is what it is". Maybe the initial lessons learned in our FIRST lifetimes as a sociopath (if male) or borderline (if female) suffice to teach us our soul's gender specific issues.

One other possibility for the explanation of borderline personality disorder is that the condition does not exist at all, and that they are actually narcissists with bipolarity. That is, they have all the insecurities of a narcissist, but have the mood lability, intense anger and suicidality of a bipolar patient (see borderline criteria....4.5,6,8,9.... very similar to bipolar). I'm quite certain that there are many suicidal patients in society who were inappropriately diagnosed borderline when they were in fact bipolar. This is a shame because the latter is highly treatable as we have learned.

The last legitimate personality disorder I would like to address is "the dependent personality". Dependents are a Cluster C disorder as mentioned. Although they are not included in Cluster B, I still believe they can fit into my paradigm. Children aged 7 to 14 tend to act just like these dependents (as it pertains to the concept of GROUP and not parents). Since this "disorder" represents my metaphorical "7-14 years" stage.... they really aren't that reprehensible and the term dependent personality should simply be a descriptive term and not necessarily be a term of pathology. They aren't unfair, just a bit self-deceived and unsure of themselves. They are searching to understand themselves just as a similarly aged youngster might attempt to do (any age 7- 14 years roughly). It's a "what am I" search not so much a "who am I" search (the latter is more of the sociopath/borderline/narcissist quest). A "who am I" search is far more desperate and self-centered.

If my theory actually exists, "dependent" people would probably represent a fairly large percentage of the world's population because of the many years that have passed since man's initial "creation" as sociopaths. Dependent personalities, like 7-14 year olds, depend upon social affiliations and conformity within a group. They enjoy the sense of belonging that being identified with a certain group offers. Dependent personality's have difficulty making everyday decisions without support or guidance from others. Just like a child in latency, they request to be told what to do. In addition, they have difficulty expressing disagreements within a group for their fear of loss of approval from others. This also correlates with the time of life that is dictated by "rule bound" behavior (as the above developmental scheme shows). It's possible that social networking sites such as "Instagram", "Facebook" and "Twitter" might be huge beneficiaries of this group as it provides a sense of belonging and connection. I'm guessing that our human soul pool AS A WHOLE has "grown up" and finally evolved collectively INTO the need for such social networks. For those who don't believe in coincidences, The Universe also provided technology like the internet to assist with these co-mingling services at EXACTLY the same time as the spiritually driven developmental need for it. # Freaky!

On the negative side however, a highly characteristic aspect of this phase is that these members have issues with people that are different than their identified group. This is "The Age of Intolerance" (as it pertains to characteristics OUTSIDE the group). I contend that this very large group of souls makes up religious extremists and unquestioning followers of doctrine. They would be the ones that developmentally need to conform to whatever the dictating sociopath or narcissist espouses (such as Hitler and his followers in The Holocaust). It's also quite common to see the combination of a dependent personality and a sociopath/narcissist in human pair bonding......one likes to be controlling and the other likes to be controlled.... it's a master and slave thing. Dependents are also highly rule bound and tend to let rules guide their behavior (even if those rules don't make sense.... Religious Doctrine?). They don't have enough confidence in themselves or have enough "spiritual experience" to come to their own conclusions. Religious fanatics tend to let their doctrine dictate their religious beliefs secondary to this need for rule bound guidance, AND they conform to the group where individual thought is discouraged. We see this "fish following fish" mentality in financial bubbles as well.... whether it be a housing bubble or a stock market bubble......it's all about following the leader! Although it's tempting to have contempt for them like with all other personality disorders, this group is acting totally appropriate for their souls developmental age. Personality disorders generically might behave "weird" to you, but believe it or not they are right where they should be.

We now will put "2 and 2 together" and quickly see that personality disorders (or unevolved souls) also play a huge part in the construction of societies or religions that oppose one another. A huge mass of young souls is just doing what comes naturally: searching for an identity, following a group that it thinks it's good, and opposing a group (for whatever ideological reason) that in their mind must be bad. Everybody thinks they are playing for "the good" team and fighting the "bad" one. All the while, in a tragic case of the blind leading the blind, dependents are following a person (sociopath or narcissist) who is simply in it for the unconsciously infantile need for attention. So this sets us up for the big War...Satan vs God (The Apocalypse). But who is Satan's army?....how can it exist if everybody is claiming to be good and fighting for God? (except the 15-year-old pimply gothic kid who listens to Marilyn Manson and likes to piss off his parents out of pure shock value). The answer is: there is no Satan's Army.... just people who have different ideas of right and wrong. Depending upon where you are on the "spiritual" evolutionary chart.... everybody has a different idea of what is appropriate behavior and different ways of conceptualizing The Universe. Any future wars would be better off in the name of battling "stupidity" (flawed unfair logic) rather than The Devil. The only reason the concept of Satan even exists is because our original societies by definition had nothing but the Earth's first souls and hence all had sociopathic personality disorders. As a result, their "black and white thinking" was the only way they could comprehend the licentious behavior that surrounded them (it was so twisted that the punishment FOR EVERYTHING was death). Certainly their loving God couldn't have caused or allowed this pervasive mayhem.... that's way too confusing for a "youngster". It must be a malevolent entity's doing (Satan).

This bad behavior was then perpetuated back and forth all in the name of fighting EVIL. Individuals never ever saw themselves as evil, it was always the “other” person. Clearly, most believe bad behavior IS acceptable and therefore “good” if one is defending God. This is a corollary to the statement: “one man’s terrorist is another man’s freedom fighter”. As long as the concept of “evil” (or Satan) exists, the longer bad behavior will be justified in its usage. When self-righteous people behave badly towards others they simply justify it by saying “they had it coming”. Whereas, if their enemy behaves THE EXACT SAME WAY towards them, well then ”they must be evil for acting that way”. We see a little of this type of logic during the Jan 2009 earthquake in Haiti. The evangelist Pat Robertson in no uncertain terms stated that this unthinkable event was a result of Haiti’s “pact with the Devil”. But, I think we all can agree if a similar circumstance occurred to him, he would probably explain it as God pruning or growing him. Evangelicals and other “extremists” tend to believe that if something good happens to them, it was duly deserved by “The Power of God” but If something good happens to their enemy, it was due to “The Power of Satan”. This type of logic makes me want to throw myself into traffic.

This unevolved thinking and behavior continues to this day in many of the ORIGINAL CULTURES (like the Middle East), and we have (believe it or not) “the lack of ADD” to thank for it. The original ancient cultures with their inordinate amount of young souls initially behaved barbarically (sociopath like) and supremely controlling (narcissistic like). But as the years passed, the attention deficits emigrated away leaving a propensity towards the maintenance of “traditional” behavior (see chapter Adrenaline Begets The West). DESPITE the existence of a maturing SOUL pool…. these ancient cultures remained barbaric out of TRADITION. The Middle Eastern culture for example continues to maintain a barbaric penal/retribution code (beheadings) as well as a controlling nature towards women as a direct result of these traditional non-extinguished vestigial codes of conduct. If my soul evolution theory is correct though, with time and further maturation of Earth’s souls, I think all fascist (controlling) governments will eventually become antiquated and philosophically shunned. It will become a dark remnant of humanity that became ossified just as did the sociopathic need for “human sacrifices” to appease the gods.

“Black and white” thinking (seeing others in only good OR bad terms) is seen in young children AND young souls. It identifies and describes other people (or deities) in SIMPLE terms that aren’t ambiguous for a young soul (but aren’t realistic either). You will notice this “good/bad” correlate in children’s Saturday morning programming. Cartoons frequently revolve around the concepts of fantasy and "good vs evil". Nowadays, we as a country (and planet) are technically more "evolved" by the passage of time but we still see this inability for many in the population to comprehend others (or the Universe) in a balanced and realistic color of "grey". There are still many young souls out there (personally, I think God must occasionally make and add new souls to the mix). The perception of Bill Belichick and The New England Patriots organization is a good example. Society couldn't wait to jump on the bandwagon during the 2001 "post 9/11" campaign and to a lesser degree the undefeated regular season of 2007. Primitively, I think people perceive strong, talented and powerful people as personal heroes, which in a strange way makes them feel protected, safe and important themselves. But as soon as THEIR OWN ego unconsciously grows weary of feeling "less than" (by The Patriots constantly winning) .... they seize any moment to tear down that hero to the status of a villain in order to psychologically "level the playing field" as seen in the "Spy-Gate" or "Deflate-Gate" affairs. It happens all the time in the tabloids too. One week a tabloid will exalt a star....then the next week snuff he/she out. Unfortunately, the whole dynamic exists because young souled people just can't accept the fact that good people can have bad qualities, and bad people can have good qualities (good/bad ideation). The take home lesson here is that the first person who has the unconscious need to put you on a pedestal, will probably be the first person who has the unconscious need to rip you off that pedestal.

Now enters the classic "us against them" mentality seen in social psychology. It effectively states, " I'm a good person, I don't like you, so that must make you bad and therefore I am justified to hate you". We see these self-justified divisions in rival gangs, fans of sports teams, families (like The Mafia) and rival schools. These "Good versus Bad" and "us against them" mentalities morphed together to spawn The concept of Good versus Evil. Young souls also found it impossible to comprehend that the very God that was supposed to be watching over them, actually caused their trials. The idea that The Devil imposed "ill will" upon us was much more comforting, as it completely vindicated our "Good God" from any "bad behavior" perpetrated against the ones He allegedly should love. So there you have it, the concept of "The Devil" was the perfect human solution to deal with our spiritual pains as well as our social ones. It truly is the penultimate of all defense mechanisms (a fabricated and unconscious process that assists us to cope with the daily pains of life).

Now that we have figured out how "good vs evil" originated, our discussion really can't advance unless we figure out the "mechanism of action" of how we are growing out of it. The idea of multiple lives (a soul progression theory) needs an algorithm to demonstrate how "logic" (more specifically "emotional logic") is encoded, maintained and carried through from life to life. It has been demonstrated in research that emotional arousal promotes strong memories (Joseph LeDoux....Scholarpedia...Emotional Memory Footnote 1). Now we know why we as humans have emotions.... they aid in the learning process from the painful impressions that a lesson of right vs. wrong confers. For instance, if you kill someone, you more than likely will be put in prison and learn from a life of seclusion and a painful loss of freedom as to how poor the choice was. This painful/emotional/"implicit memory", in my opinion, is what is carried from life to life. It is not the "explicit" memory of how to tie your shoe (mediated by the hippocampus). Clearly, we need to learn to tie our shoes each and every time we have a new life. I theorize that this implicit/emotional learning is mediated by the amygdala (Chart 1), a structure located close to the hippocampus in the medial temporal lobe of the brain. This location is not surprising at all. Norman Geschwind for years identified the temporal lobe as "the spiritual center" of the brain. His primary proof being that temporal lobe epilepsy is manifested by hyper graphia (excessive need to write) and hyper-religiosity (a preoccupation with spirituality). Similarly, Michael Persinger has asserted that changes in ambient electromagnetism can create a temporal lobe seizure which can produce paranormal experiences including hallucinations of ghosts. This idea of magnetism affecting our brains should not be too farfetched at this point in the book. In "The Sun of God" chapter we learned that magnetism may also affect our brain in buying and selling of the stock market.

As an aside, Alzheimer's disease will ravage the hippocampus (explicit memory...recognition of who a person is), but seems to be less initially destructive to the amygdala (the emotion they feel when they see the face of a loved one whom they don't recognize) (Footnote 2). That makes some sense to me if in fact the amygdala is actually a "spiritual" center. I hope that brings some comfort to those who are dealing with the painful experience of not having a loved one recognize them due to this cruel illness. Although they don't recognize you, they still may feel close. I can't help but think the pain of Alzheimer's is not so much a painful "spiritual lesson" of pain tolerance for the patient, as it is for their loved ones. I also wonder if the so called "life review" that some near death experiences chronicle is actually a rogue discharge involving emotionally charged remembrances from the amygdala. A reel that might be brought with and "sorted out" in the afterlife.

Just because the temporal lobe is seemingly responsible for the subjective experiences of the paranormal and spirituality.... does this actually mean that a spirit world with ghosts exists? According to my theory......yes, it may be the real deal! Between the multiple lives we endure on Earth.... what happens to our soul that awaits its next human life incarnation? I can't really say specifically, but given the plethora of ghost sightings and imaging supporting its existence, I would say part of a soul's "inter-life experience" might be a "ghost". But that's not the important part. As I hopefully have disproven the existence of evil people, I also will disprove the existence of "evil "ghosts. Remember, just as a YOUNG soul (personality disorder) can act horribly and be up to no good in the flesh, it can and will act the same way as a ghost. Another way of putting it is if the person had a malevolent PERSONALITY in real life....his/her ghost will be that way too. The ghost brings the personality disorder (spiritual deficiency) with it. If the person before was a sociopath...it will probably have significant sociopathic behavior as a ghost (domination, lying, scare tactics). There are no evil ghosts.... just unevolved ones. But remember, if the person's preceding life was manifested by brutish obnoxious behavior generated by a biological condition (ADD, bipolar, schizophrenia), the ghost will not have such behavioral vulnerabilities. It doesn't have a brain therefore it doesn't have aberrant brain chemicals. Simply put, ghosts seem to be people without bodies.

Personality disorders represent one of my Four Horsemen of the Apocalypse...."Flawed Logic"....a fundamental inability to discern right versus wrong as typically seen by youthful humans and youthful souls. It does not however include my other Horseman "Substance Abuse", which is seen in my ADD and bipolar sections. Although literature states personality disorders do have a high rate of substance abuse...I maintain this is inaccurate and represents the self-medication of a co-occurring Axis I condition. Given my multiple-lives theory, biological substances would not be perpetually abused by personality disorders as there is no biological substrate causing it. They "self-medicate" instead with the use of maladaptive primitive defense mechanisms (such as denial, projection and reaction formation) which help "numb" their reality.

As far as I'm concerned…the only "treatment" for sociopaths is prison. Just as you would send a child to their room to think through their behavior… the same concept holds true for the young souled sociopath. Prison is an appropriate atmosphere for a personality disorder to learn life's most basic lessons as it is structured, relatively distraction free and predictable…. the way a newborns learning environment should be. All other personality disorders are best treated in psychotherapy as long as they are not homicidal, suicidal or breaking any laws. Psychotherapy for personality disorders is helpful in that it provides a sense of support while these young souls gently discover reality while they stumble through life. The key is, one needs to work with a psychotherapist who also DOESN'T have a personality disorder, otherwise it's another tragic case of the blind leading the blind.

Chart 1

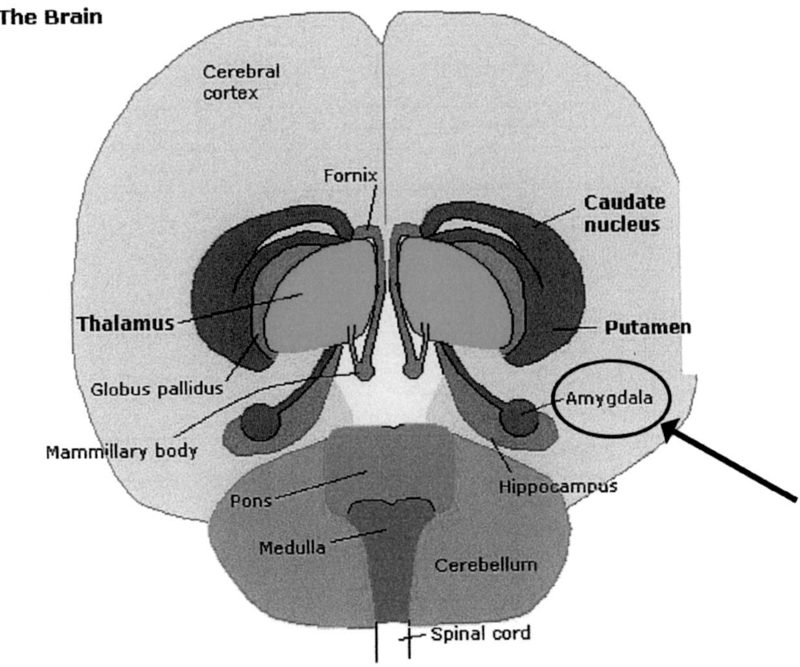

The brain as viewed from the underside and front. The thalamus and Corpus Striatum (Putamen, caudate and amygdala) have been splayed out to show detail.

Human brain in the coronal orientation. Amygdala is shown.

Original uploader of gif version was RobinH at en.wikibooks - this is Image:Constudoverbrain.gif from Commons, cropped and resaved in PNG format

Diagram showing locations of several important parts of the human brain, as viewed from the front.

6+6+6=18 1+8=9

Chapter 9

APOCALESCENCE

A Psychiatric Apocalypse implies that the battles and pains we wage here on Earth are not sent by Satan or an Anti-Christ (or Islamic Dajjal), but rather The Universe (or God) through other means. I have spent time spelling out the chemical, "spiritual" and human deficiencies that WE ALL have, which in aggregate, conspire to bring us pain. This pain however confers an emotional (amygdaloid) logic and maturity which ultimately eeeks us closer to approximating Gods Intelligence (but not necessarily His image). If God exists, He must be all about logic. If you are at all philosophical or versed in science, it is a supreme logic which must have been employed to make all the workings of The Universe. From the proper valencing of atoms, to the complex life promoting enzymatic reactions in the human body, to the physics required for galactic stability.... it's all about logic and brilliance. One might say an infinite logic would need an infinite processing unit.... I think that may be Space. Space is God's "brain". Many say God is all about love......but emotions like love only cloud logic. That's why Psychiatric "emotional" patients don't behave properly.... their emotions cloud their judgment whether it be depression, hate, irritability, mania or love. The bipolar poles of manic depression, whether high or low, create a lot of problems and this exemplifies the point. Furthermore, I've been burned by love, but never by being smart.

Love, though glamorized as being "forever" and Godly, is simply a human emotion. Its euphoric effect lights up the pleasure centers of the brain (the ventral tegmental area and medial caudate nucleus) no differently than cocaine (Footnote 1). People strive for love because it is a high. The Jerry Springer show taught me everything I needed to know about love. Jerry asks the guest why she puts up with her husband's deceit, abuse, lying and infidelity. Her response is usually.... (ok everybody, say it out loud because I want to be able to hear it) .... she says, "because I love him". She sounds like a "crack" junky who won't change her bad habit despite the problems it brings. Love fundamentally makes us put up with things that we wouldn't otherwise put up with. That's why parents were designed to love their kids so much. Aside from the feel-good feeling you receive by loving them....

you don't get a whole lot back in those younger years. Love is antithetical to logic, thus it is of no use in the basic creative process of The Universe. However it plays a huge role in humanity....it provides social glue. It also is a powerful area for learning as I will discuss.

Although emotions cloud our ability to reason, humans NEED THESE EMOTIONS to help consolidate our learning. God doesn't need emotions though.... He's already smart. So much for the concept of "God loves us" ......if He doesn't have emotions...He doesn't possess love either. If we love someone, we don't like to see them in pain (because it brings us pain). There however is so much pain on the Earth (intentionally), that I can't imagine God loves us...it would make Him too miserable to be functional. If you have ever seen anyone you love in pain.... you know the impression it leaves. The price you pay for love is pain.... whether it is from seeing someone we love in pain or actually losing something we love. It's a metaphor for most of life: "with every high comes a hangover". The "high" is love....and the "hangover" is love lost. This pain however serves as a teaching tool to "be careful". It's no different than the pain we feel when we touch a hot stove. Once we erroneously touch it, we will make adjustments in the future. Every good night of drinking is usually followed by a tough day. It's all the same thing. But this "operant conditioning" or "learning" only works if you feel the pain the lesson confers. If you tend to avoid pain, deny it, or use multiple defense mechanisms to dilute it, you are doomed to go through the same lesson over and over until you get it right. In order to learn from pain, you therefore need to feel it.

God has a myriad of alluring "booby traps" in life and they all serve as highly effective breeding grounds for learning. So once again I ask... how does Satan fit in? From what I can tell, God seems quite comfortable endeavoring all of His own stunts. Now, if this is the case, where does this leave us with the accurateness of Religious Doctrine? If Satan doesn't exist, does this also mean that Religious Doctrine such as The Old and New Testaments and Qur'an are frauds? I think the answer is yes and no. ALL these doctrines in my opinion are supernatural books and inspired by God. They have a purpose, but just not what you think. He wanted them FLAWED this way FOR NOW (I'll explain shortly). He interestingly does put some useful advice in them to keep the reader coming back for more (such as "thou shall not steal" ...good advice). In this publication, I'll frequently discredit parts of the Bible and endorse other parts. It's not in an attempt to contradict myself, but rather to highlight the parts that actually make sense, elaborate on unclear topics and pose conjecture as to how The Universe "blue prints" life. The Chairman of the Board of any private company always gets what he wants and God is no exception. He wanted our Religious Doctrine confusing because it forces us to think. The other possibility for the etiology of doctrine is that there is no God at all, and what we have here is an example of early man "gone wild" with a charcoal and parchment.

An excellent contemporary example of "confusion" and the mixed messages fostered by "The Universe" is former Florida Gators/NFL Quarterback Tim Tebow. He is the past Collegiate Heisman Trophy winner well known for his Christian pro-life stance as seen in his "Big Game" Commercial (legally I'm not allowed to say The S-word), and the Bible scriptures etched in his eye black. People seemed to have flocked to him as a defender of God's providence for his outspoken Christian views. People are like that.... if you speak the right words...their guards go down and they are putty in your hands. Did you know that during the college scouting Combine (where players are evaluated by all the NFL teams), Tim ran one of the more important drills in exactly 6.66 sec (Footnote 2)? One couldn't invent or replicate that demonic time if you tried. So then I ask....do we still put him on a pedestal or do we condemn him to hell? This is a highly confusing question for the "black and white" thinker. His jersey number was also 15 (1+5=6) and he is a left hander! (see Adrenaline Begets the West Chapter). The Universe's mixed messages, as seen with Tim Tebow, happen all of the time. Therefore, the onus is upon each individual to not fall for sentimental rhetoric or "the easy conclusion". All I can say is that The Universe clearly has a sense of humor if you are disciplined enough to look for it.

Supporting the idea that our human Religious Doctrines leave something to be desired is a list below of some of the more memorable doctrine contradictions. Many scholars or zealots will claim that these excerpts have further interpretations associated with them.... but I would say in response that God should know we are all pea brains compared to Him. As a result, anything too ornate, convoluted, complicated, symbolic, ambiguous, contradictory or requiring interpretation probably won't be useful. In fact, if the various doctrines were true instruction manuals, He would have been better off communicating them in binary. I consider myself a commoner (but educated) and part of God's alleged "target audience". If my head spins with confusion while reading these excerpts...I would imagine any other logical persons would too. If it doesn't spin after reading these follies, I'm guessing you otherwise have some invested interest in believing it's true. The following contradictions are inexcusable UNLESS of course Religious Doctrines were intentionally designed ambiguously by God to emphasize the point: "I gave you a brain now use it!". For the record, I've read and listened to much of the Bible in sections, but never from beginning to end. I've not read The Qur'an other than noteworthy topics of interest. But in my defense, I don't need 100 hours with a patient to know if they aren't thinking clearly.... just an hour.

1) Old Testament (King James Version)

Regarding Killing.

Exodus 20:13 Thou Shall not Kill.

Deuteronomy 13:15 Thou Shall surely smite the inhabitants of that city with the edge of the sword, destroying it utterly, and all that is therein, and the cattle thereof, with the edge of the sword.

Regarding Seeing God:

Exodus 33:20 And He said, Thou Regarding humility: canst not see my face: for there shall no man see me, and live.

Exodus 3:16 Go, and gather the elders of Israel together, and say unto them, The Lord God of your fathers, The God of Abraham, of Isaac, and of Jacob, appeared unto me, saying, I have surely visited you, and seen that which is done to you in Egypt.

Regarding Humility:

Psalm 58:10-11 The Righteous shall rejoice when he sees vengeance.

Proverbs 24:16-18 Do not rejoice when your enemy falls or stumbles.

Regarding the nature of God:

Proverbs 12:2 A good man obtaineth favour of the Lord but a man of wicked devices will be condemned.

Hebrews 12:6 For whom the Lord loveth he chasteneth, and scourgeth every son whom He receiveth.

2) New and Old Testament (King James Version) ....

Regarding the Nature of God:

Romans 15:33 Now the God of peace be with you all. Amen.

Exodus 15:3 The Lord is a Man of War: the Lord is His name

3) New Testament

Regarding Combat:

Matthew 5:39 But I say unto you, that ye resist no evil: but whoever shall smite thee on thy right cheek, turn to him the other also.

Luke 19:27 But those mine enemies, which would not that I should reign over them, bring hither, and slay them before me.

Regarding Judging:

John 12:47 And if any man hear my words, and believe not, I judge him not: for I came not to judge the world but to save it.

John 9:39 And Jesus said; For Judgment I have come into this world.....

Regarding Alcohol:

Romans 14: 21 It is good neither to eat flesh or drink wine, nor anything whereby thy brother stumbleth, or is offended, or is made weak.

John 2 1-11 A story of how Jesus turns water into wine at a wedding reception.

4)Qur'an

Regarding Religious Violence:

Qur'an 2:256 There is no Compulsion in Religion.

Qur'an 47:4 When you meet the unbelievers in the Jihad, strike off their heads....

Regarding Christians:

Surah 60:13 Do not be friendly with the disbelievers; they are all Allah's enemies.

Surah 5: 82 Says closest in friendships are Christians.

Regarding Alcohol:

Surah 76 21-22 ...Allah will give everyone to drink a pure Holy wine (Sharaban Tahura); these will be rewards for the dwellers of Islamic Paradise.

Surah 5:90 Says wine is handiwork of Satan.

No wonder everyone is confused. These so-called "life's principles" are positioned in opposition and undoubtedly promote the same outcome as an elaborate drinking game. Based on the previous contradictions, Religious Doctrine really ONLY seems to be perfect according to itself. The authors of these texts were some of the first people on the planet and by definition young souls. Remember what I said earlier, psychotherapy instruction with a therapist who has a personality disorder (a young soul) is the equivalent of the blind leading the blind. These young souled authors are acting like two year olds.... preoccupied with Good/Bad ideation (God vs Satan) and fraught with contradiction. Like a 2-year-old, metaphorically speaking, these authors don't comprehend that they can't play indoors AND play outdoors simultaneously (see Born as a Beast age 2 developmental chart). In keeping with behavior of a youngster, Religious Doctrine is also highly controlling and unfair (especially to women). I think anyone would agree that all of the major doctrines are supposed to be "instruction manuals" for their respective religions. However, under no circumstances, should a good instruction manual be vague, interpretable, use "symbols", or be ambiguous. It just contributes to more chaos and dysfunction than we already have. And if they were truly good instruction manuals and prophetic.... where are the sections on not smoking, on exercising regularly, and the prophecy that unhealthy "plagues" such as crystal methamphetamine and pedophiliac clergy would come to pass? Smoking kills 50 people per hour and it's nowhere to be found? But the good news though is that it does mandate that we don't work on Sundays...... ludicrous. I find it interesting that we demand logical and sensible behavior from our children, but yet when it comes to scripture, all logic goes out the window. Most people will state that "faith" is the key to overcoming these doubts about the legitimacy of scripture, but the concept of "faith" is what inspired the hi-jackers on 9/11 to perform their deadly deeds to begin with.

God is smart though. I don't think He's going to give away ALL the secrets of life in a textbook, and frankly all of the realities of life wouldn't make sense to us even if He did. It's the equivalent of trying to teach a 3-year-old to manage a Tech Company R and D meeting which would require knowledge and behavior beyond his/her developmental capabilities. The purpose of life is to LEARN your knowledge, not to be told it (and that includes this book too!). Again, the most painful emotional experience you ever had is probably the most important lesson you have ever learned. I maintain life is a better teacher than a book. Even worse, Religious Doctrine can be just another painful learning trap for the dependent personality who searches to be told what to do. For as many people who have been inspired by it, there probably have been just as many who had to learn the hard way that doctrine and life don't always align nicely. As a Psychiatrist, I am convinced homosexuality is not a choice (who would choose it?), but yet decent humble people who are homosexual are plagued by the guilt of defying The Bible daily. What a waste of energy that is. Another example is former members of cults. They are usually well meaning souls who are trying to understand life and God, but easily twisted scriptures at the hands of a hyper-religious manic depressive (who is also a sociopath or narcissist) go onto take advantage of their naivety and ruin their lives (as possibly seen in the Jeffrey Lundgren, Warren Jeffs and FLDS cults for example). It just goes to show, having good intentions really doesn't amount to much if your faulty reasoning results in bad decisions. We all glorify youth as "the age of innocence". However, another word for "innocent" is "naïve", and another word for "naïve" is "stupid". As a result, very good people can find themselves in tough times if there is a lesson to be gleaned from their flawed logic (such as involvement in a cult or nonsensical religion). That's why bad things happen to good people.... it's all in the name of personal spiritual growth. I'm guessing that IF God "allowed" (or even instigated) torture to His Son, it probably served as a lesson to Christ too. And if God was "pleased" with the pain inflicted upon His Son (Isaiah 53:10), why is it so much of a stretch that pain on Earth pleases Him too? He makes animals eat other animals in the wild, so I'm not quite sure He operates out of sentimentality. Anything goes if there is something to be learned. Some may see it as Divine child abuse.... but unfortunately for all of us its more useful than that.

On Earth you earn your knowledge of common sense through suffering. The painful learning process is an Earthly consequence of your faulty thinking and decisions for the most part. When we love someone, we don't like to see them in pain. Parent's often "shelter" their children from discomfort because they don't like to see their kids uncomfortable (it's a natural instinct). But this isn't really helping them. Children need a little discomfort as an "immunization" against future adult difficulties. Another example of "pain avoidance" is seen in "The Secret". "The Secret" was originally a film that tried to illustrate that thinking positive thoughts "attracted" positive and desired outcomes. The idea that we can somehow attract joy into our lives makes no sense if my theory stands as correct. Bad things WILL happen to you but it's for your own good and growth. As they say ...."it's not happening TO you, it's happening FOR you". "The Secret" reminds me of a bunch of children at dinner demanding ice cream and cake as sustenance. Not only will these food stuffs not allow you to grow properly, but they will also probably make you sick. I don't know whatever happened to the popularity of "The Secret", but I'm guessing a lot of people wanted their money back during the painful Recession of 2007-2010. "The Secret "won't work because pain neurologically imparts more of an impression on the amygdala than joy (Damage to The amygdala impairs fear conditioning...Scholarpedia "Amygdala" Footnote 3).

Nobody ever learned or matured from getting exactly what they wanted, and that's easily identified in people who have been pampered especially in youth. People who demand pleasure or simply have no tolerance for pain are in for a frustrating life. Humans in general (but especially personality disorders) are notorious for the avoidance of pain as manifested by the primitive defense mechanisms that they use. For example, if you are in denial that your husband is cheating, it is sure to come out in unconscious anxiety which in turn will cause you to over-eat, which in turn will make you fat, and then you have a whole new set of problems on your hands. I could name hundreds more of these similar "trickle down" scenarios. The same applies to prayer as well. Giving thanks in prayer seems reasonable, but to think God has no idea what is going on and somehow needs our advice makes no sense. Who's smarter anyway.... The Being who manages the Multiverse or the ding dong who just pushed "reply all" by mistake? Isn't prayer just another way of being controlling? The fact is, many good things have happened to you that you never prayed for, and many bad things have continued to happen to you despite your prayers. If something needs to be fixed.... use your God given brain to think your way through it. Though not perfect, think of your brain as your Bible (but for God's sakes learn from your mistakes or it doesn't work).

There however is and will continue to be pain that you never deserved, such as natural disaster, illness or loss of a loved one. Despite not deserving it, you are still going to have that confrontation. Unfortunately, it all serves to shape and mature us and it's fair game. The Apocalypse allegedly will have this type of pain. The adage "that which does not kill you makes you stronger" comes to mind. No person or book can teach you the highly maturing "amygdaloid" type emotional learning that comes from these tribulations of everyday life. I'll repeat, Life is the best teacher. A new patient once asked me "what life was" ....and my only truthful response was "pain and anger management in the pursuit of figuring out right vs. wrong". If my memory serves me correctly, I don't think she came back for a follow up visit.

The original scriptures were sufficient for where we all were as young souls over the last several thousand years. God wanted it this way because that is all we were capable of comprehending. But God also knew that our souls would COLLECTIVELY grow older through multiple passings of reincarnated lives. This would eventually require a NEW and more age appropriate dialogue......enter The Apocalypse (as predicted in Christian, Mayan, Hindu, Hopi Indian and Egyptian Prophecy). Or what I like to call: Apocalescence. The time in our collective evolution where "The Age of Lawlessness" /self-gratification (our first lives as sociopaths), "The Age of Self Glorification"/ self-centeredness (our middle lives as narcissists), and "The Age of Intolerance" (our later lives as dependents) are as a COLLECTIVE MAJORITY in our past. Roughly 2000 years after The Bible's authorship, we are NOW old enough to "get it". It took a few generations but it finally happened. Think of the Apocalypse as a GRADUATION from childhood into adulthood and commencement STARTS on Dec 21, 2012 (numerically...12/21/2012 adds to "11" [1+2+2+1+2+0+1+2=11].... the number of "Revelation"). It is a deliverance TO fair play, reasonability (reality) and tolerance towards one another. It is an "unveiling" of truth as described by the early Greeks. No more magical thinking that "repentance" somehow miraculously gets you "a pass" for your transgressions. No more assigning your neighbor as "evil" just because they are different or a New England Patriots fan. No wonder "reality shows" are craved now in the "end days", we as a species are evolving naturally out of scripted fiction (fantasy) and into fact (reality). It's almost as if we are in the midst of a profound evolutionary upgrade in which the idea of fiction is somewhat insulting to our intelligence. The age of Apocalescence therefore means we collectively no longer need to subscribe to any more magical thinking or good/bad ideation as believed by the younger souls. The concept of Santa Clause is appropriate at an earlier age…but wouldn't we all agree it's kind of creepy and maladaptive at later ones? Santa's idea of being "naughty or nice" is highly simplistic and doesn't tell the whole story does it? I guess one could say that just like the concept of Santa served a purpose for a child, so did the concept of The Devil for a young souled society. Now that I'm looking at it..."Santa" is a spelling jumble of "Satan" …. how perfectly appropriate. The myth of Satan has reached its expiration date and if my theory of soul evolution is correct, many of you have already suspected this for some time now. In fact, if you subscribe to the concept of "karma" or "God doesn't give you more than you can handle" …. you are automatically disqualified from believing in The Devil. Both beliefs describe the USE-FULNESS of pain in The Universe.

This modern-day Greek is trying to accomplish what my ancient Greek progenitors accomplished many millennia ago….integration through observation. Let's investigate the planet Venus for a moment. Both Venus and the Earth rotate around The Sun but at different angles and different speeds (Chart 1). As a result, there is a time in its revolving cycle that Venus can only be seen in the morning (The Morning Star) and times when it can only be seen in the evening (The Evening Star) (Chart 2). Prior to Pythagoras, scientists believed that what we now know as Venus was actually two different celestial bodies. But Pythagoras (a Greek mathematician) proved that they were one in the same. Not too dissimilar from my attempts to unify "good and evil". The Mayans used to worship Venus and its pattern of orbit. The scientific knowledge of this and other celestial occurrences has contributed to the assignment of the date of the start of the The Apocalypse as 12/21/2012. (Astronomically, it was the day the Sun aligned with the center of the Milky Way galaxy forming a "cross" …this happens every 1 out of 26,000 years). Christianity however condemned this pagan activity of planetary worship as occult "devil worship". It was likened to worshipping a false idol (3rd commandment). Consequently, Venus was seen demonically. Did you know Satan is known as "The Angel of The Morningstar" due to Venus's "brilliance" in the morning sky (Lucipher = Bearer of Light)? Did you know that the complete orbit of Venus is divided up into conjunctions divided by sixteen "36 Day" segments? If one adds all the numbers between 1 and 36 it equals 666 (like the roulette wheel in Chapter 2). And finally, did you know that the pattern of Venus's orbit relative to Earth forms a pentagram (a common shape associated with Devil worship) (Chart 3)? Don't forget however it was God who put this Grand Celestial/ Astrological Plan together not Satan: "In the beginning.... God created the Heavens and The Earth". I kept this in mind when Venus eclipsed The Sun on exactly 6/6/2012. "The Devil" CROSSing "The Sun (Son)" on 6/6 (see cover of this e book)....bravo maestro!

The CEO of The Universe knew exactly what He was doing with similar ironies in the 2012 sporting world as well. SB "Big Game" XLVII, which represented the 2012 season, pitted two teams whose coaches were brothers ......Jim and John Harbaugh. Matthew 01-21 specifically alludes to "brother against brother" in the so-called "End of Days". In The National Hockey league, The 2012 Stanley Cup pairing was The New Jersey DEVILS vs The Los Angeles KINGS (The King of Kings = Jesus). Thus: The Devil vs. Jesus. In the 2012 National Basketball League Final...the pairing was The Miami Heat (heat comes from Hell) versus The Oklahoma Thunder (thunder comes from Heaven). Thus: Heaven vs. Hell. Who knew He had a penchant for sports? Major League Baseball however was conspicuously left out of this 2012 highlight reel (Big Guy apparently not a baseball fan). I can only imagine all the planning and energy that it takes to actually pull all that off. I'm guessing, amongst other things, He has some extra time on His hands. The whole idea of "celestial wars" of "good battling evil" occurring while God has all this extra energy to "punk us" is really quite laughable. He had so much extra time that in 2012, He also saw to it that a snake (symbolic of Satan) had an IMMACULATE CONCEPTION producing SIX snakes at The Louisville Zoo (Chart 4). I don't know about you, but it kind of sounds like He's "dissing" his own Son on that one. Or, please recall the events of October 14, 2012, when Felix Baumgautner jumped from Space. His sponsor was Red Bull energy drinks. Did you know the logo for Red Bull is a "red bull" which looks EXACTLY like Satan (Chart 5)? Did you get it yet? It's a reenactment of Satan falling from The Heavens in the year of The Apocalypse! And then in a true testimony of how much extra time He has to burn, the very day that Man was breaking the sound barrier, the Space Shuttle Endeavor was moving at a snail's pace through the streets of Los Angeles (ANGEL) to its new home at the California Science Center.

The Universe just might have awesome plans for all of us. On that day, in an epic act of paradox, mankind switched places with a rocket.

He had further given us similar evidence of His prankster nature two years prior on Jan 12 2010. I find it ironic (but Pat Robertson probably doesn't as per last chapter "Born as a Beast) that an Apocalyptic Earthquake by anyone's standard occurred in Haiti. Haiti is a phonetic identical to the word "Hades" (another word for Hell) and it occurred 16 miles away from Port-Au-Prince (The Devil is "The Prince Of Darkness"). Undoubtedly this walloping earthquake is considered an "End of Days" event and these little "reminders" grab our attention if we know what to look for. The bottom line is, if you keep your eyes open, you will see Gods finger-prints everywhere, no matter how seemingly insignificant the matter might be. He leaves mixed messages galore to confuse those who only parcel life into black and white thinking……these are important life's lessons wrapped in well calculated satire. How He does it is amazing…… I literally have problems just getting out of bed in the morning.

So, if there is no Satan, then logically there is probably no Hell either. Just like "who needs Satan when we have God performing all of His own stunts"….I also ask, "who needs Hell when we have Earth?". In my opinion, the best way to torture a soul is to put it in flesh and that's what we have here on Earth. It is here where all the painful learning occurs. From illness, to loss, to poverty….all the pain is here. The punishment for your "sins" is here as well. Your "bad deeds" on Earth will be punished on Earth. If you drink excessively…you are not going to hell…you are going to get a DUI or alcoholic cirrhosis of the liver or make any series of bad intoxicated decisions. If you are in self-inflicted terminal debt….you aren't going to Hell, you simply have your credit revoked here on Earth which in turn causes bankruptcy and a withdrawal of future monetary freedom. If you steal… you aren't going to Hell……you are probably going to prison where you have no freedom and unspeakable things happen to you.

Sometimes I think God simply sees Earth as a gigantic episode of "Jackass"...where people wonder how they found themselves in pain after they electively decided to do something stupid like shoot a bean-bag into their abdomen for amusement (from an episode of "Jackass: The Movie"). But remember…these poorly thought out decisions are typically from four sources...mental illness, substance abuse, hormones and flawed logic (my Four Horsemen). All of which are either directly or indirectly from God's creation. So, it would follow, God doesn't hate sin, He pretty much expects it but unfortunately it is you and I who have to pay the Earthly price for it. And then, there is the issue of suicide. In my opinion, most people who commit suicide are highly Psychiatric and for the most part are not thinking properly. As mentioned, our brain is from God and so are our aberrant brain chemicals. I can't imagine God punishes people for "spilling the milk" after He has poured it so close to the rim. My guess is...the departed soul gets right back into line for another go of it. However, if you don't want to have an identical struggle again in the next lifetime, get it taken care now. Pay now or pay later.

So....is just about everyone maximally offended yet? Is there any sacred cow left standing? I think there is a little something special to offend everyone in this book, but such is the battle with newness. The birthing struggle is painful but don't blame me....I'm just commenting on what I see given the fact that I'm in the business of fixing the organ that approximates the soul. I'm not saying my postulations are fool-proof either. Everyone should raise an eyebrow to any new concept that sounds preposterous such as multiple lives. Truth be told, the most logical explanation for The Universe is that there is no God. He chose to be invisible, I don't think He really cares if we do or do not think He exists (as long as we behave appropriately). The only problem however, is that there really doesn't appear to be a consensus estimate of what constitutes "appropriate" behavior. The only reason I personally believe in God is that, from my observations, He conceptually exists similarly to a "Black Hole". We can't see a Black Hole (its black), but we know it's there based upon its effects and perturbations on the other things around it. I guess you could call it an existence "by proxy". Although I don't agree with atheists, I do credit them for at least being honest with themselves and the people around them despite having an unpopular belief. There is nothing more self-deluded than someone who says they believe in an "accounting system" but behaves otherwise.

I expect that many people will be angered by this book because it will attempt to change their core beliefs. Our core beliefs are those beliefs that define and buoy up our sense of self...... so this is to be expected. We as humans are quite predictable and pleasure seeking. We gravitate towards concepts of love and God, not because they make sense, but because they make us feel euphoric and powerful. Suggesting that love is strictly a human emotion, and that God really doesn't love us (but rather has invested interest in us) will leave a religious junky looking like an addict without a fix. This is why religion is such a touchy and emotional topic for many. Don't mess with an addicts buzz…they get angry! The conviction that God loves us is simply anesthesia for the masses. We as humans have much more of a need TO BE loved than He has the need TO love.

In addition to the concept of God and love, the non-existence of Satan is also a buzz-kill for many too. When confronted with this, the stout believers of evil feel a crisis of personal righteousness and confidence….it's one less entity to condemn, therefore a crushing defeat to their sense of superiority. These tend to be the same people who believe that when something bad happens to them…..God is testing them........but if something bad happens to someone else, it's God doling out a punishment. People have this need for self-exaltation at the expense of others. All I can say to that is; the greatest lessons of life revolve around humility….so strap yourself in.

Oh…and before I forget….my Sixth Sense hasn't clued me in that I'm an Anti-Christ either. I'm writing this book to make adjustments to my own life….the 2008-2009 recession made changes for me as it did everyone else. But given my highly controversial beliefs, I did take the time to research the criteria to be an Anti-Christ and I did get a kick out of this reading from Nostradamus Century 6 Quatrain 33 in reference to Alus ("Ali in The US" ….. a supposed antichrist….Ali-apoulios?)(Chart 6....John Hogue):

> His hand through the bloody Alus,
>
> He will be unable to protect himself by sea:
>
> Between two rivers he will fear the military hand,
>
> The black and angry one will make him repent it.

"Dr. Apocalypse" also sang in the acapella group known as The Beelzebubs and worked as a "bouncer" in Babylon, New York (Babylon: symbolic of "evil"). As far as I know, those associations, and my love for heavy metal music, constitute my only alleged kinship with Satan. I'd be stunned to think a small-town shrink was destined to "steal, kill and destroy" as referenced to the Antichrist in John 10:10.

6 is the number of man (please see number chart)….not Satan. Man was created on the 6th Day. The carbon atom is the centerpiece of life's existence on Earth: 6 neutrons/6 protons/6 electrons. We act like Beasts be-

cause of our God given limitations....especially when it comes to the most complicated system known to man....The Brain. The Apocalyptic battles that we wage here on Earth are not with Satan, but with God's Nature and ourselves. If you must believe in Satan,...then so be it....Satan is you. It's the way God intended.

Chart 1

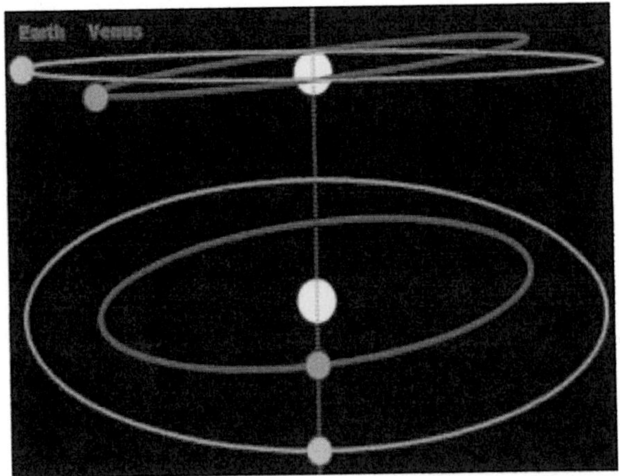

Diagram of transits of Venus and the angle between the orbital planes of Venus and Earth

Chart 2

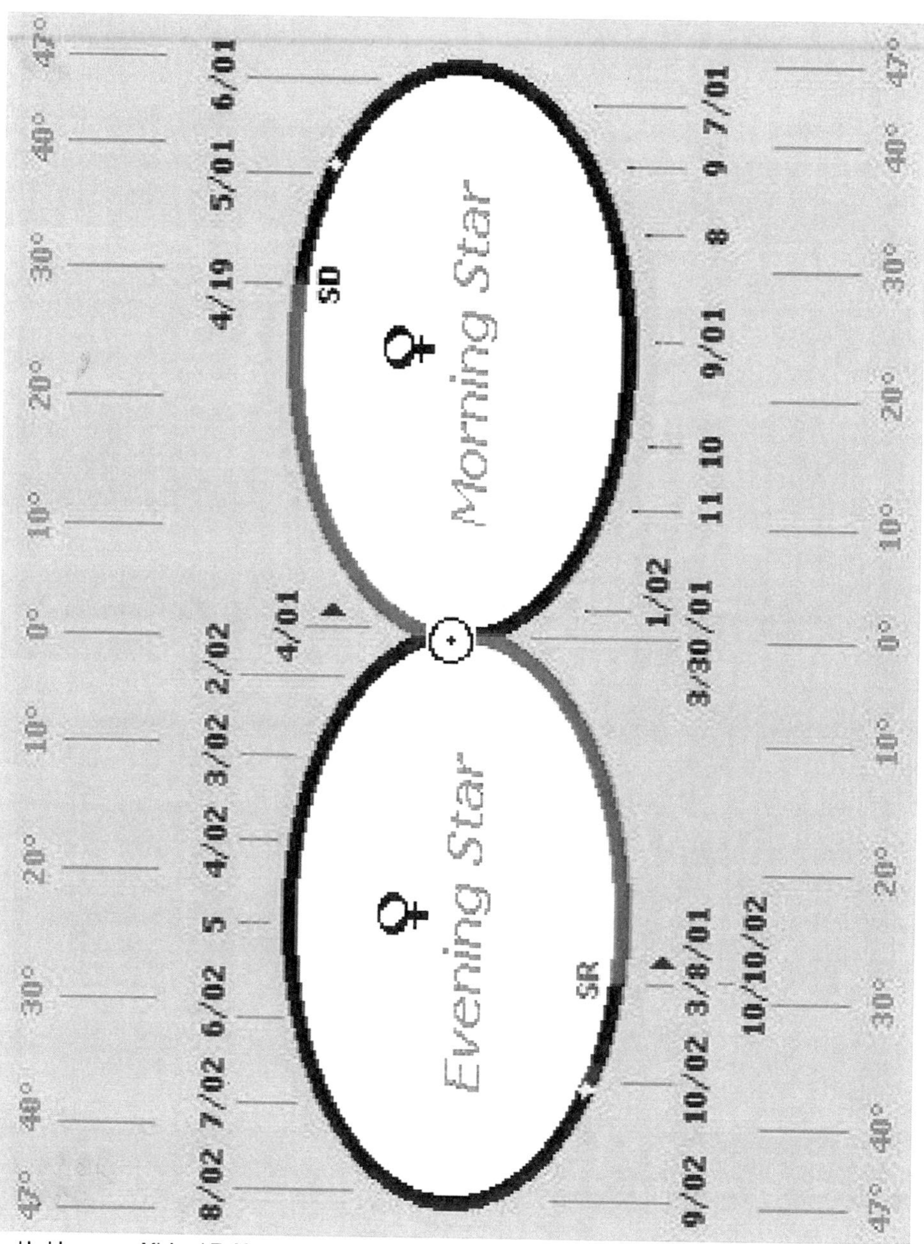

khaldea.com Michael R. Meyer

Chart 3

Compare this with the pattern of Venus's inferior conjunctions between 2001 and 2007.

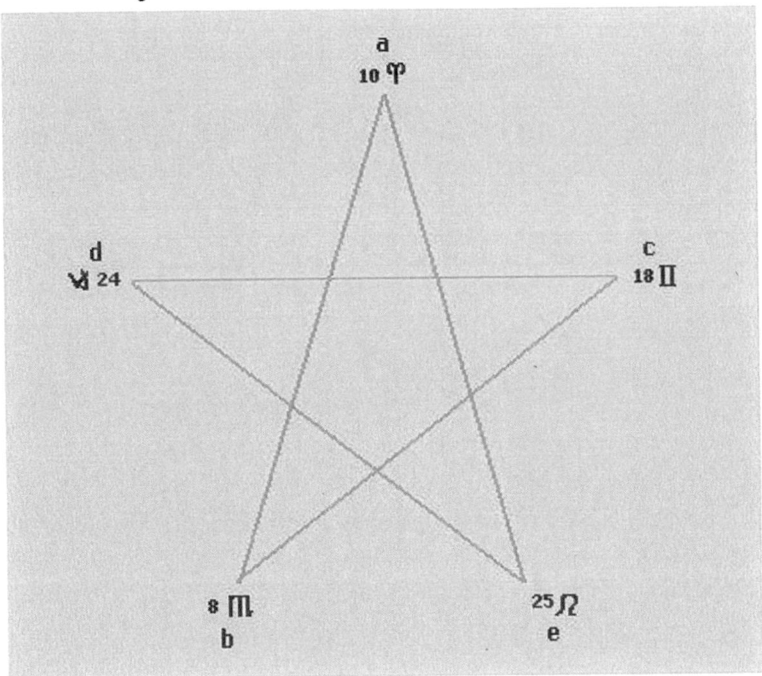

Chart 4

Python babies the result of 'virgin birth,' zoo confirms

The Louisville Zoo posted this image of 'Thelma,' the reticulated python on their Facebook page on Thursday, Oct. 23, 2014.

Chart 5

Chart 6

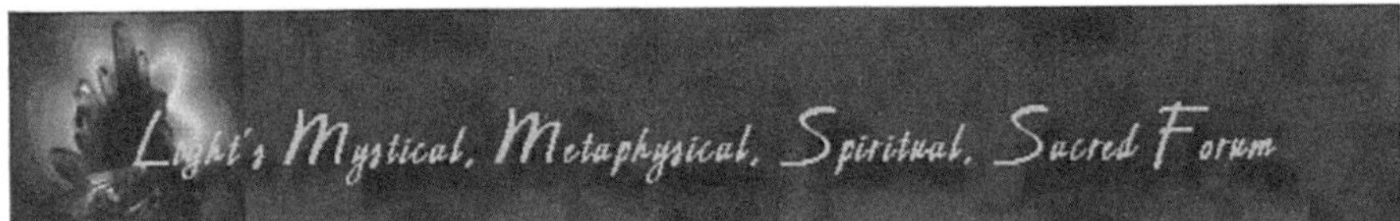

Nostradamus

Iraq Message (full) (continued)

Iraq Message

His hand(*) finally through bloody Alus,

He will be unable to protect himself by sea.

Between two rivers he (**) will fear the military hand,(*)

The black one will make the angry one repent of it.

(*)Hand meaning power.
(**)Sadam Hussein (?) was between the Euphrates and Tigris rivers when pulled from the "spider hole."

continued......

It is thought that "bloody Alus," the "angry one" is referencing Saddam Hussein. American Reporters and President Bush told us that Saddam was captured in his hometown of Tikrit, which is between two rivers that run through Iraq.

Now, putting aside any personal beliefs of the media's error of reporting on this matter, the question remains who is the "black one"? Certainly, President Bush nor the US Military is not being referred to as this, so who do we know of that could fit this description?

First, lets take a look at "bloody Alus." Nostradamus was known for placing multiple meanings and hidden messages in his predictive quatrains. Could this be a pun and suggesting someone other than Saddam? Someone is getting power *through* "bloody Alus." This could imply any number of incidents. Someone could be coming into power because "bloody Alus" dies an untimely, messy death, or because Alus assists somehow and is one of the Shia who participates in a common devotional ritual (to pay homage to Ali [Alus], [the grandson of Muhammad] for his martyrdom) by scoring their forehead and allowing it to bloody their upper body or by flogging their back until it becomes bloody. "Alus" could be the combination of Ali and the US, being that the US is in the land of the religions which worships Ali. What if, the new leadership formulating in Iraq insists on the sentencing of Saddam, as the Dictator, prior]* ←

(Footnote 4)

1+0=1

Chapter 10

IN THE NEW BEGINNING

When Medical students apply for residency programs (their "hands on" training for their chosen specialties), they are required to send an application with an essay. Since I really disliked reading (ADD!), it would follow that I also disliked writing, and hence I was clueless as to how to proceed with my essay. I remember I asked a Psychiatrist what topic I should write on and he gave me better advice than I could have ever dreamed……"just tell the truth". I had spent a summer prior to Medical School bartending and "bouncing" in an unruly club in New York, so I went on to write an essay on how being a bartender and a bouncer was similar to being a Psychiatrist. I was really proud of it and I had hoped that most of the open-minded evaluators of my application would like it as well (especially on the West Coast where I ended up being accepted). East Coast Psychiatry programs didn't like it so much….not formal, TRADITIONAL or scholarly enough. Not a surprising outcome given my observations in "Adrenaline Begets the West". I learned early-on that not everyone would appreciate or understand my quirky thinking.

My quirky thinking has only gotten "quirkier" though. I'm quite confident that this Psychiatrist, with a pharmacology bent, will be chastised for commenting on Theological topics. I'm also quite certain my physician ratings on the internet will probably plummet too. These topics are sacred to many, but the idea of spirituality is meant for EVERYONE and I guess I'm entitled as anyone to render an opinion. I'm not claiming I'm right…. just attempting to give explanations for spiritual concepts from a scientist's point of view. Remember, Psychiatrists treat the human organ that approximates the soul ….The Brain.

I originally wrote this book through Chapter 9 Apocalescence. However, after reading it through several times, I felt the reader would have experienced significant "battle fatigue", and frankly, I was ready to assume a fetal position in the corner too. So I elected to add an extra chapter to at least make the text in totality a "feel good" story. I personally don't think The Apocalypse is a bad thing. The Apocalypse is the "Labor" before the Birth.

For the most part, I don't care how people live their lives or what they do..... that's between them and their conscience, and them and their Maker. What I thought I would do though is simply add a section on how people can maximize their life's experience should they choose to. These hopefully helpful tenets can be employed whether the reader believes in any of my unconventional theories or prefers to pass on them. It's not meant to be a narcissistic replacement for anyone's Religious Doctrine, just a self-help "companion text" for "Born as a Beast". It is a practical summation of my soul progression theory and common sense AS I SEE IT as a practicing Psychiatrist. Common sense of course differs from person to person….and hence it remains the seed of most disagreement and conflict. My advice is derived for the most part similarly from the method of diagnosing a patient based upon their drugs of choice….it's the concept of working backwards through extrapolation. If there is a God, and I can't say definitively there is or isn't, maybe He would want us to act in a way which is opposite to a young soul (as described in Born as a Beast). The goal would be to EVENTUALLY aspire to the qualities of an "old soul." I think amongst other things, God must be an "Old Soul," so it's an effort to approximate His Logic. Figuring out what an "old soul" stands for however requires some thought. We need to figure out the behavior we should want, based upon the behavior that we don't want. As I mentioned, I think all of life's lessons mature us, and the lessons I will site might help us all regardless of where we stand philosophically and religiously. My goal is that this particular "common sense" makes sense from anyone's perspective. I'm far from adequate, and have taken my share of "left" turns in my life, but I do try to improve myself daily with them.

1. Humility. The greatest lessons of life are those of humility. Even if one is humble….more lessons of humility are on the way. We become humble through experiencing pain and loss. It assures that we keep our rightful place on Earth….we are all EQUAL but not the SAME. Once we have navigated painful seasons, we are one step closer to being FAIR with others as we no longer feel superior to them. Humility aids in the process of being less self-centered as well. For some reason I keep thinking that if God exists… His primary concern is how humbly or civilly we will actually act without certain knowledge or sight of Him (He chose to be invisible for a reason!). I also think he might be keeping a ledger on our behavior despite the alleged promise of a "pass" through the act of repentance. Conveniently, I find those who have been the most

"sinful" are the ones counting on that "pass" the most. Interestingly, the most Churches I've ever seen in one place is definitely in Vegas. Anyway, we need to act humbly but having said that, we can't be door mats either. I'm not demonstrating contradiction when I say we need to be humble but courageous simultaneously. They are two separate concepts that are not antithetical.

2. Courage. As previously mentioned, the definition of life as I see it is "pain and anger management in the pursuit of figuring out right vs. wrong". What I mean by that is, if we have faulty logic, we in turn will produce faulty decisions which ultimately get us into trouble. When we get into trouble, we need to be courageous enough to feel the pain of that particular lesson so we can learn from it. Courage means we need to feel our pain in life or else we are doomed to go over the same painful lesson until we get it right. If we touch a hot stove but don't feel the pain of the stove, we in the worst-case scenario are doomed to lose a hand. Anything that impairs our sensation of pain will eventually harm us and prevent us from growing. Defense mechanisms are constructions that personality disorders ROUTINELY use to distort reality in an attempt to not perceive life so painfully. An example of a defense mechanism is denial. If we deny that something painful exists, the problem never gets fixed. Denial or the "blunting" of pain is also seen with substance abuse. The euphoric effect of substance abuse particularly in youth only delays the maturation process. Substance abusers never quite learn any common sense if they are "high" during those formative years. Medications we use in Psychiatry, on the other hand, should not (in proper forms or doses) produce a euphoric alteration of reality. Patients tell me that the medications don't "kill the pain" of life.... but rather it allows them to think clearly and functionally despite it. Courage also means that we should be careful not to use religion as a euphoriant. I find the people who are most preoccupied with "their place in Heaven" and "the after -life" are the same people whose Earthly life is so painful that they would rather not deal with it. They ignore their Earthly woes, and as a result their lives become a hot steamy mess. It's as if they've given up on this life and just focus on their next one. Religion should be used to enhance our lives, not escape from it.

3. Reasonability. Reasonability is simply the knowledge of Truth. The more reasonable we are, the better grasp we will have of life.

In turn, when we are better informed, our lives are easier due to better decision making. Younger souls (personality disorders) live a "magical" (fake) life in their head, so their idea of reality is much different than someone who is more evolved. Older souls, just like older people, are simply more aware of reality. Two people can come away with two totally different conclusions from one singular event because of this discrepancy in evolution. We all have different viewpoints based upon the "evolutionary" lenses we are looking through. The acquisition of Universal knowledge is ones key to growth. This is EMOTIONAL KNOWLEDGE and not concrete knowledge (Born as a Beast). The way we acquire this knowledge is to TRUST OUR INSTINCTS, BUT LEARN FROM OUR MISTAKES, AND TAKE RESPONSIBILITY FOR OUR FAILURES. It's best we trust OUR own instincts, because if we listen to someone else's and they are wrong, the only lesson we learned was that the other person is an "idiot". We didn't learn anything about ourselves. We just become resentful of the person we listened to. But if we make a mistake AND LEARN FROM IT, we assimilate the new lesson into our NEW instincts so we can make a better decision the next time around. This goes on and on throughout ALL our cosmic stages as we accumulate emotional knowledge and slowly graduate out of those personality disordered lifetimes that we all have had to go through. The spiritual journey of a soul is certainly a long one as we evolve in and out of flawed logic. Interestingly, the word "enLIGHTenment" is peripherally antithetical to the word "darkness" (an analogous word to "evil").

Psychotherapy for example can often help people make sense of their lives by helping them learn from a lifetime of faulty decisions. Some may say the objective of psychotherapy is "happiness" but I don't entirely agree with that. Often times in therapy, patients are confronted with the reality they have created for themselves and as a result they become bitter. The objective of therapy therefore is not necessarily to be happier....but rather stronger and SMARTER than when you started. But even in psychotherapy, it's important to listen to other's input, but it's more important to come to your own conclusions.

4. Flexibility. Undesirable events will happen to all of us...you can't escape it regardless of your prayers or where you THINK you stand with God. When bad things happen to us, I've hopefully put

forth a good argument that it isn't "The Devil's" doing, but it's just the "rules of engagement" of being a human being. When they do occur, we have to decide for ourselves if it was somehow related to a bad decision we made, or simply the result of The Universe acting like a thug to an otherwise "innocent" victim ("bad" things happen to "good" people). We need to know the difference because in the former case, we must learn from our mistake and integrate it into our new instincts. If it's the later, we are just going to have to suck it up (be FLEXIBLE) and deal with something we didn't ask for or deserve (death of a loved one for example). When we are flexible with the pains we can't change, we become more adaptive to life, as opposed to life adapting to us (which rarely happens). People with personality disorders like to control their environment, because they are generally speaking quite inflexible to the vicissitudes of life. As a result, they are constantly stressed because life is not quite going as planned.

As a corollary to this notion, everyone will be confronted with people whom they simply don't like, and for the most part there is no changing the other person unless they want to change. People who we don't engage well with should probably just be avoided (not killed). Ongoing confrontations with said person just end up with more dysfunction and emotionality (that's why Bravo's "Housewives" series is so popular…it features the logical emotional conclusion of forcing a group of women together who otherwise would probably have nothing to do with each other). If we can't avoid said undesirable people, and they are not our responsibility, we then need to be TOLERANT. Tolerance is the flexible acceptance of others. If a person has undesirable qualities, it's the Universe's job to change them through their own path of trials and tribulations…..not yours. The difficult part here is that sometimes the Universe uses PEOPLE to teach other people lessons, and I'll be damned if I know what behavioral alterations of others is justified and not justified. In prison, child molesters are often targets for belligerence by fellow inmates. I think The Universe might "sanction" said belligerence towards these particular offenders as it serves as a lesson learned for an abominable Earthly act. However, the perpetrator of the belligerence is still responsible for taking the law into his own hands ….so the whole mess turns out to be a painful lesson for everyone: from victim, to family, to criminal, to vigilante justice doer. Again, this tsunami of pain is just as God intended, no matter how senseless it may seem to us. He's got us coming and going and it only makes sense to Him. Often times it

EVENTUALLY only makes sense to us many years after the fact when the smoke has cleared. At that time, we see how a painful destiny changed us… usually for the better. People tend to glorify the notion of destiny ("we were destined to meet each other"), but destiny unfortunately isn't always pretty.

5. Self-Reliance. Self-reliance gives us freedom and freedom is one of our greatest gifts….especially in the US. The reason freedom is so important is that without it, we can't pursue our dreams on our own terms or enjoy the things we love. Freedom means….no one can control us. An extreme example of this loss of freedom is being in prison. Being prison bound drastically changes how we can happily live our lives on our terms. As I've hopefully emphasized, there is also no shortage of personality disordered people who would developmentally speaking love to control us as well. The way we avoid others controlling us as individuals is self-reliance. This is not just financial self-reliance, but also emotional. Financial self-reliance is pretty straight forward….when someone pays for us they own us. That means, it is in most people's best interest to do what they can do to be educated, innovative and productive. This will ensure our freedom and right to choose, via being gainfully employed. Having said that, there are many people, especially those responsible for caring for the household, where this simply isn't possible. My only response to that is, I hope your spouse isn't controlling. The other type of self-reliance is emotional. We all have relationships with ourselves. Unfortunately, if we don't like ourselves we tend to not like to be BY OURSELVES because WE DON'T LIKE THE COMPANY. As a result, we tend to choose any partner that simply relieves us from being alone. We might hate the other person, but as long as we hate them less than we hate ourselves we stay with them. The problem is, when we stay with someone with whom we aren't compatible …life becomes very difficult and painful. The key then is to be emotionally SELF RELIANT in order to enjoy our own company and thus avoid participating in dysfunctional relationships. The same can unfortunately be said for love. If we love someone TOO much then we lose control of our own sense of peace and welfare. If that person elects to leave or they die, we need to be emotionally self-reliant enough to move forward and not feel sentimentally bankrupted. In this life unfortunately….YOU ARE ON YOUR OWN…. so it's in your best interest to get used to (and accept) your own company. Our loved ones always eventually

leave us either by volition or by death so we all need to be strong, prepared and self-reliant. The issue of love is challenging because we as humans were designed to love. This is especially difficult for mothers. Mothers need to have enough emotional self-reliance to allow their beloved children to grow and LEAVE as nature intended. Once again, the Universe has us coming and going. Welcome to Earth…God's olive press.

6. Health. This is a doozy of a lesson. If we aren't healthy or we are self-indulgent, life gets much harder. If we have a mental illness but choose to self-medicate it with alcohol….we will eventually have to deal with a whole host of other medical issues including cirrhosis of the liver, cardiomyopathy, esophageal cancer and/or dementia etc. The same applies for stress. If we don't solve problems in our lives…we will suffer the physical ramifications of stress such as lowered immune function, gastritis, hypertension or even a myocardial infarction. Once major health issues enter our lives, we immediately lose a substantial amount of our personal freedom. The lesson here is to be honest and courageous enough to know when there is a problem so it can be aptly taken care of. In addition, we need to be proactive with our health even before there is trouble. Make well thought out decisions in life, so the stress of a bad decision is avoided or minimized. In addition, be disciplined enough to avoid unhealthy and immediately gratifying foodstuffs. The "payback" from this indulgent joy could result in a stroke and any physical limitation thereafter. It takes effort to exercise, but exercising will not only improve your overall health, but will also improve your disposition and confidence which in turn will result in overall peace of mind. The term "Health" also applies to the Gifts The Universe has given us. Caring for the health of animal welfare and the environment not only makes us responsible stewards, but also ultimately makes our lives easier and more enjoyable. Ignoring the health of the environment by being inefficient with its resources only make our lives harder and less fun.

In my opinion, The Universe (not its inhabitants!) operates in complete efficiency. Efficiency is HEALTH. I used to look at all the silly "stupid human tricks" we all perform as globally inefficient and mechanistically slowing of the overall System. But with time I revised my opinion and now I find it's actually quite healthy for our "firey" human non-sense to exist. That fire is what teaches us right vs. wrong and maturity. Efficiency is also seen in the concept of "soul progression" and "multiple lives" as well. Rather than making exorbitant numbers of "new souls", I think "God" primarily re-uses existing souls in the same way we might recycle a plastic water bottle. I think we can all agree that the later example is responsible and efficient, and hence the former may be as well. The concept of multiple lives is therefore energy conscious.

7. Industry. Industry means that if we are able....we must be productive. This assures that not only does the species move forward, but also we as individuals develop emotionally and physically. The easy way out is to simply be lazy or have other people do it for us.... there is clearly a sense of narcissistic entitlement with that. However, the greatest lessons in life usually involve humility....so this approach usually promotes pain one way or another in the long run. In life, we can either pay now (like by going to school for example)...or pay later. The choice is yours. Industry can mean many things... education, work, exercise, or helping others. Destiny will find you either way, but my guess is you are much more likely to find a more rewarding and interesting life by being productive. For meaningful things to happen to you, you need to show up. Some people however are physically or mentally unable to be as productive as others. That's OK...the key is trying to the best of our ability as this increases the chance of some type of success. With success comes confidence, and with confidence comes acceptance of self.

I consider myself an industrious person but I never would have written this book if it were not for the support of family and friends. For years they have listened to my inane theories and for years have encouraged me to write a manuscript expressing them. I'd like to thank them for insisting on this publication as it not only provided me the chance to consolidate my own understanding of Psychiatry and humanity, but also gave me a chance to inform others of the deliberateness of The Universe. Contextually, my musings would have never been actualized if I hadn't had the appropriate education and I'd like to thank those who were generous with their knowledge. Finally, Life is our best teacher, and it was my patients who taught me the difference between the brain and the mind. The brain is just chemicals, but the mind incorporates a soul, so it has a deeper and more inclusive web of meaning and experience. I still hope we all get visited by aliens one day....we then will finally realize that we as humans are more alike than different. We all share the same house and attend the same school. See you at Graduation......I'll be the one with the glazed look, holding a participation trophy, wondering what the #!?% just happened....

COPYRIGHT REFERENCES

Cover: Venus Transit of The Sun on 6/6/2012. NASA. SDO
Book cover design, content layout, and original charts by Rachel Burgo.

Chapter 1: In the Beginning
Chart 1. National Violent Death Reporting System, US.
Chart 2. The Human Brain. Credit: Udaix Shutterstock
Chart 3. Axis Formulation . Original chart.
Chart 4. Diagnostic Criteria for PTSD from DSM-IV-TR. American Psychiatric Association. Behavenet.com

Chapter 2: Thou Shall Not Be Bored
Chart 1. Diagnostic Criteria for ADHD from DSM-IV-TR. APA. Behavenet.com
Chart 2. Prefrontal Cortex. Polygon Data from Bodyparts 3D. Wiki. Credit: Database Center for Life Science.
Quote: Homer Simpson from "The Simpsons". Created by Matt Groening.
Chart 3. Adrenaline Formation. Credit: GFDL and Creative Commons.
Chart 4. ADD/ADHD Medication List. Original Chart.
Chart 5. Consequences of ADHD. A Handbook For Diagnosis and Treatment. 1998. Barkley RA. Originally from American Journal of Psychiatry. Biederman et al 1995. Teenmentalhealth.org

Chapter 3: John's New Revelation: Adrenaline Begets the West
Footnote 1. "The Epidemiology of Adult ADHD" from CNS spectrums. Adler, Spencer, Stein, Newcorn.
Footnote 2 and 3. The Worldwide Prevalence of ADHD. Polanczych , Silva de Lima, Horta, Biederman, Rohde. American Journal Of Psychiatry. June 2007. Psychiatryonline.org
Chart 1. World Cocaine Usage. World Health Organization. World Mental Health Survey Initiative. Awarenessblog.com
Chart 2. World Tobacco Usage. World Health Organization. World Mental health Surveys in PLOS Medicine. Stranger.com
Chart 3. Domestic Crystal Methamphetamine Usage. National Drug Survey on Drug Use and Health. June 2007. Oas.samhsa.gov
Chart 4. "Monster Drink" . Google Trends software.
Chart 5. Number Chart. Original Graph.
Chart 6. Foreclosures. "Realty Trac". USA Today. Motherjones.com
Chart 7. Isomers. Wiki. Credit: Neurotiker. (with modifications)

Chapter 4: Thou Shall Not Be Moody

Chart 1. Diagnostic Criteria for Major Depression from DSM-IV-TR. APA. Behavenet.com
Chart 2. Diagnostic Criteria for Schizophrenia from DSM-IV-TR. APA. Behavenet.com
Chart 3. Antidepressant List. Original Chart.
Chart 4. High Energy/Low Energy Bipolar. Original Graph.
Chart 5. Diagnostic Criteria for Mania from DSM-IV-TR. APA. Behavenet.com
Chart 6. Diagnostic Criteria for Mixed episode from DSM-IV-TR. APA. Behavenet.com
Chart 7. Self-medication of Bipolar. Original Graph.
Chart 8. Proper Treatment of Bipolar. Original Graph.

Chapter 5: John's New Revelation: The Sun of God

Chart 1. Solstices. Original graph.
Chart 2. Melatonin Synthesis. Wiki. Credit: Adicorr7.
Chart 3. Melatonin Function. Wiki. National Institute of General Medical Sciences.
Chart 4. Suicides by Month. Wiki. Creative Commons Attributions Share Alike 3.0. User Credit: Citynoise
Chart 5. A Counter Intuitive Corollary. American Journal of Psychiatry. April 2003.
Chart 6. All Suicides vs Time. Original Graph.
Chart 7. "Psychiatric" Suicides vs. Time. Original Graph.
Chart 8. Artist Suicides (Mood Disorder equivalent) vs Time. Original Graph.
Chart 9. Suicide Data. Original Graph.
Chart 10. Suicide Omissions. Original Graph.
Chart 11. "Assisted Suicide". Google T rends Software.
Chart 12. Aurora Colorado Massacre: James Holmes mug shot. Arapahoe Detention Center.
Chart 13. 1 Year Dow Chart. Yahoo Finance Software. Original Graph.
Chart 14. 5 Year VIX Chart. Yahoo Finance Software. Original Graph.
Chart 15a. "Sex". Google Trends Software.
Chart 15b. Bitcoin investment trust (GBTC) 6 month chart. Yahoo Finance Software.
Chart 16. Sunspots. Solarscience.msfa.nasa.gov. Credit: Hathaway 2009.
Chart 17. Market Perturbations Relative to Historic Sunspot Cycles. Solarscience.msfc.nasa.gov. Credit: Hathaway 2009. Modified.
Chart 18. 10 Year Dow Chart. Yahoo Finance Software. Original Graph.
Chart 19. Sunspot Cycle. NASA. Credit: Hathaway. Solarscience.msfc.nasa.gov

Footnote 1. December 2008 Solar Minimum. Joseph D' Aleo. Rightsidenews.com
Chart 20. Census Bureau. Haver Analytics.
Chart 21. 20 Year VIX. Yahoo Finance Software. Original graph.
Chart 22. 6 Month (YTD) Dow Chart. Yahoo Finance Software. Original Graph.
Chart 23. 7 Year Dow Chart. "Spring Market Peaks". Yahoo Finance Software. Original Graph.
Chart 24. 2 Month Sunspot Number: May 10 "Flash Crash". European Space Agency. NOAA. space-env.esa.int
Chart 25. 3 Month VIX Chart. Yahoo Finance Software. Original Graph.
Chart 26. Proctor and Gamble Logo: 666. Credit: Proctor and Gamble. Nightmaregirls.net. Prison Planet Forum.
Chart 27. 30 Day daily Sunspot data. US Dept of Commerce. NOAA
Chart 28. 2 year Ap Geomagnetic Index. European Space Agency. Space-env.esa.int
Chart 29. 1 Month VIX Chart. Yahoo Finance Software. Original Graph.
Chart 30. Solar Cycle Chart. Credit: Ole Humlum. climate4u.com
Chart 31. Similar Amplitude Solar Cycle Comparison. Credit: Ole Humlum. climate4you.com
Chart 32a. Search term "Happy". Google Trends Software. Original Chart.
Charts 32b. Heroin Overdoses. Clearbrook Inc/ Clearbrook Treatment Centers. The CDC: Centers for Disease Control and Prevention
Chart 33. "Flickering". 2 Month Sunspot Number. European Space Agency. NOAA. space-env.esa.int
Chart 34. Suicides/Homicides During Descending Phase of Great Depression Solar Cycle 16. Centers for Disease Control. suicidemethods.info
Chart 35. 26 year VIX. Yahoo Finance Software. Original Graph.

Chapter 6: Thou Shall Not Cast Stones at That Hormone

Chart 1. Epinephrine/Cortisol/Glucagon. Chemistry.gravitywaves.com
Chart 2. Chemical Pathway for Sex Hormone Production. Original Graph.
Chart 3. Anatomical Pathway for Sex Hormone Production . Original Graph.
Chart 4. Effects of Testosterone. Original Graph.
Chart 5. USA Suicide Rates: Gender. National Center for Injury Prevention and Control.
Footnote 1. "A Profile of Pedophilia". Mayo Clinic Proceedings.
Footnote 2. Bureau of Justice Statistics. 1989
Chart 6. Reasons for Commitment by Gender. Texas Youth Commission Annual Report 2004. images.google.com
Chart 7. Testosterone and Aggression. Flyfishingdevon.co.uk. Credit: Redrawn from Wagner et al (1980)
Chart 8. Effects of Estrogen. Original Graph.
Chart 9. Menstrual Cycle. www.sydneyivf.com

Chart 10. Hormones Menopause "All About Menopause". Credit: Ryan Andrews.
Chart 11. Hormone Crash. Credit: Tucker 1994. Classes.ansci.uiuc.edu. Modified

Chapter 7: Thou Shall Not Act Like a Child (Unless You Are One)
Chart 1. Diagnostic Criteria for Paranoid Personality Disorder. DSM-IV-TR. APA. Behavenet.com
Chart 2. Diagnostic Criteria for Schizotypal Personality Disorder. DSM-IV-TR. APA. Behavenet.com
Chart 3. Diagnostic Criteria for Schizoid Personality Disorder. DSM-IV-TR. APA. Behavenet.com
Chart 4. Diagnostic Criteria for Avoidant Personality Disorder. DSM-IV-TR. APA. Behavenet.com
Chart 5. Diagnostic Criteria for Passive Aggressive Personality Disorder. DSM-III. APA. pttypes.com
Chart 6. Diagnostic Criteria for Obsessive Compulsive Personality Disorder. DSM-IV-TR. APA. Behavenet.com
Chart 7. Diagnostic Criteria for Dependent Personality Disorder. DSM-IV-TR. APA. Behavenet.com
Chart 8. Diagnostic Criteria for Histrionic Personality Disorder. DSM-IV-TR. APA. Behavenet.com
Chart 9. Diagnostic Criteria for Antisocial Personality Disorder. DSM-IV-TR. APA. Behavenet.com
Chart 10. Diagnostic Criteria for Borderline Personality Disorder. DSM-IV-TR. APA. Behavenet.com
Chart 11. Diagnostic Criteria for Narcissistic Personality Disorder. DSM-IV-TR. APA. Behavenet.com

Chapter 8: John's New Revelation: Born as a Beast
A non-footnoted reference is made to Otto Kernberg. He determined Borderline Personality Disorder patients have the characteristics of a 6-36 month old infant.
Footnote 1. "Emotional Memory". Joseph LeDeux. Scholarpedia 2 (7) 1806.
Chart 1. Amygdala Anatomy. Image: Constudoverbrain.gif from Creative Commons. Credit: RobinH at en.wikibooks
A non-footnoted reference is made to Norman Geschwind who identified the temporal lobe as "The Spiritual Center" of the brain.
A non-footnoted reference is made to Michael Persinger. He studied the effects of a magnetic field on the temporal lobe.
Footnote 2. Amygdala Sparing in Dementia. "Brain" Volume 131:12 pp 3266-76. Dec, 2008.

Chapter 9: Apocalescence

Footnote 1. Love Activates Same Brain Areas As Cocaine. The New York Sun. Highfield, Aron, Brown, Fisher.

Footnote 2. 2010 NFL Scouting Combine results. Tim Tebow. Deadspin.com

Footnote 3. Amygdala in Fear Conditioning. Joseph Deleux. Scholarpedia 2008.

Chart 1. Transits of Venus and Earth. Wiki. Credit: Theresa Knott.

Chart 2. Venus Orbit. Credit: Michael Meyer. Khaldea.com

Chart 3. Pentagram. Credit: Michael Meyer. Khaldea.com

Chart 4. Python Virgin Birth. Credit: Photo from Louisville Zoo. Angella Mulholland. CTVnews.ca.

Chart 5. Felix Baumgartner/Red Bull Logo. Credit: Red Bull Stratos. Airpigs.com

Chart 6. Nostradamus interpretation of "ALUS". Entire page Credit: John Hogue. Lightchamber.org

Made in the USA
San Bernardino, CA
25 October 2018